D1282523

OPEN YOUR EYES
Life Lessons Learned in Haiti

JEFF NEWELL

ISBN 978-1-64191-888-6 (paperback)
ISBN 978-1-64191-889-3 (digital)

Christian Faith Publishing, Inc.
832 Park Avenue
Meadville, PA 16335
www.christianfaithpublishing.com

Printed in the United States of America

Contents

Foreword

IT PLEASES ME A GREAT deal to be invited to write the foreword to Jeff Newell's book about what he and his companions have learned from the visits they make to Haiti. It is indeed a collection of wonderful stories.

I've known Jeff Newell for more than ten years. First, as his teacher for several of the Ecclesial Lay Ministry theology courses that Saint Joseph's College furnishes for the Lafayette Diocese. Then in some special ELM courses on the documents from the Second Vatican Council, as we began to observe the fiftieth anniversary of that council. Jeff became the principal advocate for the teachings of the council about social justice, sometimes chiding the instructor (me!) for not giving enough attention to this dimension of the texts. And finally, Jeff and I became collaborators for an ELM workshop on *Gaudium et spes*, the longest, the last, and perhaps the most challenging of the documents from Vatican II.

In *The Church in the World of Today* (the English title for *Gaudium et spes* or *GS*), the new approach to theology practiced in Vatican II exhibited its most mature development. It was called "theology from below," a more inductive approach to an understanding of faith that begins with how people *live* the Gospels. This is no more complicated than the old adage that "Experience is the best teacher."

Chapter 1 in *GS* seeks to answer the question: "What do we learn about what it means to be created in the image of God when we pay attention to our lived experience?" We know we have *minds* that seek to understand the whole of reality, a moral *conscience* that works at distinguishing good from evil, and genuine *freedom* to choose what we do. Most remarkably, Christians learn how these essential traits of being human can be done with perfection by observing how the Gospels present Jesus, true God and true man, to us:

> He worked with human hands, He thought with a human mind.
> He acted with a human will, and with a human heart He loved.
> Born of the Virgin Mary, He has truly been made one of us,
> like to us in all things—except sin. (GS 22 and Heb. 4:15)

How Jesus lived teaches us how to be fully human. And what staggers and astonishes the mind is that Jesus also reveals the Father to us. At the Last Supper, one of the twelve implores Jesus to "show us the Father." And Jesus answers: "Whoever has seen me has seen the Father" (John 14:9). So the theology from below learns both who we are as images of God and who God is from what Jesus says and does in the four Gospels. In more academic terms, theology is anthropology and vice versa.

The most basic connection between the divinity and the humanity of Jesus is self-giving love, the way the Persons within the Trinity relate to one another and what Jesus became human to do for us and to show to us. *GS* is very clear about love for God expressing itself through love of neighbor. "We are witnessing the birth of a new humanism, where people are defined above all else by their responsibility to their sisters and brothers and at the court of history" (GS 55). Responsibility for others—practiced with reciprocity—I see as the underlying theme of this book.

As the chapters in these pages make abundantly clear, the time spent in Haiti involved much more receiving than giving on the part of those traveling there from Indiana and, in the light of the theology from below, much more learning than teaching. Living in those very special communities produced thirty-some lessons in how to live the Gospels.

I am very grateful to Jeff for writing this book to preserve and to share the lessons learned in the field. I have learned a great deal, as something of a second-generation fellow traveler, from reading these stories; and I am confident that the many readers of this book will similarly be gifted.

Thank you, Jeff, and "Si Dye vle, m'ap avek ou." (See chapter 9.)

John Nichols, STL, PhD
Saint Joseph's College (retired)
October 11, 2016
Feast of Saint John XXIII

Introduction

It is impossible for us not to speak about what we have seen and heard.
—Acts 4:20

FREQUENTLY PEOPLE ASK ME WHAT would they do if they were to go to Haiti with me. The inference is that they don't know whether they have skills that would be helpful there. I respond by telling them that I am the least useful person to go to Haiti. I am not very fond of going to the doctor or even seeing blood or needles, so I am not particularly helpful in medical missions. I am not mechanically inclined. I can't do electrical work or rewire a generator or work on fixing anything beyond a flat tire on a vehicle. I do not have any good trade skills. My friends tease me that I am best suited to be the "dummy end" of the tape on any task requiring two people! I am not trained in masonry work, which is a vital skill to have in Haiti. Therefore, the talents I do have do not seem to correlate well with those areas that Haiti seems to need the most.

So why is it that I go and keep on going back to Haiti? Hopefully this book will shed some light on those two simple, yet powerful questions.

While I may not be "useful" in the many endeavors I just described, I do feel that I am good at spending my time with the people of Haiti. I love to walk with them, to talk with them, even to learn to speak Creole, to eat with them, to worship with them, to sing, to dance, to laugh, to cry, to comfort them and to be comforted by them, to be with them and share whatever the moment brings with them. We are told in 1 Peter 4:10, "As each of us has received a gift, use it to serve one another as good stewards of God's varied grace."

I have experienced countless wonderful situations throughout my many mission trips to Haiti. More importantly, God has allowed me time to reflect, to absorb all that has happened, and to notice even the little moments. Deuteronomy 4:9 confirms the importance of this when it says to "not forget the things your own eyes have seen nor let them slip from your memory as long as you live." God has given me insights that hopefully make me a better person in all facets of my life. My reflections on each of these trips and experiences have taught me so many wonderful lessons about life in general.

I also think that I am good at coming home and sharing those many wonderful experiences with anyone ready to listen. I have written a lengthy journal after every trip I have taken to Haiti and shared those journals with others willing to read them. I suppose that writing this book is an extension of my desire to share my experiences and what I have learned over the past two decades.

After all, Jesus instructs us to do so at Mark 5:19 when he says, "Go home to your family and announce to them all that the Lord… has done for you."

While my mission experiences have come from my many trips to Haiti, the life lessons I have learned could have just as easily been acquired wherever mission work occurs, from inside your own home and community to as far away as a developing country in another part of the world. Ultimately, we are called to mission everywhere. Pope Francis reaffirmed this worldwide calling at the closing of World Youth Day in 2013 when he said, "Where does Jesus send us? There are no borders, no limits. He sends us to everyone."

Wherever it is that you choose to follow God's calling, remember the words from the following Franciscan Benediction. They fit perfectly with doing any such endeavor:

> May God bless you with enough foolishness
> to believe that you really can make a difference in
> this world, so that you are able, with God's grace,
> to do what others claim cannot be done.

1

Mission: What Does that Mean?

The first task in approaching another people, another culture,
another religion, is to take off our shoes, for the place we are
approaching is holy. Else we find ourselves treading on people's dreams;
worse, we may forget that God was there before our arrival.
                                                    —*Bishop Kenneth Cragg*

PROBABLY THE MOST IMPORTANT LESSON I have learned deals with answering this question: "What is mission?" After all, if I am going to go on a mission trip, what is it that I am trying to do?

If you asked me before my first trip, my answer would most likely have been simply, "To help those in need" or "To put my faith in action." Those reasons sound worthy and even seem to dovetail with the Golden Rule of doing unto others as you would want them to do for you. However, my answer today would be much different and much deeper. It has taken a lot of reading and reflection on this simple question after many visits to Haiti for me to form my current view.

Any thought process on mission should begin with Jesus. What did He do? Who did He help? Sinners, the blind, the deaf, the lame, the lepers, the poor, the widows, and orphans. These people were at the forefront of whatever Jesus did and thereby taught us to do. His ministry was defined by helping those who were least able to help themselves, the marginalized and often forgotten in society.

We have many "Gospel calls" throughout the Bible, each giving us our "marching" orders to do mission. I know the Bible is replete with many more examples of such "marching" orders, but I will list three of my favorite mission verses, the ones that speak the loudest to me. The first is found at John 13:15. Jesus has just finished washing the feet of the disciples after the Last Supper when he says, "I have given you a model to follow, so that as I have done for you, you should also do." Seems simple and straightforward, doesn't it?

A second "Gospel call" is the Golden Rule, which can be found in two places, at Luke 6:31 and Matthew 7:12. Both essentially say, "Do to others as you would have them do to you." While these callings may not be complicated to understand, they are much tougher to implement daily.

My third example, and my favorite instruction on mission, comes from chapter 25 in the book of Matthew. We all know these verses. They involve the judgment day when the sheep are separated from the goats. What separates them from each other for eternity is their feeding of the hungry, giving drink to the thirsty, welcoming the stranger, clothing the naked, and visiting the sick and imprisoned. Summing up their acts of mercy, the Lord says, "Amen, I say to you, what you did for one of these least brothers of mine, you did for me" (Matt. 25:40). Likewise, He adds to those who did not do any of those things, "Amen, I say to you, what you did not do for one of these least ones, you did not do for me" (Matt. 25:45). Many homilies, books, and treatises have been written on these verses of the Bible.

Recognizing Jesus in such situations reminds me of what we are taught in Hebrews 13:2. "Do not neglect hospitality, for through it some have unknowingly entertained angels." Better yet, to adapt it to Matthew 25, unknowingly entertained Jesus!

It seemed my initial aim of "helping those in need" was the calling that I was being led to do. It was very easy to want to simply give some assistance to the many worthy needs we encountered. We didn't have to look very hard when we were in Haiti as they were everywhere. In the beginning, that was what we did.

However, it took much contemplation for me to realize those Gospel calls were the starting points for mission, not the end goal of mission. To do mission in the spirit in which it was intended, more is required. Being a missionary cannot be a one-way endeavor. It can never simply be about the "haves" giving to the "have-nots." If it is, the mission will eventually die out and fail. A proper foundation must first exist. I know that is a topic often found in the Bible. For example, see Matthew 7:24–27 and 1 Corinthians 3:11.

Mother Theresa put this idea of a proper foundation in perspective for me. She said, "Let us not be satisfied with just giving money. Money is not enough, money can be got, but they need your hearts to love them. So, spread your love everywhere you go."

The cornerstones for setting that proper foundation are a profound focus on relationships and mutual respect. You cannot see yourself as bringing Jesus to others *but* rather you must see Jesus in the others and then draw yourself to them. Then true missionary work can begin.

Former British prime minister Benjamin Disraeli encapsulates this idea of mutuality well when he said, "The greatest good you can do for another is not just to share your riches but to reveal to him his own." This mutuality theme can also be found in Booker T. Washington's comment, "When you want to lift up yourself, lift up someone else."

Seeing Jesus in others is a skill that takes a lifetime to develop. I found a simple tool that helps me. When my oldest son, Justin, was in third grade in St. Mary School, he was at a school garage sale fundraiser. He bought a small wooden carving that spelled J-E-S-U-S. There were raised areas that were a different color than the background of the rest of the block of wood. To the untrained eye, those raised areas looked more like Japanese letters than English letters. The word "J E S U S" was not obvious when you first looked at it. You had to study it to find it. The letters spelling J-E-S-U-S were what were behind the raised portions that were there merely to divert your attention.

When he first brought it home, we had to mark the back side of the piece of wood so we could figure out which direction to hold it so it would be easier to discover "J E S U S" the next time we looked at it. Without those cues, we struggled to find the letters. It took us many attempts to find "J E S U S" before it began to become easier to do. What is amazing to me, I now have a difficult time looking at it and not seeing "J E S U S."

I loved the symbolism of this simple piece of wood. Once you learned to block out the interferences of the false raised letters and look past them, what was left was "J E S U S." Too often in our lives we train ourselves to see the wrong things. We typically look at the surface, thereby missing Jesus in the situation. Just like with the piece of wood, you must learn to look past the distractions to find what is important. It is always there, just rarely is it obvious! Think how much better Christians we all could be if we were better at looking beyond the interferences and finding Jesus. Just like with the piece of wood, think how much better we could become in finding Jesus in others with some practice. Maybe we could get to a place where it was more difficult to not see Him than to recognize Him in others.

Gaudium et spes was the final document approved by Vatican II in December 1965. It espouses this thought well in paragraph 93 by saying, "It is the Father's will that we should recognize Christ our brother in the persons of all men and women and should love them with an active love, in word and deed thus bearing witness to the truth."

Mahatma Gandhi takes this recognition of Jesus in others to a higher level when he challenges us by saying, "If you don't find God in the next person you meet, it is a waste of time looking for him further."

I don't know why but it was much easier for me to see Jesus in others when I was in Haiti. I think part of it was because everything I encountered was so new. I did not have a lifetime of third world experiences tempting me to focus on the wrong things, so it was easier to look beyond the distractions. Since everything was new to me, no interference was strong enough to divert my attention!

After further reflection on this, I realized that I have never been to Haiti without feeling that I was there to be at God's service, to do whatever He led me to do. I never have had the illusion that I was in charge of anything when I was there. My dominant type A personality disappears while I am in Haiti. When something does not go as anticipated while in Haiti, I often think, *God, what are you trying to teach me now?* I am quite certain that has never been true for me while in the United States. When I am here, it seems that I don't turn to God for help until I have exhausted everything I can do and have come up empty. In Haiti I go to Him first, not last. With that as my mind-set, it is easy to understand why it is much easier to see Jesus in others while I am there. My challenge now is to carry that priority over to the rest of my life and not just while I am in that tiny Caribbean nation.

Another reason it is easier for me is that I am truly impressed with every Haitian that I have met. My whole life I always had electricity, running water, indoor plumbing, a house that did not have dirt floors or thatched roof, paved roads, and a nearby grocery store. The list could go on forever! Most Haitians do not have any of these things that we would consider routine or expected. In Haiti, they would be luxuries, especially in the rural mountain areas.

In addition, I have backpacked many times in my life. I know how difficult simply not having clean drinking water readily available can be and how finding it can take an inordinate amount of your time and energy. So the Haitians quickly had my admiration for being able to live their entire lives in a way we would consider very difficult, if not impossible, and not merely survive a few days of voluntarily "roughing it!"

Frederick Ozanam, the founder of St. Vincent de Paul, summed up my feelings well when he wrote: "Assistance to the unfortunate honors when it treats the poor with respect, not only as an equal, but as a superior because he is suffering what perhaps we are incapable of suffering."

Ad gentes divinitus was another document approved near the end of Vatican II in 1965. It summed up being a missionary in paragraph 8: "Missionary activity is nothing else, and nothing less, than the manifestation of God's plan...thus missionary activity tends toward eschatological fullness."

A final thought I have on mission comes from Julie Lupien, executive director of From Mission to Mission. I have heard her speak several times and love when she says, "When the God in me meets the God in you, great things will happen."

Great things will happen when a solid foundation is laid for the mission. You don't have to go thousands of miles to do it. You can see Jesus in the next person you encounter, wherever you happen to be! As Bishop Cragg's words so aptly remind us, He "was there before our arrival."

Wood carving with the hidden "J E S U S." Can you see Jesus?

2

So What Do We Do in Haiti?

People don't care how much you know until
they know how much you care.
—*John C. Maxwell*

I AM REPEATEDLY ASKED, "WHAT do you do in Haiti?" My response always is, "We build relationships!" That can be a difficult concept for most Americans to grasp or appreciate. After all, we are doers. We like to take charge, assess the situation, fix the problem, and then go on to do something else.

We like to keep score and quantify results. We always tally how many patients were seen or how many vitamins were passed out or how many houses were built. You name the endeavor, and we can measure it somehow!

Results are difficult to quantify when your goal is to build relationships. In fact, it is nearly impossible. Before each trip, I tell all the first-time travelers to Haiti that the most important thing we do is build relationships. To help satisfy that American need to keep a tally, I also tell them that they will have a successful trip if at the end, they know the name of ten different Haitians and that those ten Haitians know their name. This cannot occur without spending time and effort getting to know them, which is at the core of building a relationship with someone.

"Koze mande chez" is a Haitian proverb that is directly on point. Translated, it means "A conversation requires a chair." The chair symbolizes time. A true conversation, as opposed to a mere chat, takes time. Obviously, a conversation lasts longer if you are sitting than if you are simply passing by one another. The same concept applies to building a relationship. It can't be accomplished in your spare time. A relationship needs an intentional investment of your time and energy to fully develop.

I know the notion of the importance of building relationships is not easy to grasp, but nearly everyone begins to comprehend it the longer they are in Haiti. Many that have traveled with me have come up after a few days and said, "I am up to six!" or "I am up to twelve!" The highest number anyone has told me they achieved was thirty. They are typically beaming with their newfound understanding of this concept.

There are two profound early experiences that helped define the importance of building relationships for me. Each took more than one year to fully develop. The first began on my initial trip to Pendus in March 2000. We went in mid-March so we could celebrate the Feast of St. Joseph (March 19) with the parishioners of St. Joseph Church in Pendus, Haiti. The celebration of this feast day was different than our similar Feast of the Immaculate Conception (December 8) at St. Mary Cathedral in Lafayette, Indiana. The biggest difference was that the Haitian feast lasted the entire weekend and the entire community was involved. It truly was a party with food and music, joy and laughter, praise and festivities.

Everything was new to me. All my senses were being bombarded with new sights, sounds, smells, tastes, and touches. I was not used to seeing machetes, the big bladed knives that looked more like a weapon than a common everyday tool. Many men and women would carry them as they walked, holding them hanging down toward the ground as they moved around.

There was one middle aged man at the feast. I never did learn his name. He was very slightly built, standing not much taller than five foot. He wore a Civil War rebel hat, which I found very curious.

His clothes were big on him, and he was barefoot. He was also a deaf-mute. He could only communicate by grunting, none of which I thought discernible by anyone as none of it was Creole, just guttural sounds. He was very animated when he tried to communicate with anyone, waving his arms and making as much noise as he could. I suppose most folks simply had ignored him for most of his life. Those machinations were necessary for him to gain anyone's attention. And he did get my attention, but it wasn't with the flailing of his arms or the decibel level of his grunting. What grabbed my attention was his machete! He carried his upright, not hanging down by his side. By holding it up, it seemed to be right in your face as you meet him. When he tried to get your attention, his arm movements included the machete waving in the air too. I know he was not threatening me with it, but I was unnerved a little nonetheless.

During that first trip, we passed out rosaries to everyone at the feast day Mass. The church was more than packed. There were people standing outside looking through the concrete block windows since there was no more room inside. I had no idea who everyone was that received one, just that we gave out all that we had brought with us.

I did not see the deaf-mute man after that Mass, nor did I see him during the next year's trip. The following year, our group hiked up a mountain to the chapel at Mayombe for the first time. It was a very tough hike. We each climbed the rocky path at our own pace. This means that we were all strung out along the way up. Therefore, I was essentially hiking by myself. About an hour into the hike, another path from the other side of the mountain merged with my path. Right at that juncture I came face-to-face with the man that was the deaf-mute.

By now I was beginning to learn some Creole. My first instinct was to greet him and finally ask him his name, but I quickly remembered that he could not understand me, nor would I understand his response. However, there was instant connection on both our parts. I do know that he recognized me as someone he knew from the expression on his face, and I am positive he could read my face and know the same from me! Father Bob Klemme was walking about twenty to thirty yards behind me. Father was also on the first trip two years earlier. I turned to him to tell him to hurry and come meet this man again. However, when I spun back toward the man, he had already pivoted around and was hurrying back down the path toward his thatched roof home about one hundred yards below.

Father caught up with me about the time the man went into his home. I explained who he was. Father said he recalled him from that initial trip. Before we could turn away and continue our journey to Mayombe, the man came back out of his house. I could see him staring up at us. He was waving his hand over his head and grunting as loud as he possibly could. It was loud enough that I could hear him. He kept waving his hand back and forth, like you would do to gain someone's attention during an emergency. However, there was no emergency other than his desire to communicate with me. He was holding a white rosary. I *know* he was telling me in the only way he knew how that he remembered who I was because he associated me with him getting that rosary two years earlier!

Sadly, I have never seen him again over the next decade and a half, but he did teach me a very valuable lesson on relationship building. I was building a relationship even when I did not know I was doing so, even when I was a little intimidated by him, his inability to speak, and his machete!

Another powerful example of the importance of building relationships began in December 2000. That was my first trip to Haiti with my wife, Sharon, and son, Kyle. Our travel from Port-au-Prince (PAP) to Pendus was slowed by poor roads and several flat tires. It was dark when we arrived at the rectory in Gros Morne. Even though it was only about ten miles from Pendus, it would take over an hour to drive there over the dirt mountain road. Father Ronel Charelus decided that it would be safer if we spent the night at the rectory and finished our journey the next morning in daylight.

The next day we were up and on our way before sunrise. We had been in Gros Morne less than twelve hours and had slept for most of that time. There was an older gentleman at the rectory. He seemed to me to be the butler there. Better yet, he was the security system, as he seemed to know who came and went and who should or should not be there. Because we were at the rectory so little time, I did not know any more about him other than he lived there.

The following year we did not have any car trouble, so we arrived in Gros Morne in midafternoon. There was still plenty of daylight left in the day. However, it had been raining a lot several days before our arrival. There are five rivers to cross between Gros Morne and Pendus. None of those crossings had a bridge at that time. One would simply drive their vehicle down the bank of one side of the river, through the flowing river, and up the bank on the other side. Due to the recent rain, two of the rivers would be too deep and the water flowing too fast. It would not be safe to take a vehicle through them that day. Again, we would have to spend the night at the rectory in Gros Morne and hope the water levels receded by the next day.

Sharon was the first from our vehicle to get out and carry her suitcase around the corner of the building to the back entry into the rectory. She was greeted warmly by the same elderly gentleman. She did not understand him other than he greeted her as Madam Jeff and somewhere in his greeting he mentioned Jeff. She simply pointed back to the vehicle where I was still unloading.

Moments later I rounded the corner dragging my suitcase behind me. Smiling, he welcomed me as a long-lost friend. Instead of calling one of the interpreters, I wanted to try the few bits of Creole that I had learned so I simply asked him, "Kouman ou rele?" or "What is your name?" He gave me an answer that was as incomprehensible to me as supercalifragilisticexpialidocious from the movie *Mary Poppins.* Nothing in his response sounded like any name I had ever heard before. I did not know how to say that I did not understand him, or to speak slower, or to simply repeat his answer. So I again asked him, "Kouman ou rele?"

After asking the same question four times and getting the same long-winded response from him, one of the interpreters came over to me and said, "He has been telling you his name is Fessen. He remembered your name, how come you did not remember his?"

I felt awful. I had never even bothered to learn his name the year before, let alone try to remember it. I did recall him being at the rectory, but that was all. My "mission" was in Pendus, not in Gros Morne, so I did not have myself in "mission mode." I was tired, and it had been a long day. We weren't at the rectory very long! How could I have been expected to know and remember his name? I meet lots of new people every day when I am in Haiti! All of them were good excuses to me, but not truly valid ones, nor were they ones he would have understood or even mattered to him.

Fessen did not want, or need, anything from me other than the respect and human dignity that comes with being noticed and of being a person worthy of being remembered. Nothing else mattered to him. He had remembered my name. I did not reciprocate that gift back to him. I can honestly say that I have never let that happen again. I have been back through Gros Morne and the rectory many times since then. I always get out of the vehicle and find Fessen and greet him by name and with a hug.

If I learned nothing else from my many trips to Haiti, this lesson alone would make it all worthwhile. Building relationships is the heart and soul of being in mission mode or better yet trying to do Christ's work. You don't go into mission mode like turning a light switch on and off. It must become part of every moment of your life. You are making an impact on everyone you meet wherever you may be and however little time you have with them. I learned that it does not take great deeds to make an impact either; that even the simplest acts of kindness can have a lasting effect. There always is time to make a positive, lasting impression and one you may never know that you made.

For me there are two very challenging aspects from learning this lesson. First and foremost, I must be able to take my revelation back home with me and try to use it every day in all areas of my life. It is not worthwhile to learn a lesson and then never use it! It is challenging to implement this lesson daily.

Second, lessons are difficult enough to master when they develop in one relatively short period. They can be hard to grasp when the learning opportunities take such a long time to unfold. You must keep paying attention. God can be very subtle in his teaching. Reflection on what has happened is the best way to tie the events together to catch what is being taught! It can be very easy to miss.

I always find Fessen when at the rectory in Gros Morne.

3

Haitian History and Perspective

We cannot escape history.

—*Abraham Lincoln*

Many times, there are misconceptions about why poverty prevails in a county, especially when it exists for an extended period. It was important for me to learn some of Haiti's history and background to help understand its current situation.

I will not attempt to give a complete recounting of Haiti's history. For a great book on this subject, read Paul Farmer's *The Uses of Haiti,* the first book I read before I became actively involved in our Haiti ministry.

Haiti's Independence Day is January 1, 1804, but its "modern" history goes back to Christopher Columbus who first set foot on the island shortly before Christmas in 1492. It was not his first landfall in the New World as it followed his historic October 12, 1492, landing in San Salvador, which now is part of present-day Bahamas. Columbus's flagship the *Santa Maria* later sank after running aground on the Haiti's northern shore on his maiden voyage across the Atlantic. An anchor from that ship is on display at the National Museum of Haiti in Port-au-Prince (PAP). It was reported that Columbus said that this island was the most beautiful of all the new lands that he discovered.

The island was originally named *Insula Hispana,* which meant the "Spanish island." Over the years that name evolved to its current name Hispaniola. It was under the control of both the Spanish and the French at various points in time. Today, Haiti is the western third of the island with the Dominican Republic the eastern two-thirds.

The Taino were the indigenous natives who lived on the island when Columbus arrived. Initially they were tolerant of the Europeans. Colonization of the island began in earnest in 1493 with the arrival of 1,300 men from Spain, who then established themselves near present-day Santo Domingo, Dominican Republic. However, in less than twenty-five years, the Taino were virtually wiped from existence. Many of them died due to exposure to new European diseases, such as smallpox, from which they had no immunity. However, a significant number also died from harsh treatment from enslavement by the early colonists. The island was then essentially repopulated with slaves from Africa.

By the late 1600s, Haiti was under the control of the French, who renamed it Saint-Domingue. Because it became the richest and most prosperous colony in the West Indies, it was nicknamed the Pearl of the Antilles. Sugarcane, coffee, and mahogany were some of its most desired exports back to Europe and helped to enrich both Paris and France.

Slave trading continued to be a prominent part of Haiti's history. While exact numbers are unavailable, many estimates show there were nearly fifteen times more slaves than the estimated thirty thousand white ruling class members by the end of the eighteenth century. In 1791, a slave insurrection began a struggle for independence from France that transpired over the next dozen years. A natural military leader, Toussaint Louverture, led this push for independence. However, he was captured in 1802 and sent to a prison in France, where he eventually died.

Haiti's extended conflict with France had a great influence on the growth of the United States. France sold the Louisiana Purchase to Thomas Jefferson and the United States in 1803 in part to finance its continuing battle with Haiti's slave revolt. In addition, Napoleon realized that if he could not protect and control a small Caribbean island, there was no way to defend the nearly landlocked territory west of the Mississippi River. This acquisition nearly doubled the size of the USA at the time.

Jean Jacques Dessalines was selected commander in chief to continue the fight for independence after Toussaint's capture. He was part of the final battle with France, which occurred at Vetieres near Cap Haitien on November 18, 1803. However, the legend of that battle belonged to Francois Capois. He led a charge toward the French amid a rain of bullets. His horse was shot and fell under him. While many around him also fell, Capois grabbed his sword and continued to lead the charge on foot. French General Rochambeau watched this transpire from afar and issued a sudden cease-fire. He sent a mounted officer toward the insurgents. He dismounted and saluted the Haitian warriors and purportedly said, "General Rochambeau sends his compliments to the general who has just covered himself with such glory." He then returned to his position and the fighting resumed. Ultimately the French were defeated. Today there is a bronze monument near Cap Haitien remembering this battle. It consists of a statute of Capois, his fallen horse, and several other soldiers moving forward.

Under Dessalines's leadership a formal cessation of the revolution and acknowledgment of Haiti's independence was pronounced nearly six weeks later in Gonaives on January 1, 1804. Dessalines restored the name Haiti to the newly independent country as a tribute to its indigenous roots. *Haiti* was a Taino word that meant "land of high mountains."

The French flag is a mixture of red, white, and blue. It was reduced to only red and blue with a crest over it to become the new Haitian flag. This new color scheme symbolized the "whites" being removed from Haiti.

In his book *The Uses of Haiti*, Paul Farmer said:

> There exists outside Haiti no other case of an enslaved people breaking its own chains and using military might to defeat a powerful colonial power. Haiti was more than the New World's second oldest republic, more even than the first

black republic of the modern world. Haiti was
the first free nation of free men to arise within,
and in resistance to, the emerging constellation
of Western European empire. (p. 63)

Dessalines was assassinated in 1806 (which went unpunished).
Thereafter, control of the country was temporarily split between
the north and the south. Henri Christophe led the north from Cap
Haitien and Alexandre Petion led the south from PAP.

To help protect Haiti from a possible return by the French,
Christophe built the Citadelle, a massive stone fortress built on the
highest point in Haiti. It provided protection of the Cap Haitien harbor and a lookout for miles around, yet was located about five miles
inland south of Cap Haitien.

It took more than twenty thousand men over a decade to build
this mammoth fortress. The walls at the base were up to twenty-five
feet thick and were built with a mortar that consisted of a mixture of
lime, sugarcane, molasses, and cow's blood. It was fortified with over
350 cannons, some of which had a range that could accurately reach
the Cap Haitien harbor. Through the years, the Citadelle has withstood several earthquakes and hurricanes. It was named a UNESCO
World Heritage site in 1982.

Early leaders for the young country all seemed to have different
titles, such as emperor of Haiti for Dessalines, president of the republic for Alexandre Petion, and king for Henri Christophe.

After Haiti gained its independence, it was the single biggest
trading partner with the young United States of America for the next
twenty-five years, even more than England, France, Spain, and other
European countries. No wonder France fought so long to try and
keep it. Despite this, the United States did not officially recognize
the sovereignty of Haiti until after the Proclamation Emancipation
was issued in 1863. I suppose our leaders were fearful of a similar
slave uprising in our country.

In 1825, the king of France demanded and obtained from Haiti
a "restoration" fee of 150 million francs to former plantation and slave

owners as well as to France for the costs of the war. In exchange for these sums, France finally agreed to recognize Haiti's independence as a nation. That sum was later reduced to ninety million francs in 1838. In today's prices that would amount to over fifteen billion dollars! These payments to France over the next 120 years greatly hampered Haiti's economy as it took much of Haiti's annual budget just to pay the obligation and its interest. From nearly the beginning, it was impossible for Haiti to escape its destiny as a debtor nation.

There were many different leaders throughout the ensuing years as well as a period of US military control from 1914 to 1934. Francois Duvalier, also known as Papa Doc, was elected president in 1957 and ruled until his death in 1971. His nineteen-year-old son Jean-Claude "Baby Doc" Duvalier succeeded him as president for life. He led the country until his ouster in 1986 when he fled to exile in France. A generation later he returned to Haiti for a couple years before his death at the age of sixty-three in 2014.

In December 1990 a former Catholic priest named Jean-Bertrand Aristide was elected president for a five-year term. That term was cut short by a coup in 1991. Aristide was later restored as president in 1994 to complete that initial term. The new constitution did not allow for him to run for a second consecutive term, so Rene Preval was elected in 1995. He completed his five-year term without incident. Aristide was then returned to the presidency in 2000. Once again, there was a "removal" of Aristide in 2004 where he was forced into exile to Africa. The next election saw Rene Preval reelected a second time to the office of president.

The 2010 election was delayed over ten months due to the devastating earthquake in January 2010. Michel Martelly was the final run-off presidential winner in March 2011.

Writing for the Ontario Historical Society during Haiti's bicentennial in 2004, Dr. Eric Pierre summarized as follows:

> The colonial powers quickly realized the significance of our [Haiti's] independence. They viewed it as a dangerous precedent and vowed to

keep the liberation disease from spreading. They quarantined the new nation. Cardinal Talleyrand called Haiti a 'haven of barbarian piracy' until France granted conditional recognition to the independence in 1825 upon payment of the first installment...it took the United States 60 years to recognize Haiti's independence...No foreign heads of state set foot on Haitian territory for any extended visit before President Franklin D. Roosevelt in 1934 at the end of the American occupation.

While all these names and changes may seem confusing, the history of leadership of Haiti gives me greater admiration for the constitutional formation and history of leadership in the United States. When Preval stepped down after his first term, he was the first ruler to peaceably continue to live in Haiti after his tenure as the country's leader. The rest either died while in office or were killed or exiled. That covers a period of over two hundred years after Haiti's independence!

Despite its natural resources, it was economically handicapped and faced with international isolation from the start. Add to this mix, the freed slaves that formed the new country were not very educated. The slave masters did not want them to think, just to work. With this brief historical summary, it is easy to see why Haiti never had a very good chance to thrive and grow as a young country.

⤜⇒●●⇐⤛

The island of Hispaniola is the twenty-second largest island in the world and the second biggest in the Caribbean after Cuba. It is located southeast of Cuba with the closest point of Haiti being only fifty miles from the southeast corner of Cuba. The country of Haiti is approximately the size of the state of Maryland and currently has a population of nearly ten million people. One of the more unique facts about Haiti is half of its population is eighteen years old or younger!

Per statistics from the United Nations, Haiti's maternal and infant death rates are the highest in the western hemisphere and among the highest in the world. Often this is due to lack of adequate health care, especially in the rural mountain areas of Haiti. Haiti health ministry lists Haiti with 59 infant deaths per 1,000 births as compared to only 7.5 infant deaths per 1,000 in the USA. The maternal mortality rate for Haiti is 160 per 1,000 births as compared to only 12 per 1,000 in the USA.

One of my pet peeves concerning Haiti is how it usually is referenced. Most people say "Haiti, the poorest country in the western hemisphere." It is as if that last phrase is part of the country's name! While it is the poorest, with an annual income of approximately $500 per person, it still is a country that is rich in its heritage, history, and culture.

———

Creole is the language spoken in Haiti. Creole is defined as a stable natural language that has developed from a simplified mixture of languages. This is precisely what happened in Haiti. Through the centuries, the slaves that were brought to Haiti came from many parts of Africa and thus had different language backgrounds. Often those slaves were intentionally separated upon arrival in Haiti to keep their ability to communicate to a minimum.

For years, the common language the slaves heard spoken was the French of the slave masters, many of whom were not the most linguistically proficient Frenchmen themselves. The slaves were not educated either and therefore could not read and write, so the Creole that they spoke was all learned orally. Therefore, it began as a phonetic language that was not written down until much later.

Unlike the French that it was based upon, it is very simplified. First, there are no silent letters. Every letter, or letter combination, is pronounced the same every time it is used in a word. Once you know what those sounds are, you can easily pronounce words that are unfamiliar to you. That is very different from French and other Latin-based languages. Creole also does not have conjugations to learn. A verb is the same no matter who the subject is in the sentence! Creole nouns also are not gender based, meaning there is no masculine and feminine to memorize and master. These facets help make Creole an easy language to learn!

Even with these characteristics, it still takes a lot of work to master speaking it. I have been trying to become fluent for a long time and have yet to do so. My problem is I am only in Haiti for relatively short time frames. By the end of my stay I am feeling better about my ability to communicate. Then I go home and don't use Creole until I return the next year. Like everything else in life, practice make you better and the same applies with learning a new language, even a simple one like Creole!

Despite Creole's widespread use in Haiti by most the population, French was the official language of Haiti until the constitution of 1987 when Creole was finally recognized as a co-official language. It was even later in the 2000s that Creole was actually incorporated into curriculum and taught in the schools.

>➤●◄<

St. Mary Cathedral is twinned with St. Joseph Church in Pendus, Haiti. Pendus in Creole is pronounced "Pawn-due." It is in the northwest mountains of Haiti in the Artibonite Department, one of ten departments in the country. That department coincides with the Gonaives Diocese of the Catholic Church as well.

Because there are not enough priests for every village in the rural areas of Haiti, many such areas simply become chapel areas to a more centrally located and more populated church. A chapel is a satellite to the core church, meaning the chapel relies on the priest stationed at the central church. St. Joseph Church has six such chapels surrounding it. The two that are physically closest to Pendus are the two that are accessible only on foot and not by vehicle, Massacre and

Mayombe. The other four chapels are in Berard, Kayimit, Savanne Carre, and Montbayard.

St. Joseph School in Pendus is a primary school. It has classrooms through sixth grade. The closest secondary school, the equivalent to our middle and high school grades, is in Gros Morne located about ten miles away. However, if a child was fortunate enough to continue his education beyond the primary school, he might wind up attending a school much further away, such as in Gonaives, Port-de-Paix, or even Port-au-Prince. Often the determining factor in where a child would continue school is where his or her extended family lives so he could stay with them.

———⋙◆⋘———

As I have mentioned, building relationships is the most important aspect of our twinning partnership in Haiti. We have made many lasting friendships over the years. The names of many of those friends will appear throughout this book. As a simple introduction, the following are just the tip of the iceberg of those who have played a critical role in facilitating our visits.

Father Ronel Charelus was instrumental in starting our twinning relationship. Everyone lovingly calls him Father Cha Cha! In Creole, *Cha Cha* is pronounced "sha-sha." The *ch* in Creole is pronounced like the *ch* in *Chicago*. Born June 14, 1958, in the northwest part of Haiti, he was ordained a Montfort priest on December 28, 1992, and was the priest responsible for St. Joseph Church in Pendus, Haiti, through June 2004. Thereafter, he has been stationed at St. Louis du Nord in Port-de-Paix; St. Bridget Church in New York City; and now at Notre Dame du Maillais in Le Marillais, France.

While St. Joseph Church has always had six satellite chapels, St. Joseph was not yet a stand-alone parish in the early years of this twining relationship. It was under the umbrella of Our Lady of the Light Church in Gros Morne, which is located about ten miles from Pendus. The rectory where the priests then resided is also in Gros Morne.

Father Wilner Donecia was our second priest, beginning in July 2004 through the end of 2010. He was born December 28, 1950, in northern Haiti and was ordained a Montfort priest on April 25, 1982. He continues as pastor at Our Lady of the Light Church in Gros Morne, Haiti.

Father Joseph Telcin was the third priest at St. Joseph in Pendus. The oldest of seven siblings, he was born on October 11, 1975, and ordained a Montfort priest on April 15, 2007. He took over in December 2010 and was there until reassigned to a brand-new parish on the southern coast of Haiti in mid-2012. Sadly, Father Joseph died in a motorcycle accident in the southern mountains several months later.

The fourth and current priest at St. Joseph Church is Father Sylvio Jean. He was born December 27, 1959, and ordained a Montfort priest on April 28, 1996. He was assigned to St. Joseph in May 2013. Shortly before that time, St. Joseph became a stand-alone parish, meaning it would have Father Sylvio on a full-time basis and would be fiscally responsible for itself and its six chapels. It would also mean that Father Sylvio would now be the first priest to live full time in Pendus.

Sister Jackie Picard and Sister Pat Dillon are both women religious in the order of the Religious of Jesus and Mary (RJM for short). Both were born in the USA but were living in Gros Morne at the beginning of our twinning relationship. They both are still there at the time of the writing of this book! Sister Jackie was born in Rhode Island and is a nurse. Before moving to Haiti in September 1997, she did extensive work in elderly nursing homes and with homeless people with AIDS. She currently is instrumental in running Alma Mater Hospital in Gros Morne. Sister Pat was born in the Bronx and worked for twenty-four years for Northwest Bronx community and clergy coalition before moving to Haiti in February 1998. She has a passion for and worked at length in various agricultural and forestry projects in Haiti. She also helps in translating reports and obtaining funding for local parish schools and is responsible for overseeing a primary school of 550 students run by her congregation.

There have been several interpreters for us through the years. Each has been much more than an interpreter. They have all become valued friends and trusted advisors. Those young men have grown up with us over the years were Their names are Fritzner Guerrier, Sergo Castin, Roody "Octa" Pierre, Serge Fortune, and Rueben "Benedict" Remy. I have devoted an entire chapter later for both Fritzner and Benedict.

Madam Marcel Garson is the nurse that runs the dispensary in Pendus. She also is the head cook for each of our groups that go to Pendus. I have elaborated more on her several times throughout the book. She is such an integral part of Pendus that we often refer to her as Mama Pendus, which translates as "Mother of Pendus." Madam Marcel Garson is not her given name. It simply means Mrs. Marcel Garson. Culturally that is how a married woman is referred to in Haiti. It took me nearly fifteen years to learn that her given name is Cetoute Celianise Garson.

The concept of the Parish Twinning Program of America (PTPA) began in Nashville, Tennessee, over fifty years ago through the efforts of businessman Harry Hosey. He first saw the plight of the poor in Haiti while on a pleasure cruise ship visit there. He dedicated his efforts to improving conditions for the poor in Haiti through his Nashville parish of St. Henry. Later in 1978 he took Theresa Patterson, also from Nashville, on her first visit to Haiti.

The idea of parish outreach by other churches germinated from that trip. The ministry began slowly. PTPA was not officially incorporated as a 501(c)(3) tax-free entity until 1992. Initially the focus was entirely on Haiti but has grown to include all the countries of the Caribbean, Latin America, and the Philippines. Its purpose is to provide linkages between churches in the United States and those other countries.

The PTPA picked "twinning" to describe what it does because it "implies a coming together in a close relationship. Through this coming together, the twin parishes are joined in their search for an ever-deepening faith and in their shared struggle to lend hope to poor parishes." When a twinning relationship is established, it becomes "a bridge whereby the love of God flows in both directions as parishes learn to care, share and pray for one another."

Under the tutelage of Theresa Patterson, the only executive director the PTPA has had through all these years, the PTPA has grown. Today there are over three hundred twinned relationships actively involved in Haiti and approximately another fifty throughout the other parts of the world.

Neg Mawon is to Haiti what the Liberty Bell is to the
United States. The bronze statue commemorates the
end of slavery in Haiti as the former slave blows on a
conch shell to announce his new found freedom.

4

My Personal Background

*Trust in the Lord with all your heart, rely
not on your own understanding.*

—*Proverbs 3:5*

THERE IS A HAITIAN PROVERB that translates to "One sees from where one stands." I will expand further on that idea in a later chapter. However, I think it is important to know a little of my background to better understand my experiences in Haiti. It just might help you appreciate the vantage point from where I have stood in my lifetime.

I firmly believe every lifetime experience becomes part of the foundation for what is to come later in your life. Even if the experiences do not seem to be related, God somehow draws them all together. The first and most important foundational experience for me was my family. I was born in Lafayette on May 30, 1955. My parents are James D. and Theresa Newell.

My earliest childhood memories revolved around a strong sense of family and church. Both of my parents came from large rural Benton County families. There were ten siblings in my mother's family and nine in my dad's. Between the two families, I had over seventy first cousins and many more second and third cousins. I have great memories of family get-togethers, many of which revolved around church functions such as weddings, baptisms, first communions, and funerals.

I took this strong family connection for granted, assuming everyone must have had the same experience. My mother's side of the family was all Catholic. My dad converted when they were married in 1950. However, if he didn't tell you that he converted, you'd never know he wasn't a cradle Catholic.

Dad didn't talk about God and religion much, but he showed you how you were supposed to live it. Without using words, he taught me about working hard, being proud of a job well done, helping others, being honest and loyal, and treating others like you would want to be treated. He also wanted me to earn a living using my head and not my back like he had to do his whole life.

My mom instilled in me a strong sense of self-confidence, the importance of a good education, a "penny saved is a penny earned" mentality, and the ability to plan for tomorrow and not just for today. She made sure we attended Mass faithfully every week and received all our sacraments along the way.

I truly had a storybook childhood. One great blessing was our family never had to move. My parents bought their house on a Friday, moved in on Saturday, went to the hospital on Sunday, and I was born on Monday. Dad still lives there today as did Mom until her death in 2014. This provided me with a well-established sense of roots and stability.

I am the oldest of three siblings. My sisters, Jana and Julie, are four and eleven years younger than me. We each were blessed with many successes in our lives, academically, athletically, and socially. We have supported and attended each other's events our entire lives.

My love for sports led me to do football and basketball radio broadcasts for my high school radio station. That experience opened the door for me to work as a sports journalist for the *Journal & Courier* newspaper during my four years of undergraduate studies at Purdue University. The communication skills honed while doing something I enjoyed proved to be valuable in law school, in my subsequent career as a lawyer, and now as I write this book.

I met my wife Sharon while we were in high school. We began dating near the end of our senior year and even went to the prom together. On our first date, she asked me three questions: "Do you drink? Do you smoke? Do you believe in God?" I must have answered correctly as three years later we were married between my junior and senior years at Purdue. More solid building blocks for my life's foundation were being added as my family experiences continued to grow.

God blessed Sharon and me with differing personal religious styles as well as different religions. Sharon grew up Lutheran and went to a Lutheran school through eighth grade. She was always more prayerful and open to talking about her relationship with God than I was. She clearly was much more ready to share her faith with others. While I was prone to keeping my religion personal and not likely to openly share it, I was more set in my faith. Sharon would call it stubborn, such as never missing church on Sunday and never going to any church but a Catholic one. I didn't question things. My outlook usually was "Don't worry, things will work out." From my point of view, they always had in my lifetime. Gradually over time, the best attributes of both of our styles, my steadfastness and Sharon's openness, have rubbed off on each other. God was using each of us to enhance the other!

Without me asking, Sharon later converted to Catholicism. Changing denominations wasn't a stumbling block for her like it was for me. She was more concerned that we worship together as a family. With her parochial school background as part of her foundation, she has become an ardent defender and practitioner of her Catholic faith ever since!

The proudest moments of my life were the births of our two sons. Justin Matthew was born on March 12, 1981. Sharon immediately felt he was here for a special purpose. Our second son Kyle Andrew was born October 8, 1983. Both were a gift from God. Our faith grew as we tried to teach them about God.

Sharon and I conscientiously tried to be as involved in our kids' lives as we possibly could, with each activity bringing its own set of adventures, friends, and memories. While our boys' extended family was not nearly as large as what I grew up with, they did have their grandparents living close by and being actively involved in their lives.

Family get-togethers, especially during the holidays, were moments to treasure.

We attempted to install ritualistic family times together, whether it was meal time at holidays, family ski trips, summertime at a cottage in Michigan with our great friends, or merely a family campout at many of Indiana's state parks. In addition, our family vacations took us to many parts of this country. However busy our lives got throughout the years, we could always count on these special times together.

Justin and I were blessed with many personal times together as well. Two of those times came in the summers of 1994 and 1995 when we went camping in the Florida Keys and backpacking in the Appalachian Mountains. The views we shared of God's creation, from snorkeling in Loo Key to sitting high atop John's Rock, were spectacular! As it says in Romans 1:20: "Ever since the creation of the world, his (God's) invisible attributes of eternal power and divinity have been able to be understood and perceived in what he has made."

However, my "perfect" storybook life came to a screeching halt in January 1996 when Justin died as a result of an accident at our home. Normal was never going to be the same for us.

Those next few days were the most difficult for Sharon, Kyle, and me. Thankfully we had good friends and family to support us along the way. That support was especially evident at the visitation as over two thousand attended the wake. Many were close friends; some were mere acquaintances. Many drove a great distance only to be with us for but a moment. Their presence was what was important to help sustain us through that time.

The outpouring continued the next day at the funeral Mass, the gravesite, and the meal back at St. Mary Cathedral. The church was packed as were the cemetery and school gym. The words of Paul come to mind from 1 Corinthians 10:13: "No trial has come to you but what is human. God is faithful and will not let you be tried beyond your strength; but with the trial he will provide a way out, so that you may be able to bear it."

Since Justin's death I have read the Bible a lot, many times more than I did my first forty years combined. Now, it seemed like God was speaking to me, or maybe I was simply paying closer attention. C. S. Lewis once said, "God whispers to us in our pleasures, speaks in our conscience, but shouts in our pain. It is His megaphone to rouse a deaf world." I had an insatiable desire to learn more about my faith. I did not like the uncomfortable feeling of not knowing the details of the many stories of the Bible. I wanted to be better equipped to get into a discussion on any matter regarding the Bible or my faith and be able to carry on a dialogue with others accurately and insightfully.

Another part of God's "providing a way to bear it" placed a men's Christ Renews His Parish weekend at St. Mary one month later. This religious retreat was well-timed to help keep my jump-started spiritual life going. It gave me an opportunity to know other men from my church on a level I had never experienced. I knew their favorite Bible verses instead of their favorite athlete. We shared our life stories and faith journeys. I no longer felt compelled to keep my beliefs to myself. The change in me wasn't immediate, but it eventually evolved. Sharing my experiences, struggles, and my faith began to feel natural to me.

As an outgrowth from that retreat, we formed a men's Bible study group that has continually met at 6:30 a.m. weekly for the past two decades. My continued search for understanding also led me to take and complete a three-year curriculum in Ecclesial Lay Ministry from our diocese.

Over the past several years I have had many chances to talk to various groups about various aspects of my faith and my life journey. I have relished those opportunities. I know that would not have happened before Justin died. As it says in 1 Peter 3:15: "Always be ready to give an explanation to anyone who asks you for a reason for your hope."

Raising your child in faith is one of a parent's most important functions. What is more remarkable is when a child can enhance a parent's faith. Maybe that was Justin's special purpose Sharon always talked about.

My absolute favorite passage in the Bible is Proverbs 3:5, which says, "Trust in the Lord with all of your heart, rely not on your own understanding." While we are not prohibited from trying to understand God's ways, we are told not to lean or rely on our ability, or better yet our inability, to make the pieces fit. After all, Isaiah 55:8 says, "For my thoughts are not your thoughts, nor are your ways my ways, says the Lord."

Three years later the opportunity for St. Mary's Haiti ministry arose. Not only did I have Sharon's support to go, my faith journey had prepared me to take that next step, which was more like a leap of faith. God truly wove an intricate pattern with the many threads of my life to prepare me to travel to Haiti.

An eagerness for this ministry quickly developed within me. As I am writing this book, I am amazed that I have completed my twentieth trip to Haiti. What makes this ministry extra special for me is the fact that I share this newfound passion, and most of the experiences set forth in this book, with both Sharon and Kyle.

The Newell family in Pendus, Haiti: Jeff, Sharon and Kyle

5

Highway to Heaven

Faith never knows where it is being led, but it loves and knows the One who is leading.

—*Oswald Chambers*

ST. MARY CATHEDRAL BEGAN ITS twinning relationship in Haiti in mid-1999. Two new priests had recently arrived at St. Mary, Father Dave Hellmann as pastor and Father Bob Klemme as associate pastor. Both had a passion for outreach ministries, especially in Haiti. Father Bob had either started or enhanced twinning relationships at the two prior Indiana churches he was stationed.

Sharon was on the parish council at that time when St. Mary agreed to establish a twinning relationship with a church in Haiti. Early in the summer of 1999, Father Bob contacted Theresa Patterson in Nashville, Tennessee, to get that process started. He knew that the PTPA's primary objective was to match Catholic churches in the United States with Catholic churches in Haiti.

Father Bob requested only two things for this new relationship. First, he wanted the church in Haiti to welcome us as visitors on a regular basis, and second, that the church in Haiti would have a school since St. Mary also had a school. Theresa said within days of Father Bob's call she got a call from Father Ronel Charelus of Pendus, Haiti. He was looking for a US church to twin with St Joseph Church in Pendus. He told her that it was more important to him that the church would make regular visits to Haiti than to simply send money. He also added that St. Joseph had a primary school! *Bingo*. That may have been the easiest match for Theresa Patterson to make out of over 350 twin church relationships currently established by PTPA.

Arrangements were made for Father Cha Cha to visit Lafayette in August 1999. I distinctly remember Father Bob bringing Father Cha Cha to meet me and Sharon for the first time at a downtown basketball tournament that August. Little did any of us know what the future would have in store for us. Father Cha Cha told me that he vividly remembers preaching from the Magnificat at St. Mary that weekend on the feast day of the Assumption of Our Blessed Mother. Talking about the newly formed twinning relationship, he quoted Mary by proclaiming, "The Lord has done great things for me and holy is his name" (Luke 1:49).

Father Bob put together a committee to plan St. Mary's first team visit to Pendus for mid-March, 2000, to coincide with the Feast of St. Joseph in Pendus on March 19. Sharon could not go. It was very difficult for her to get any vacation during the school year where she taught. However, she greatly encouraged me to go.

Including Father Bob, there were eleven on the initial St. Mary team. I knew all but Karen Sullivan and Jane McCaslin, as both were from other parishes. They came because they knew Father Bob. Of the group, only Father Bob and Karen had previously been to Haiti, so there were many first-time experiences being shared on this trip.

The whole visit provided sensory stimulation on a level I had never experienced. There were several things that stuck out in my mind from just my first few hours in Haiti. First, I faced the gauntlet of people as we exited the airport. There was no fence or rail keeping anyone back from the door as we exited the airport. There were over one hundred people pressed up against our group as we tried to walk from the building to our waiting vehicle. It was already dark, and my personal space was immediately violated! I was uncomfortable with everyone grabbing at my suitcase. No one wanted to take anything or even hurt me. They simply wanted to "help" so we would give them a tip.

There were also a few that were begging. One man was saying that he was hungry. Another said he had six children. Another man on crutches had one leg missing. I knew I would encounter poverty in a manner I never had before. I just wasn't expecting it so quickly and so up close and personal!

My next impression came from the drive to our guesthouse. The road was bumpier than most off-road excursions in the United States. The potholes often caused the bottom of our vehicle to scrape the ground. *Shanties* seemed to be a better name for most of the "homes" we passed along the way. Food stands lined the route as well, with some of the food being cooked over open fires. I could smell and see trash being burned along the edge of the road. People were walking in many of the roadways. I never did see a stop sign or a streetlight anywhere. Most of the streets were no wider than two lanes, but often there would be three cars abreast trying to pass each other in the most unexpected stretches of the street. It all seemed to be chaos!

We finally reached our guesthouse. There was no electricity there that entire night, which we learned was not unusual in this capital city of Port-au-Prince. It was called a rolling brownout as the entire city was not dark. The evening was very humid, yet the fans did not work, neither did the showers or the phones.

Despite these problems, we enjoyed the evening on the third-floor terrace overlooking the parts of Port-au-Prince that still had electricity and were all lit up, talking with each other, tasting our first Haitian Prestige beer, and enjoying the gentle Caribbean breeze.

Before we retired for the night, Karen pulled me aside. She said she had something she wanted to tell me but didn't know if she should. I did not know her prior to this trip, so I could not imagine what it was she wanted to say. She told me that her first trip to Haiti was in January 1996 with Father Bob. She got a message while in a village outside Port-au-Prince to return an emergency phone call to her husband. As any parent would be, she was anxious about what could be wrong at home. Once she got to a phone back in PAP, she found out her daughter was distressed over the death of one of her friends from school, our son Justin. She needed her mother's consolation. Now here Karen was on her second Haiti trip, and it was with me! What an impact it was to think that the news of my son's death would travel so quickly and as far away as rural Haiti. In some way, Justin actually beat me to Haiti and possibly led the way for me to go! Father Bob later said he remembered this happening too, but he did not know either Sharon or me at that time.

The final initial experience came throughout the night, listening to the many night noises such as a rah-rah band, engines backfiring, singing, roosters that crowed the entire night, dogs barking, some snoring, mosquitoes buzzing, and something that sounded a lot like gunshots!

Quite an end to an eye-opening day for me.

The next morning, Jane McCaslin approached me. She was the other person on the trip that I did not know beforehand. She said that her sister was a St. Mary parishioner. Since they had different last names I had not made the connection. Her sister was the mother of Justin's best friend! I had been in Haiti less than twenty-four hours, and I already had two encounters concerning Justin, who had been deceased for over four years by then! I was ecstatic. Nothing makes me happier than for someone to remember him and talk with me about him. I never imagined that would happen once in Haiti, let alone twice! How ironic was it that the two people I did not know were the ones with these connections to Justin? God was making me very comfortable to be on this trip. I knew then that I belonged in Haiti!

We took this first full day in Haiti to get acclimated and see some of Port-au-Prince and discover more about Haiti's history. First, we went to Visitation House (now Matthew 25 Guest House), where we learned about the Haitian Stations of the Cross. There was a beautiful mural depicting fourteen key historical events that have shaped Haiti's history through the present. The significance of each event was explained in a chronological order. It was very informative. We could also buy handcrafted wooden pieces as well as hand-painted artwork made by local artisans in PAP.

The most impactful part of the day came next, a visit to Mother Teresa's Sisters of Charity Children's clinic. We were barely inside the door when we were greeted by smiles and outstretched arms of the Haitian children that were well enough and old enough to walk! Everyone in our group held at least one child during our stay there. Some of us even held two at a time! One young boy led us to a back room where the younger, and sicker, children were. There were so many children there that many of the cribs had two babies in them. Many in our group held the smallest children and even helped to feed them. It was so amazing that they would stop crying as soon as they were picked up. They clearly were starved for human contact. It was very tough for all of us to leave that morning.

The next stop was St. Jean Bosco Church, which was burned during the massacre there on September 11, 1988, in an attempt to kill Jean Bertrand Aristide. He did manage to escape. It was never repaired and had been left as a memorial to that day's event. Next, we drove by where Fort Dimache once stood. It was a prison that had a painful history of torture and death. It had since been torn down. We then drove through City Soleil, the poorest section of Haiti. Literally built on a trash dump, that one square mile of real estate has one of the highest density populations of anywhere in the world. It was hard to imagine that humans could, or would, live there.

Other stops that day included the Catholic Cathedral and the Episcopal Cathedral. The latter contained gorgeous Haitian murals depicting many of the stories in the Bible with each of the characters being Haitian and not Caucasian. We also drove by the National Palace, the equivalent of the White House in the USA. (Unfortunately, all three of these beautiful places were destroyed a decade later in the 2010 earthquake.)

The next day we needed three vehicles to drive us from Port-au-Prince to Pendus. I was in the lead car driven by Father Cha Cha. I sat in the front passenger seat and had a great talk with him as we headed north on the highway that paralleled the coastline for the first couple of hours. Eventually we made a "bathroom" stop literally along the side of the road. When I got back into my vehicle, Sister

Jackie Picard got in to drive. I asked, "What happened to Father Cha Cha?" She replied matter-of-factly, "He is much too careful a driver. We will never get there!" I responded, "Did I just witness my first Haitian coup?" She tried hard not to laugh, but I finally got a big grin from her. I knew instantly that we would become good friends! I also learned quickly that she would be using the horn on the vehicle much more than the brakes the rest of the way!

The road that we were traveling on is Highway 1 in Haiti, which connects the two biggest cities in the country, Port-au-Prince and Cap Haitien, located further north on the coast. However, to call it either a road or a highway would be very misleading to most Americans. For openers, it was not all paved and it was the busiest and most important highway in Haiti. There were many stretches of the road that were gravel or even dirt. Potholes were everywhere. Where there was pavement, there were no lines, either in the middle of the road or along the edges.

Often a driver would take a line of travel on the opposite side of the road, thinking that portion to be better. Better simply means less bumpy to drive upon. At the same time the approaching vehicle would also be on its opposite side of the road doing the same thing. It always amazed me that both drivers thought the other side was the preferred side to drive on. Usually the two vehicles would wind up on the correct half of the road by the time they eventually passed each other, but not always! To make matters more exciting, this road dance often involved three or four vehicles, each jockeying for the smoothest portion of the roadway!

Because of the deplorable condition of the road, there would be stretches where you could not get out of second or third gear, so travel was very slow. What struck me as odd, there would often be a big speed bump on stretches of the nicer sections of the road to keep vehicles from going too fast. I found it humorous that the literal translation for speed bumps in Creole was "sleeping police." Many of the speed bumps were so big that a car, truck, or bus would have to come to a complete stop before proceeding over it. Many times, Haitian merchants, usually selling drinks or food, would be there to hawk their wares to the momentarily stopped vehicles and often with success. The passengers would simply transact the sale by reaching out the window to the waiting vendor. This concept sure beats the heck out of a drive-through!

What is most amazing is what I have just described was the best part of the road we traveled on that day! In the mountains, it got worse! Once we passed through Gonaives along the coast, we turned off Highway 1 and headed inland and upward. That route climbs through the mountains northwest toward Port-de-Paix.

From the moment, we turned off Highway 1, there were no more paved roads the rest of the way to Pendus. In addition, there were almost no gravel sections. Most of the way, the road was simply dirt. There was lots of evidence of recent rain in the area. When the road would get soft from the moisture, deep ruts would be left from the tires passing through. Traction could be very difficult in the mud especially as you tried to climb in elevation, making the indentations deeper. However, the aftermath of the rain seemed to me to be much worse than the mud. Once the road dried out, those big ruts hardened, almost like concrete. Navigating around those ruts was difficult and dangerous. Some were deep enough to damage a car or worse yet possibly tip a car and hurt the passengers. Car jockeying for the better lane of travel was ratcheted to a new level of importance!

There also were some huge potholes, big enough that all four wheels of our vehicle could rest inside at the same time. Several of those depressions still had water in them. I chuckled at the thought that we may have to roll up the windows to go through them! Without air conditioning, the windows had to stay rolled down or it would get too hot inside. Of course, you also had to deal with the dust from the road, especially whenever an oncoming car passed by. So you had to pick your poison, either endure the dust or the heat!

Our vehicle chose the dust, leaving our windows down. By the time we reached Pendus, we all looked like we had aged. The dust coated our hair, making us look much grayer and older than we were! Good thing that "gray" was easy to wash out!

When we reached the rectory in Gros Morne, we had to switch to two four-wheel drive vehicles for the final ten miles. That distance would take us another hour to traverse! Because the vehicles were smaller, several of us sat on top the luggage in the bed of the truck. The bumpiness intensified, both due to where we were now sitting as well as the continued worsening of the road. I now fully understood how a drive of only 120 miles—from Port-au-Prince to Pendus—could take eight to ten hours of drive time! Through the years, experiencing this road has prompted some memorable comments. One member once vividly described this drive as ten hours of riding over railroad tracks! Another simply said, "I'm glad my hemorrhoids are in remission!"

However, when we finally reached Pendus, we were warmly greeted, mainly by swarms of children but also by many of the villagers. I was embraced by one young boy before both of my feet hit the ground as I got off the back end of the truck! There were plenty of smiles, hugs, and laughter. It was exhilarating to receive such a heavenly welcome—from people we did not yet know.

There were also many introductions, meeting our new friends in Pendus! A key one was Madam Marcel Garson, a woman of many hats. She is both a nurse who runs the local clinic and the cook in charge of fixing our meals during our stay. She welcomed us with a feast she prepared for us upon our arrival. My sensory overload now included my taste buds! The meal, as all her meals are, was very good!

Despite the harsh travel conditions, I labeled the road from Gonaives to Pendus the Highway to Heaven. My analogy was, like life, the road was full of lots of twists and turns, ups and downs, and potholes but the struggle to reach the final destination was worth every effort it took to get there. Besides, the welcome we received in Pendus has to be a precursor to the welcome awaiting us one day in heaven!

The Highway to Heaven is my name for the dirt road stretching from coastal Gonaives to Pendus, located in the northwest mountains of Haiti. Originally there were five river crossings along the way. Progress is being made as there are now bridges on all but the final river near Pendus.

6

Wisdom Found in Haitian Proverbs

Not to know is bad, not to wish to know is worse.
—African Proverb

ONE OF MY FIRST MEMORIES of going to Haiti was learning of the existence and the incredible wisdom of Haitian proverbs. These great sayings, often no longer than most bumper sticker slogans, shed a great insight into the culture of Haiti. These sayings can break down life situations into a simple, easy to remember, yet very powerful concept. More importantly, they are equally applicable to learning about life whether you are in Haiti, the United States, or anywhere else. Many of these proverbs are at the core of building relationships.

The first Haitian proverb I ever heard was "Fòk ou nan plas yon moun pou'w konprann sa lap viv," which translates to "One sees from where one stands." Right away I couldn't help but think of our similar saying "Don't criticize another until you've walked a mile in their shoes." I think it struck such a deep cord within me because I was surrounded by sights, sounds, smells, tastes, and situations I had never experienced before!

It seemed to me that many people, including me, have opinions about third world countries such as Haiti. Yet how many of those opinions were formed with accurate knowledge and background? How could I begin to know anything about Haitians or their way of life, especially if I have never been there? But being there isn't enough either. I can't really "know" anything unless I lived there. Even that may not be sufficient. My background and relative affluence—and my skin color—would never allow me to experience life the same as a Haitian! However, being there is still better than not being there! And trying to learn and absorb all that I can is better than not trying at all. Hopefully the vantage from which I see will improve because of the variety of new places I will be standing during my time in Haiti!

There is another similar proverb on point that I like as well: "Woch nan dlo pa konnen doule woch non soley." This means "The rock in the water does not know the suffering of the rock in the sun." While we may all be "rocks," where we are determines our perspective. We, as Americans, have been in the comfort of the water much more than we have been in the heat of the sun!

These proverbs go two ways. It is not just me who is learning something from a new perspective from my being in Haiti. The Haitians learn from us too. The last night of one of our early visits to Pendus, Benedict was sitting alone in the school yard under a beautiful full moon. He was sad that we were leaving. I went over to comfort him and assure him we were coming back. It was a fact I knew he knew, but he was sad nonetheless. I got Fritzner to come translate for me. I told Benedict that we could have a connection despite the two thousand miles that separated us. I told Fritzner to tell him that whenever he was lonely, Benedict could always look up at the moon and know that I would be looking at it too. That was something we could share. Instead of translating for me, Fritzner turned to me and said with all seriousness, "You mean it is the same moon?"

By Haitian standards, Fritzner was very educated. He had completed high school. That is an accomplishment in a country where barely 40 percent of the children attend school and a vast majority rarely get past the elementary level. Still, it shocked me that Fritzner would not have realized there was only one moon or that it could be seen in other places besides Haiti. It made me realize just how our world vision is shaped in so many ways by so many circumstances, most of which are truly beyond our control.

⟫●⟪

Another early proverb that impacted me was "Dèyè Mon Gen Mon," which means "Beyond the Mountain is a Mountain." My first visit to Haiti taught me that adage is true both literally and figuratively. It is true literally as it took us nearly ten hours to drive the 120-mile trip from Port-au-Prince to Pendus, Haiti on our first visit. That is roughly five times longer than needed to traverse that same distance in the United States. The biggest reason it took so long was the mountains. It seemed like there was an unending chain of mountains to get past to reach Pendus. Every time we climbed up and around one mountain there was another standing in front of us and another looming after that as well! My initial encounter with these mountains was by car. Most Haitians do not have a vehicle. They have to walk in these mountains. Imagine how daunting they become when you are on foot!

In addition, it was true figuratively. Most Haitians do not have access to good medical care; over 50 percent of the children do not attend school; infrastructure such as paved roads and bridges, especially in rural areas, are uncommon; good clean drinking water is not readily available; and the list could go on and on. Other troubles such as natural disasters, hurricanes, cholera, Zika virus, and political instability also seem to constantly loom on Haiti's horizon, one after another! Haiti never seems to catch a break in avoiding problems.

⟫●⟪

I learned the proverb "Sa Bondye sere pouw, lavales oa ka pote ale" on my first hike up to Mayombe. Translated, it means "What God has brought us, no flood can take away." It was a difficult, two-hour hike up the mountain from Pendus. The chapel that existed upon our arrival was only about twenty feet by twenty feet in size

53

with an uneven dirt floor; palm-woven sides; and a roof that was part palm leaves, part tin roof, and part missing, meaning gaping holes, that provided no protection at all.

As we began to interact with the townspeople that came to meet us, I attempted to give a young boy, maybe two years old, a piece of candy. He kept hiding behind his mother, grabbing onto her leg to keep his mother between me and him. His mother apologized saying that he had never seen a white person before. Using the interpreter, I asked, "When was the last time a white person had been in Mayombe?" Three of the matriarchs in the chapel conversed with each other before one replied that a French priest had been there about ten years earlier. I then asked, "When was the last time an American had been in Mayombe?" Once again they conversed, and their answer was "Never!" The feeling that I may have been the first American to be there overwhelmed me! I had never experienced that before!

We were ready to hike back down the mountain when one of those matriarchs uttered the above proverb. Why did she say that? We had not brought anything, other than some candy! We had not promised to do anything for Mayombe. We had not even promised to come back! Yet she felt that our mere presence was something significant. What we brought to the people of Mayombe was hope. Someone from far away now knew about Mayombe, and now possibly cared about Mayombe. How else could they explain why Americans that had never before stepped foot there had exerted so much energy just to come and spend but a few moments with the people of Mayombe! Clearly to them, our presence was a gift from God and not from us. There was now a hope that could not be swept away by any means.

———⟫◆⟪———

Both civil unrest in the early 2000s and several subsequent natural catastrophes have caused severe hardships in Haiti. The most immediate hardship usually is hunger. Either type of calamity leads to either a spike in the cost of food or a total shortage of food that is available. After one such event, Father Cha Cha sent me the proverb "Sak vid pa kanpe," which means "An empty bag cannot stand." Clearly he was referring to the many people that were hungry.

While most of those disasters or political events did not occur in the northwest mountains of Haiti, the repercussions were being felt in Pendus. Whether it was civil strife or storms causing the problem, commerce often was slowed or even halted. Gas prices would quickly inflate, making it tougher and even more expensive to get such staples as rice and cooking oil. With an average annual income of much less than $2 per day, the poor were barely getting by before such troubles arose. The fate of one without adequate food would be much worse than simply "not standing."

During several of these times St. Mary Cathedral spearheaded relief efforts for Pendus and its chapels. Because there would never be enough to feed everyone in each of these areas, the priests would typically use the money we sent to feed the children a meal while at school. Unlike in the United States, the schools in the Pendus area did not have a school lunch program to feed the children. Father's solution seemed strange to me at first, but he explained that a child that ate at school would then skip eating when at home. That would then allow more food at home to be shared by the rest of the family. It broke my heart to hear this, but that was a simple fact of life in Haiti.

We were in Haiti during one of these food shortages. I saw some of the school children receiving their bowl of rice and beans at school. There were several younger siblings that did not attend school standing at the doorway, anxiously watching just a few feet away. Without fail, the older siblings all walked over and shared their daily portions with the younger ones. That sharing simply occurred by scooping a couple spoonful of rice into an outstretched hand that was both eager and thankful to get even that meager amount!

When translated, "Demen ap pi bon" means "Tomorrow will be better." Haitians have an uncanny ability to focus on what they have, even if all they have is hope for tomorrow! To me, they almost will themselves not to be burdened by the many obstacles that I see them confronted with daily, such as lack of food, water, medical care, education opportunities, adequate roads, and more.

I have witnessed Haitians exhibit joy and thankfulness rarely seen in the United States. They truly have a hope for the future, an outlook that is very uplifting to witness. That is just one of many lessons I very much wanted, and needed, to learn from my time in Haiti. Vatican II embraced the notion that there are lessons to be learned from places like Haiti. *Gaudium et spes* expressed it well in paragraph 15, saying, "It should be pointed out that many nations which are poorer as far as material goods are concerned, yet richer in wisdom, can be of the greatest advantage to others."

This acknowledgement by Vatican II truly shows that mission work is not just a one-way endeavor but rather a mutual opportunity for both sides to be of great benefit to each other. When that does happen, tomorrow will be better!

There are several other Haitian proverbs to which I have dedicated an entire chapter in this book to their meaning and impact they had on me. In addition, there are many other proverbs that I don't have stories to go along with but nonetheless they still contain lots of wisdom. Some of those that I especially like are the following:

> "Kay koule tronpe soley, men li pa tronpe lapli"—The house that leaks can fool the sun but it cannot fool the rain.

> "Se nan malè ou konnen bon zanmi"— Good friends are recognized in adversity.

"Padon pa geri maleng"—Sorry doesn't heal the scars.

"Bay kou, bliye. Pote mak, sonje"—The one who gives the blow forgets. The one who gets hurt remembers.

"Memwa se paswa"—Memory is a sieve.

"Depi se fanm kap separe, tout moun ap jwen"—When women dish out the food, everyone eats.

"Wont pi lou pase sak sel"—Shame is heavier than a bag of salt.

"Byen pre pa lakay"—Very close is not home yet.

"Promes se det"—Promises are debts.

"Bel anteman pa vle di paradi"—A beautiful burial does not guarantee heaven.

"Avan ou ri moun bwete, gade jan ou mache"—Before you laugh at those who limp, check the way you walk.

"Chemen bezwen pa janm long"—The road to need is never long.

"Kote y'ap plimen kodenn, poul pa ri"—Where they pluck turkeys, chickens don't laugh.

"Le w'ap neye, ou kenbe branch ou jwenn"—When you are drowning, you hang to the branch you reach.

"Lespwa fe viv"—Hope makes one live.

"Regle jis pa gate zanmi"—A fair deal does not spoil friendship.

Mayombe's original chapel was in dire need of repair or replacement. This is where the woman told us "What God had brought us, no flood can take away."

7

Rainbow as a Sign

Therefore, the Lord himself will give you this sign.
—Isaiah 7:14

HAVING EYES TO SEE AND ears to hear is a theme that is repeated often in the Bible, particularly in the New Testament. Sometimes you simply need eyes of faith to see what can literally be right in front of you, especially when it comes to seeing God in a situation. For example, take the rainbow. It is simple to see as a human, but it can also have a spiritual connotation. For our family, it has an added personal meaning and connection.

God gave all of us the rainbow as a sign of his covenant with Noah. "I set my bow in the clouds to serve as a sign of the covenant between me and the earth" (Gen. 9:13). However, the rainbow had become a great and wonderful sign for our family even before we started going to Haiti. Still, we have many special stories of receiving the gift of a rainbow while in Haiti as well.

Before he died in 1996, Justin had been the sound and light technician for Greater Lafayette Civic Theater. He worked the Youth Theater performances for several years. In addition, he was also beginning to fulfill the same role in the adult shows as well, even though he was not quite fifteen years old yet! When he died, I often said that God needed help with special effects for such things as beautiful, sweeping sunsets. It gave me hope for a way to continue to connect with Justin.

Our family vacationed in Michigan for nearly fifteen years before Justin died. We traveled to Portage Lake in Onekama with our best friends Rod and Linda Ray multiple times each year since our children were born. Their two children were the same age as ours, and they grew up together there. Our first family outing without Justin came just a few months after his funeral, and it was to these cottages on Portage Lake with the Rays.

As was our custom, we would leave after work on a Friday and drive the six hours north to the cottages, not arriving until nearly midnight. Both our sons loved to immediately run out to the dock to check out the lake, even before unloading anything from the car. On this trip, we took a family walk out to the lake. It was a beautiful night with a full moon and no clouds in the sky. The lake was like a sheet of glass, reflecting the moon above.

I then saw something I had never seen before or since. There was a complete 360-degree rainbow encircling the full moon—at midnight—with the cloudless sky. It was incredible. It was like a rainbow halo. I know I was not simply seeing things as Sharon, Kyle, and the other families that were with us also walked out onto the dock and witnessed this blessing from above. Immediately it became our sign from God that Justin was with us.

A couple of years later we were vacationing out west, driving through the desert in Arizona. It was a nice sunny day. There was no threat of rain. Suddenly there was a huge arching rainbow stretching across the Arizona sky. Again, we took it as confirmation that Justin was there with us! While these are the two most spectacular—and unexpected—examples of rainbows, we have seen them on nearly every family vacation we have taken since he died.

On our very first family trip to Haiti, we did not even get out of the United States before we saw a rainbow. We had just taken off after our first layover. To keep travel costs low, we leave Indianapolis and have a short layover at one of several different places—Atlanta, Charlotte, Dulles, St. Louis, Cincinnati, Pittsburgh, or Chicago—before reaching Miami. From there it is a short hop over to Port-au-Prince, Haiti, only an hour and forty-five-minute flight. I find it interesting that Haiti is that close to the United States. In fact, Miami is nearly twice as far from Indianapolis as it is from Port-au-Prince.

We were all excited about what was in store for us, yet we also had normal apprehensions associated with traveling to a new and different place. Kyle had a window seat on this flight while Sharon and I were together in the middle section of the plane. Shortly after takeoff, Kyle said, "Mom, you have to come and look at this!" Of course, we both got up and looked out his window. The plane was flying above the clouds, but below was a shadow of our plane on the clouds with a rainbow completely encircling it. It was as if the rainbow was protecting our travel and that Justin was going to be with us. It was our sign from God.

<hr>

There was a similar story a few years later. This time it occurred within Haiti! Pendus is only 120 miles from Port-au-Prince, so we usually drove to get there even though it took eight to ten hours to do so. The condition of the roads, and the inevitable flat tires that resulted, made that relatively short distance an all-day endeavor. However, there had been a lot of civil unrest before that trip. Father Cha Cha did not want us to take any chances driving through several of the potential hot spots along the coast between Port-au-Prince and Gonaives, so he said we could come only if we would fly from PAP to Port-de-Paix and then drive south the approximate twenty-five miles to Pendus. By traveling this way, we would be hopping over the trouble spots to safely wind up in Pendus. This was the second time that he requested we take the short puddle jumper flight instead of driving up the coast. So we arranged to do so.

Besides the civil unrest, there were several other factors that also had our group a little more apprehensive compared to all prior trips. This trip was the first time that Father Cha Cha did not come to Port-au-Prince to meet us at the airport and then travel with us on to Pendus. It was always a great comfort to see him immediately at the airport in Port-au-Prince and have him with us throughout our entire stay. There had been lots of rain in the northwest part of Haiti, and the roads were in even worse shape than normal. Since we were flying to Port-de-Paix, he would simply meet us at that airport instead.

There also had been the issue of lost luggage already on this trip. The small plane that we were to take only held twelve passengers. There were nine in our group from Indiana plus our three interpreters. To keep the plane within its allowed weight limit, all our luggage would have to travel to Port-de-Paix by separate puddle jumpers. We all were worried about having our luggage arrive, both our personal items and the medical supplies and other items we were bringing for Pendus.

Lastly, several in our group were not fond of flying in general, let alone in a small plane, in the rainy weather—in northern Haiti! The scheduled flight time was only forty-five minutes, so we were not going to get to a very high altitude on this flight. This added a bit to our collective anxiety as we would be flying low over many mountains along the way.

The clear skies of Port-au-Prince quickly turned to clouds mere minutes after taking off. Looking out my side of the plane, I saw the shadow of our small plane following behind us on those clouds below with a circular rainbow completely encompassing it! It was beautiful and comforting to see. Everything would be all right. Once again we were under God's protection and Justin was with us. I retold the significance of the rainbow, and everyone seemed a bit more at ease for the rest of the short flight!

By the time we landed in Port-de-Paix, it was raining and had been for twenty-four hours. But Father Cha Cha was there at the end of the gravel runway to meet us, standing under his umbrella, smiling, as he warmly welcomed us.

⸻⸻

The best Haiti rainbow encounter occurred on Sharon's first hike to Mayombe, one of St. Joseph's six satellite chapels. It is located about two miles east up the mountain from Pendus. The year before this story unfolded was the first time that Father Cha Cha took anyone from our group up to Mayombe. Sister Jackie Picard had warned us that it was a very difficult climb and that our whole group should not attempt it, so only a few of us did. Sharon and several others stayed behind. However, having made it there the year before, I was convinced that she and everyone else in our group could make it this year.

There was an extra incentive to go to Mayombe as well. St. Mary had sent money to Father Cha Cha since the prior trip to Pendus. It was designated to build a new Mayombe chapel. This would be our first glimpse of the finished construction! In addition, Father Cha Cha was going to celebrate the first Mass in the new structure. Sharon did not want to miss out on that! Neither did anyone else in our group.

While I was sure everyone could make it to Mayombe, it would still be a test of our endurance and our will to get there. To get to Mayombe, you first walk east through Pendus and wade across the Pendus River. Once up the bank on the other side, you turn right for a short distance and then back east again.

From there the hike begins its ascent in earnest! It is nearly a forty-five-degree-angled slope for the greater portion of this hike. Unlike many of the other hikes we have taken in Haiti, this path has lots of rocks. The rocks can make the climb difficult for a couple reasons. First, they are slicker when they are wet. It is easier to lose your footing, to slip or even fall. Second, a rocky path does not allow you to take your normal stride or step. Imagine walking up a stairway verses a ramp. You can take as short or long of strides that you are comfortable with on the ramp whereas the rise of the steps on the stairs is already predetermined for you. When rocks are involved, the elevation of each step is often greater than what is a normal or comfortable step up. You must be careful every step of the way. In addition, the challenges or dangers of going up are different than they are hiking down!

To complicate the situation even more, Sharon has asthma, which will be a factor more on the climb up than on the way down. The physical exertion necessary in climbing the mountain will push her lungs to their capacity.

We got a late start on that morning because it had been raining, which would also mean that the path would be muddier and the rocks slicker. As we walked, I heard Sharon saying the Hail Mary prayer over and over. I assumed she was saying the rosary to help her climb this mountain, and she was! We made sure that we took many breaks along the way up so we all could catch our breath.

Luckily, it never did rain on us during our climb that day, and the mud was not nearly as bad as I anticipated it would be due in large part to a steady breeze that helped dry things out for us. The clouds also kept the sun from beating down on us, keeping the temperatures more comfortable for us as well.

After over ninety minutes of climbing, Sharon finally said that she could not go any further. We had reached a plateau where we could look down both sides of our path. At that point I told her that she had finished the most difficult part of the hike, the up portion! The new blue chapel could finally be seen. It was only a couple hundred yards away, and the rest of the walk was on nearly level ground on that ridge of the mountain!

Sharon said, "I don't know how I made it!" I told her that I did and to turn around. We were standing at the top of this mountain with a big valley behind us. She turned around to see the biggest, most vivid double rainbow we had ever seen. The colors were so distinct, and there were two rainbows. They were so close that you almost felt that you could reach out and touch them! But they weren't arching across the sky. We were standing above them as they filled the valley between where we stood and the mountain beyond. It was incredible. I had never seen an entire rainbow arc like this from this vantage point, from above, at least when I was standing on the ground and not in an airplane!

It says in Sirach 43:11–12: "Behold the rainbow! Then bless its Maker, for majestic indeed is its splendor. It spans the heavens with its glory, this bow bent by the mighty hand of God."

We both instantly knew how Sharon had made it to the top— that her prayers were answered on that day and that God and Justin once again were with us!

To show you just how grueling that hike was, Sister Maureen Colleary, who was part of our St. Mary group that year, also struggled on this climb as well. She was pushed even more to her limit. She had a person on either side of her the whole way up to help her with the slickness of the path. Once she reached the Mayombe chapel, she had one of the best one-liners of the trip, facetiously saying as she finally sat down, "This would be a great place to die!"

⸻⟫●⟪⸻

We have seen a rainbow on every trip to Haiti but our next to last one. We often tell our group about our rainbow story and its special significance in our lives. Time and time again someone from our group will come running to either Sharon or me, saying, "Come see the rainbow we found!" These are always great Kodak moments for me. I have lots of beautiful photographs of rainbows in Haiti, even the one of the rainbow circling the shadow of the small plane!

We have seen rainbows while in Pendus, arching from one mountain on our left across the sky to another mountain on our right. We have also seen them as we drove around in the mountains. One year another brilliant rainbow was nearly above us as we were driving toward Pendus. It looked like we were approaching an archway. Of course, we never quite made it through that archway, but it sure appeared to be that close to us.

Maybe the reason we did not see a rainbow on the 2015 trip to Haiti was because we no longer need the reassurance that God and Justin are with us when we are there. We already know that to be true.

This is the double rainbow Sharon saw stretching
across the valley below Mayombe's chapel.

8

The Bible Comes Alive

All scripture is inspired by God and is useful for teaching...
—2 Timothy 3:16

"Every happening, great and small, is a parable whereby God speaks to us. The art of life is to get the message!" That quote was from Malcom Muggeridge, a British journalist and author who lived in the twentieth century. I love that quote. God is speaking to us every day in many ways. We just need to learn to pay attention.

Sometimes God must be shouting as his "message" comes through louder and clearer than others. There have been many of those times for me while in Haiti, times when certain verses of the Bible have truly come to life for me. They were so applicable to what was happening that it seemed that those words were written just for me!

The most vivid occurrence happened on my third visit to Pendus. This was the trip where we had to wait in Gros Morne overnight to give the rivers a chance to recede after several days of rain. There were only two vehicles available that morning to take us the last ten miles to Pendus and over the final five rivers. Unfortunately, we needed three vehicles to complete our trip, so one driver would have to make a second trip to get the twelve of us, our luggage, plus our three interpreters, Father Cha Cha, and Sister Jackie Picard to Pendus. So Father, Sister, and two of the interpreters, and a few of the suitcases stayed behind as the rest of us took off at 8:00 a.m.

We did not get very far before encountering our first problem. There was a traffic jam at the first river just north of Gros Morne. There were no bridges at any of the five rivers we were to cross this morning. Therefore, traffic simply had to drive down the bank of one side and into the river. Our drivers knew the route so well they even knew where the shallowest portions of the river bed were located. They would follow that route across. Often that route was not the most direct path across, but it would be the safest when driving through a flowing current of water! Once across to the other side, we would climb up that bank and back onto the dirt road awaiting us on the other side.

There was a large pickup truck that got stuck trying to get up the other side of the river and was blocking any traffic from going either direction. There were dozens of vehicles standing still in the water waiting for a chance to continue. In addition, there were hundreds of Haitians that were walking, trying to cross the rapid current on foot. Only the pedestrians were making any progress. Even they encountered difficulties as one older lady lost her footing and went down. Four fully dressed men quickly jumped in to help her up and get her to the other side.

After forty-five minutes of standing there and not moving an inch, a vehicle bigger than the truck stuck in the mud approached from the other side. It had a chain and was powerful enough to pull the stranded truck on up the bank and out of the water. We were on our way again!

About a half hour later, Sharon, who was standing in the bed of the second truck, mentioned that we had not had any flat tires yet on this trip. Within minutes we were stopped with the first, and luckily the only, flat tire of our entire trip! It was 9:30 by the time the tire was changed, and we were on our way again. We soon reached a very muddy section of the road. There was a natural spring in the area causing the road to become nearly impassable. One of our vehicles got stuck. There were four teenage boys in our group—Kyle, Jorge

Figueira, John Velten, and Tony VanAlstine. They got out and began to push that vehicle. Haitians are very quick to lend a hand when they see a problem and soon there were about ten helping the boys get the vehicle through the fifty-foot quagmire called a road! The four boys were covered in mud with no good place to clean up.

We continued until we reached the Pendus River, the fourth of the five we would need to cross that day. The hill down to the river is very steep, and the road going down was the only stretch of today's travel that had any concrete. It is necessary as this hill has so steep a grade that vehicles could barely traverse it when it wasn't wet, let alone when it was muddy.

The water had receded some but there still was over a foot of dirt and rocks covering the final twenty feet of the ramp's entry into the river. The river was still over four foot deep and flowing very quickly. There would be no vehicles crossing this river that day. My heart sank as I did not want to turn around and wait another day in Gros Morne. Here was where I first prayed, "God, what are you trying to teach me today?" I was guessing the lesson was patience. By the time the day was done, I am sure it was "With God all things are possible!"

Our two drivers were not going to wait around. One still had to go back to get the rest of our group and the other still had to go to Port-au-Prince, so we unloaded everything and everyone on the slope of the hill overlooking the river. Both drivers then took off. I knew we were going to be here quite a while before Father Cha Cha would possibly get here. We probably shouldn't have left the other interpreters behind, but I did not want to split up our group either, and there was no more room in the first two vehicles. Besides they were only supposed to arrive a couple hours behind us.

There were a lot of people at the river today, more than I had ever noticed before. It was a bottleneck unlike I had ever seen. I did not recognize any of the people from prior trips. All of them were on foot, and a few were trying to walk across. A couple of them slipped and wound up fifty-sixty feet downstream in an instant before regaining some footing.

There was one man at the river named Antwone. He was about five foot five. He was barefoot and wearing only his white underwear. I suppose you could say he was dressed for work as he was helping folks get across, crossing whichever direction they needed to go. His balance was remarkable as I never noticed him slip even once as he crossed the river nearly one hundred times over the next couple hours. He helped escort people across as well as carry their wares. He even led a few less-than-willing donkeys across! Whenever he would help someone across, he would lead them about forty-fifty feet upstream and begin to cross. By the time they would reach the other side, the current had pushed them downstream to where they wanted to exit the river. He obviously knew what he was doing and would get tipped for his services. With his strength, balance, and ability to fend off the flow of the water, I thought he would have made a great linebacker in football!

From our group, only Father Bob, Sharon, Kyle, and I had been to Pendus before. I knew the way to Pendus and thought we were only a mile from our destination. I wanted to go on ahead and get help. I was not yet sure what help would look like as I knew there were no vehicles on the Pendus side of the river and we had over forty pieces of luggage with us. But again, I did not want to leave any of the group alone either. I was impatient enough that doing nothing was not an option, so we decided to send Kyle and John ahead. At least the folks in Pendus would recognize Kyle even without the aid of an interpreter.

As he began to cross, John slipped slightly. Two Haitian men were quick by his side to make sure he made it across safely. Kyle then approached the river. Antwone, who was about Kyle's size, simply picked Kyle up and slung him over his shoulder like a sack of potatoes and carried him across! The incredulous look on Kyle's face as he was carried across was priceless!

The rest of us sat on the rocky hillside watching Antwone work. After an hour, we were beginning to worry about Kyle and John, especially Sharon. Surely they should have had time to get there and find help. Another thirty minutes passed. Finally, several of the young boys from Pendus arrived—Benedict, Serge, Johnny, David, and Woodley. They had seen Kyle and figured out we were stuck at the rivers, so they hurried to meet us.

Once Sharon saw Benedict she immediately got up to cross over and give him a hug! She said she had come too far to be this close and not do so, especially if we would have to go back to Gros Morne when Father Cha Cha arrived later. Antwone and another man each grabbed Sharon's arms and safely escorted her across. She said they had such good hold of her that she simply lifted her feet and was floating as they walked. I followed behind, thinking I was missing a great Kodak moment. However, I couldn't afford to be carrying my camera in this predicament! The bottom of the river was very rocky so your footing was not very secure. Add in the swiftness of the current and it was a challenge to cross without tripping and going under.

Not long after Sharon and I had crossed, Ken, one of the older boys from Pendus, arrived. He was carrying a basket of bananas courtesy of Madam Marcel Garson. She figured we had to be hungry while we waited! There was great happiness in seeing each other. We knew that we were no longer alone and that help was on its way.

Finally, two of the men from Pendus arrived, Jean Claude and Hebert. Neither of them could speak any English. However, I still understood that they were excitedly telling me in Creole that everything was going to be all right. They picked out several of the men at the river that they both knew, along with Serge and Johnny. They began to carry every piece of our luggage across the river, one at a time on the top of their heads! Not a single item got wet. It was truly remarkable to watch this caravan at work! Once the luggage was across, they paired up on the rest of our group and escorted them across the river one at a time. Again, no one went under. However, I can't say no one got wet as we were wading through four-foot depths!

Now that all of us and everything we brought was on the Pendus side of the river, I wondered what Father Cha Cha would say when he arrived in a vehicle that would still be on his side of the river. Hopefully we hadn't just made this a bigger mess! However, I wasn't going to find out as Jean Claude and Hebert immediately began directing all the Haitians to carry each piece of luggage to Pendus. Back in 2001, our checked-in bags could weigh seventy pounds. They were heavy and cumbersome to carry. One of them took two people to carry! The rest they would simple hoist on top their head and begin walking.

Even the young children helped, carrying everything including our backpacks, water bottles, and my camera! I saw several of the younger boys who acted very disappointed when all that was left for them to carry was perceived to be "too small" or inconsequential. They wanted a more important role in helping us! I stayed behind until every piece was picked up and carried by someone! I wanted to get a picture of one of the biggest suitcases being carried by one man on top of his head. He was about seventy-five yards ahead of me when I started. I figured I would get it when I eventually caught up to him. I never did catch him. In fact, I saw him jogging at one point. It was incredible!

By the time I started walking, I was sure the front of the line had to be close to Pendus. However, I underestimated the amount of trail left to walk. It turned out to be over two miles from that river crossing to Pendus. It took us about an hour to walk that last distance. Luckily, most of it was relatively flat, although as in any mountain hike there are still some ups and downs. There also was one last small river crossing. It was more of a creek. Luckily it was not much more than ankle deep and was not a problem.

Every piece of luggage made it safely. We paid each of the veteran river crossers $2 US or about 10 Haitian dollars for their help. That was double what was recommended for me to pay them, but it was more than worth it. We also gave each of them a polo shirt and thanked them profusely!

A few hours later, Father Cha Cha appeared in Pendus. He was very happy that we were already there. When his vehicle dropped him off at the river, he too had to cross on foot and hike the final portion of the mountain to Pendus.

Later the following night as we sat in the courtyard, I asked Jean Claude and Hebert what their favorite verse in the Bible was. Jean

Claude said his was Psalm 91 and Hebert said his was Psalm 23 and Psalm 91. I knew what Psalm 23 was but would have to wait until daylight to read Psalm 91 as back then there was no generator for electricity.

The next day I was up and showered before the 6:00 a.m. bells rang. I sat in the school yard and watched the sun rise over the eastern mountains and read my Bible. I wanted to read Psalm 91 since both Jean Claude and Hebert liked it so much.

A few of the verses in Psalm 91 were very familiar to me, such as verses 1–2, "You who dwell in the shelter of the Most High... my refuge and fortress, my God in whom I trust," and verse 5, "You shall not fear the terror of the night nor the arrow that flies by day." However, it was verses 11 and 12 that really spoke to me that morning, literally sending a chill throughout my body. I was familiar with those words as well. I just did not remember they were found in Psalm 91. They said:

> For God commands the angels to guard you
> in all your ways. With their hands they shall sup-
> port you, lest you strike your foot against a stone.

Did not those words describe exactly what happened at the Pendus River! God had sent his angels—all the local Pendus residents—to protect us and keep us from dashing our feet upon the stones as we waded across the river! I felt that was exactly what had happened. And for those words to come from our rescuers' favorite verse in the Bible, it was like God wanted me to read and understand them precisely at that time.

The sunrise over the eastern mountain top that accompanied this morning's revelation was equally spectacular.

<hr>

The Bible came alive for me again on our December 2012 trip. We were waiting around the St. Joseph Church courtyard area for vehicles to arrive to take us to an event in Gros Morne. There was a little girl sitting alone on the concrete ledge next to the cistern. I had never seen her before. I cautiously approached her and sat down next to her.

She was barefoot. Dust covered her face, legs, feet, and arms. She was wearing a dress that once was white but had not been cleaned recently. She sat very quietly looking straight ahead, hardly even acknowledging that I was now next to her. I did not see anyone who appeared to be with her. I tried to ask her for her name, but her response back to me was barely more than a whisper. I didn't understand any of her words.

I got out a handful of trail mix from my backpack. Without speaking any further, I offered it to her. It only took a few peanuts and M&Ms to fill her tiny little hand. She quickly ate the handful, like she had not eaten in a while. I opened a small packet of peanuts. Her hands were so small that it took four handfuls to empty that small packet, but she quickly ate all four handfuls. I then opened a small package of peanut butter crackers. She ate all of those as well. We got her an empty plastic Tampico bottle filled with water. She guzzled that too.

Paula Max got some wet wipes and gently began to clean her face, her hands, her legs, and her feet. I knew that we had brought some small girl's clothes that might fit her but they were down at the dispensary (about one hundred yards away). Danielle Morris volunteered to retrieve them. While we waited for her to return, the little girl picked up the nearly empty cracker wrapper. She shook the remaining crumbs into her hand and then licked both her hand and wrapper clean. We gave her more water to drink, and she did.

All the while, my body was tingling. It was almost like I was watching this happen from outside myself. I could not help but think of the scripture found in Matthew 25 and feel the presence of Jesus: "When I was hungry, you gave me something to eat." I also visualized the Bible passage about giving a drink to a child. However, I could not remember where it was in scripture. I needed to return to my Bible study group the next week after I got home to find this verse:

> And whoever gives only a cup of cold water
> to one of these little ones to drink because he is
> a disciple—amen, I say to you, he will surely not
> lose his reward. (Matt. 10:42)

Finally, a perfectly sized pink dress arrived from the dispensary, also some socks. Paula carefully got her into her new dress. She began to smile. It was then that I realized her mother was sitting just around the corner, watching us interact with her precious child. Without the aid of an interpreter, I learned from the girl's mother that her name was Jevela and that she was four years old.

I did not see Jevela again the rest of the trip, but I instantly knew those few moments would be the highlight of the week for me and possibly of all my trips to Haiti. It was one of those revelation moments when a Bible message unfolded in front of me in such a way that I could never forget.

Massacre, pronounced "Maw-sock" in Creole, is a chapel area that is in the mountains about two miles north of Pendus. Its French spelling and meaning probably give a clue as to some happening long ago that led to the area's name. It is one of six chapel areas that surround Pendus. It is the first chapel area that any St. Mary group visited and one that we try to visit during every trip to Haiti.

What makes it a difficult destination is that you can only get there on foot and it is a two-hour uphill climb most of the way. Beginning at the St. Joseph Church compound area, you walk east through the village of Pendus. This area is flat. On the far edge of "town," you must cross the Pendus River and turn left or north. This is the first of five river crossings en route to Massacre. The path follows the river a short distance before climbing fifty to one hundred feet above the water. It then descends to cross the river again. This repeats several times before the hike begins its ascent in earnest. During this early portion of the hike there is lots of lush vegetation, which makes sense with its proximity to the water. It gives you a feeling of being in a tropical area.

Once past the river area, the climb becomes much tougher with several steep sections. Luckily the path is all dirt, and not rocky, so it is a bit easier than a rocky climb. If you hike early in the day a large portion of the way is in the morning shade, making it a more comfortable walk. However, the hike back down typically is in the midday to early afternoon sun, making it much more uncomfortable! The vistas on the way down, however, are spectacular. You can truly see many mountains set behind each other for miles in every direction. Even the hillsides that are treeless from years of deforestation are a beautiful sight to see, especially for someone who lives in Indiana!

This hike has resulted in a couple more opportunities for a biblical story to unfold before me. Both were the result of unusually difficult circumstances making the hike extra onerous. One occurred on our first trip to Haiti as a family. We began the hike right after breakfast to catch the comfort of the early shade. Under normal circumstances, the journey to Massacre can be daunting and difficult. However, about half the way up, Sharon got a migraine headache, making her morning miserable.

We made many stops along the way to see if we could ease her pain. We tried giving her ibuprofen. We tried applying damp bandanas to both her forehead and the back of her neck. We tried having her drink water to help with dehydration. Sister Jackie Picard even massaged the back of her head and neck. Nothing worked. Sharon threw up a couple times. The climb was difficult enough without the added hardship she was enduring.

About a hundred yards from the chapel, which also doubled as a one-room school for 225 students, Sharon began to hear the children singing. It got louder the closer we got to the chapel. She said when she heard the beat of the drums and music that it felt like angels were carrying her the rest of the way!

The building was about twenty-five feet wide by forty-five feet long. It had a thatch roof, palm-woven sides, and dirt floors; and it was filled with schoolchildren in blue-colored uniforms singing loudly and proudly. We were not sure of the words being sung, but we knew that we were being warmly welcomed! As stated in Matthew 10:40–41, "Whoever receives you receives me, and whoever receives me receives the one who sent me…and whoever welcomes a righteous man because he is righteous will receive a righteous man's reward."

The singing continued even after we all arrived. Chairs arrived from out of nowhere for us to sit on. The heavenly greeting was just the medicine Sharon needed, uplifting her from her misery from the hike.

The principal of the school spoke first and welcomed us. Through the interpreter, he said, "Just like Jesus climbed the mountain to bring the good news, our friends from St. Mary have done the same today." Sharon was not the only one in our group that was now teary-eyed. After all, who were we? We had struggled mightily to get up the mountain; all we had done so far was try to catch our breath! However, merely our presence in their worship space was enough to make an impact. They knew we were not used to climbing mountains at our home, that such effort was not simply a way of life for us as it was for them. The fact that we struggled made it that much more significant to them. We came anyway, and that was what was important to them.

The principal's thoughts reflected the words found in Luke 8:1: Jesus "journeyed from one town and village to another, preaching and proclaiming the good news of the kingdom of God."

———⟫●⟪———

The second Massacre climbing experience arose a couple years later. It had been raining quite a bit, making the path very muddy. I learned a new phrase that day, *anpil labou*, which means "lots of mud."

Many times in the past there would be some mud, but nothing like this. In those times, you could often simply step around the mud along the route by being careful where you stepped. This was especially true in the lower portion of the trail along the river, as it was much wider with more choices for where to step. However, the path was only a couple of feet wide at best in most of the elevated portions of the trail. When oncoming people or donkeys approached, you had to be very careful in passing, especially where there was either a row of cactus or a steep drop-off on either side of the path. Both such hazards were very common most of the way up!

This mud was unavoidable on this hike to Massacre. Most of our shoes were completed caked in mud. The mud on me covered both of my entire lower legs below the middle of my shin. It looked like I had dipped my feet into a gray paint bucket.

The chapel compound at Massacre is located adjacent to the path up the mountain. However, the building itself sets down the side of the mountain enough that its roof is about the same elevation as the walking path. There are about ten concrete steps with an iron railing that lead down into the front entry into the chapel. I always thought it quite ironic that the only concrete within miles covered the last few steps into the chapel, after most folks had walked long distances over very rough terrain to get there without concrete or railing anywhere else!

After we all arrived at Massacre, we sat on those concrete steps and removed our shoes and socks so not to make a mess inside the chapel. Amotese Amilcar is the elder statesman from the village. He is the founder of the school at Massacre and still teaches there. He is a longtime leader in the community. He suffers from elephantiasis, a deformity of his right foot making it nearly three times as large as his left foot.

He had brought a bucket of water and an empty bowl with him. As we all removed our shoes and socks, he bent over and washed our feet for us, gently holding our feet over the bowl as he poured water and rubbed the mud away. The bowl would catch the water and dirt so as not make a mess on the steps. It was very humbling and immediately brought to mind the Last Supper when Jesus washed the feet of the disciples.

Amotese clearly comprehended the query found in John 13:12 when Jesus asked, "Do you realize what I have done for you?" Jesus continued at John 13:15, instructing us by saying, "I have given you a model to follow, so that as I have done for you, you should also do." Amotese clearly followed that example and brought the lesson home to everyone in our group!

This was simply another wonderful example of one of the stories of the Bible being played out before us, with us being participants! It is a blessing to be able to see these stories come to life.

St. Augustine once wrote: "Faith is to believe what we do not see; and the reward of faith is to see what we believe."

Amotess washes Michelle Ray's feet after
a muddy hike to Massacre.

9

Dependency on God

A gem cannot be polished without friction,
nor a man perfected without trials.

—*Confucius*

HAITIANS HAVE TAUGHT ME MUCH about total reliance on God and of the power of prayer. One of the toughest questions for anyone to answer is "Why do bad things happen?" That question is especially pertinent for a country that has been beset by more than its share of "bad things." Just in the relatively short time I have been going to Haiti, there have been coups, civil unrest, a devastating earthquake, multiple hurricanes (with four in a one-month span), a cholera epidemic, and now the Zika outbreak. None of these disasters include the normal struggles Haitians face daily due to lack of infrastructure and deprivation of many of life's basic needs.

Why does God get credit when something good happens but not the blame when something bad does? Why doesn't prayer seem to work all the time? These questions are frequently asked. The answers are rarely understood.

Matthew tells us at 7:7–11:

> Ask and it will be given to you; seek and you
> will find; knock and the door will be opened to
> you. For everyone who asks, receives; and the one

who seeks, finds; and to the one who knocks, the door will be opened. Which one of you would hand his son a stone when he asks for a loaf of bread or a snake when he asks for a fish? If you then, who are wicked, know how to give gifts to your children, how much more will your heavenly Father give good things to those who ask Him?

It sounds so simple, doesn't it?

Did God give me a loaf of bread or fish or did I get a stone or snake when my son Justin died?

The Bible is replete with verses telling us to "trust in the Lord" (Prov. 3:5, Sir. 2:6) Yet even God's only Son is not spared from suffering and death. Evidently trusting in the Lord won't deliver us from "bad things happening." Just as Jesus's passion and death did not make any sense to his disciples at the time, neither does it make sense when today's bad things happen to us.

Often people are quick to openly thank God after a seemingly miraculous occurrence (such as the return of a POW) or a wonderful event (such as winning a championship). Rarely does anyone ever give the same thanks after an equally painful experience, and if they did, would they be believed? When the family of a returned POW expresses the evidence of the power of prayer upon their loved one's return, what is the family of the soldier killed in action supposed to think of the power of prayer.

I have struggled with these issues. However, over the years I have witnessed Haitians, who have had tougher lives than I could ever imagine, exhibit recognition of God being in charge. Not just occasionally but every day. There is a heartfelt thankfulness that goes along with that dependency as well. It has been a very simple and subtle lesson for me and one that has resulted in me thinking more about it.

Once you begin to understand some Creole you will frequently hear the phrases *si Dye vle* and *gras a Bondye* being used in routine conversations. Both constitute an innate understanding of where God has been in their lives and where he will continue to be. *Gras a Bondye* means "by the grace of God." It is a looking back, with gratitude and thanksgiving, of some way God has blessed you. For example, I might simply ask, "How are you?" which in Creole would be "Kouman ou ye?" Frequently, the response is "Gras a Bondye, mwen byen" or "By the grace of God, I am good."

Si Dye vle translates into "If God is willing" and encompasses a looking-forward attitude. For example, if I am in the United States, I might ask a friend, "Are you going with me tomorrow?" His response might be, "Yes, I will go with you." However, in Haiti the response more likely would be, "Si Dye vle, m'ap ale avek ou," which translates to "If God is willing, I will go with you." It might only be a slight difference in response, but those few extra words say volumes about where God fits into their lives.

Both phrases are really small prayers. Unlike the common Haitian responses, prayer often isn't the first thing that occurs to me when I'm faced with a problem. Usually, it isn't until I have done everything that I can, explored all the options, and exhausted all possibilities that I resort to prayer.

At my time of most need, when our son Justin was in the ICU at Riley Hospital, I sat just outside his room. There wasn't anything else I could do, so I tried asking God's will be done. All the while, I knew full well all I wanted was for Justin to be all right. I was okay with God's will if it looked like mine too! I wasn't sure how I would handle any other scenario. Yet, somehow, I knew God would make him all right. I did not know how or what to pray for, so I tried saying the rosary, using my knuckles as the beads. As Paul said in Romans 8:26–27:

> In the same way, the Spirit too comes to the aid of our weakness, for we do not know how to pray as we ought, but the Spirit itself intercedes with inexpressible groanings. And the one who searches hearts knows what is the intention of the Spirit, because it intercedes for the holy ones accordingly to God's will.

Remember, God will not give you more than you can handle. Paul tells us that in 1 Corinthians 10:13: "No trial has come to you but what is human. God is faithful and will not let you be tried beyond your strength, but with the trial will also provide a way out, so that you may be able to bear it."

I have learned that in ancient times, a potter would not test defective clay jars as he knew they would break. He would only test the sound ones! I suppose if the same were true for God that I should be thankful that I have been tested. If he only tries us to our limit of our own strength, it would mean he didn't think me to be very strong if I didn't have my cross to carry. However, I also understand Mother Teresa's sentiments when she said, "I know God only gives you what you can handle; I just wish he didn't trust me so much!"

Jesus tells us in Matthew 11:28–30: "Come to me, all you who labor and are burdened, and I will give you rest…For my yoke is easy, and my burden light." This never used to make sense to me. Then I learned that the Greek word for *easy* is "christos," which translates better to "well-fitted." Somehow, it is more palatable to say "My yoke is well-fitted" than "easy." That means God's plan is specific to me and not haphazard. There is some consolation in that!

Jesus touched on these issues while talking to his disciples about why a man was born blind. They perceived that it was someone's fault that caused a "bad thing" to happen. Jesus said that neither the man nor his parents had sinned. Rather, he said, "It is so that the works of God might be made visible through him" (John 9:3). Again, it is comforting to me to realize God is using the situation for good, even if I may never know what that good is!

Besides Jesus, who in the Bible was tried more than St. Paul? Repeatedly, he tells us to rejoice in the sufferings (Col. 2:24) or boast in our afflictions (Rom. 5:3) or to consider the sufferings of the present as nothing compared to the glory to be revealed to us (Rom. 8:18). Paul adds in 2 Corinthians 4:17–18 that his "momentary light affliction is producing for us an eternal weight of glory beyond all comparison as we look not to what is seen but to what is not seen."

True prayer, the one that is always answered, is not praying for what I want. True prayer is not praying for the cup to pass. God did not promise that nor did He grant it even to his own Son. In fact, God "knows what you need before you ask him" (Matt. 6:8). Prayer doesn't change God's mind. Prayer changes my heart. Wouldn't it be wonderful if we could all occasionally say, "God, I don't know why you want me to carry this load? I can see no good in it, and it's awfully heavy. But if you want me to carry it, I will."

It can be difficult for me to remember that prayer is a conversation with God and not simply me placing an order. Think about it. If you are conversing with God, shouldn't He be doing most of the talking, not you? That is why the Bible continually tells us to slow down, to wait, to be still, and know that He is God (Ps. 46:10).

Being still and waiting are not typical human characteristics. However, only when we do slow down and wait are we able to hear God's whisper. Haiti has given me many opportunities to slow down and block out my normal worldly distractions and listen and contemplate on what I was experiencing. That may well be one of the best blessings I could ever receive!

Summarizing her thoughts on prayer, Trina Wurst, one of many daily reflection writers for St. Monica Church in Indianapolis, said it best when she said, "Usually I'd be better off if, instead of me trying to let my *brain* find the way to God, I left my *heart* open so God could find me."

If my heart is open and God indeed finds me, then accepting his will and the answers he sends to our prayers becomes a simpler task. Maybe, just maybe, that is when the "yoke is easy and the burden light."

Often, I am asked why so many "bad things happen" in Haiti and "why don't prayers seem to help." It has taken me many years of visits and reflection on those experiences to reach my newfound conclusion. God already knows the poor of the world will spend eternity with him. The poor of the world are there to see if we notice and then do something. They are not being tested, the rest of us are. Maybe that is why they can accept God's will so much easier than me.

St. Paul sets forth this paradox well in his first letter to the Corinthians. In chapter 1:18 he bluntly tells us, "The message of the cross is foolishness to those who are perishing, but to us who are being saved it is the power of God." He concludes at verses 27 and 28 by saying, "Rather, God chose the foolish of the world to shame the wise, and God chose the weak of the world to shame the strong, and God chose the lowly and the despised of the world, those who count for nothing, to reduce to nothing those who are something."

Jesus told us as much himself. In fact, his opening words in the Sermon on the Plain, found in Luke's Gospel, were "Blessed are you who are poor, for the kingdom of God is yours" (Luke 6:20).

Haitians have taught me many lessons about being dependent on God, who they recognize to be present in their everyday lives.

10

You Can't Out-Give God

The same Lord is Lord of all, enriching all who call upon Him.
—*Romans 10:12*

SHARON AND I ALWAYS DREAMED of going to Hawaii for our twenty-fifth wedding anniversary. When we began going to Haiti we had been married for twenty-two years, so we were getting close. However, we had not yet begun to save specifically for that long-awaited Hawaii trip.

By the time we reached our silver wedding anniversary, I had been to Haiti three times and Sharon and Kyle twice each. That is seven total plane tickets we had bought to go to Haiti. In those early years, the plane tickets were much cheaper than now, averaging between $350–400 per round-trip. Had we not gone to Haiti and simply saved the cost of those seven tickets, we would have banked $2,650 toward our dream getaway.

I had a wonderful travel agent in those early years. She called me in early December, a few weeks before we were scheduled to fly to Haiti. Our flight from Indianapolis to Miami was ticketed through American Trans Air and then from Miami to Port-au-Prince on American Air. She said she had an opportunity to get us free tickets if we agreed to get bumped on the American Trans Air leg. She said the free tickets were good for anywhere within the USA.

I promptly had two questions for her. First, was she sure they were good for travel anywhere in the United States and not just within the continental United States? Most free ticket scenarios do not include Alaska and Hawaii. Second, would the bump involve our entire group? I did not want us to get separated in our travels to and from Haiti. She assured me that the bumped tickets were eligible for travel within all fifty states and that American Trans Air had flights to and from Honolulu! She also guaranteed the bump would be for everyone in our group and that the new arrangements would keep us together throughout our trip. As a bonus, we would arrive in Port-au-Prince at roughly the same time as we were already scheduled! Therefore, I immediately jumped at this opportunity.

Later in the year, I did book a family trip to Hawaii to celebrate our twenty-fifth anniversary. Kyle went too. Not quite the romantic getaway for just the two of us, but when your son is ready to go to college, you take every opportunity to spend more time with him too. The amazing part of this story was the three tickets to Hawaii that we received free from American Trans Air would have cost us $2,650 if we had to purchase them.

Those coincidences just don't happen! Luke 6:38 says, "Give and gifts will be given to you... For the measure with which you measure will in return be measured out to you."

We got another chance to be bumped in advance again the next year. Again, we happily took advantage of that opportunity. However, that scenario has not happened again after my travel agent retired! It would now be virtually impossible to bump an entire group at the check-in gate at the airport. However, I still had my proof that you could not out-give God!

Oddly enough, there is a Haitian proverb on point that says, "Si se bondye ki voye, li peye fre ou," which means "If it is God who sends you, he will pay your way."

Over the years, God has far out-given me in many other, non-monetary, ways as well. First, I was blessed to have both my wife and son share this ministry with me every step of the way. He also blessed me with the many insights I have come to appreciate and attempt to recount for you. I have also have had the honor to travel to Haiti with well over 140 different people throughout the years.

Each person brought a new vantage point to our shared experiences and became my lifelong friend if they weren't one already!

The biggest blessing Sharon and I have received from our years in Haiti was having Benedict Remy become a vital part of our lives. I have devoted an entire chapter later in this book to him. It was difficult to only spend a few days each year with him, but we did watch him grow from a young boy into a mature, goal-oriented, hardworking adult.

Another huge blessing for us was when Andre and Josee Angrand came to St. Mary Cathedral in 2005. Our Haiti ministry benefited greatly when they got involved. Since they were born and raised in Haiti, they could add insights and perspectives from both sides of the ministry. My appreciation, understanding, and love of Haitian culture, Haitian cuisine, Haitian history, and Creole language were greatly enhanced through their involvement.

However, the absolute best examples of not being able to out-give God belong to Michelle Ray and to Kelly Krueckeberg.

Michelle is the daughter of our best friends Rod and Linda Ray, but we always claimed her as our daughter too! She went with us to Pendus twice. On one of those trips, she also got the free ticket to anywhere in the United States for voluntarily getting bumped.

Like we did with our free flight, she used her ticket to take a trip to Hawaii to fulfill a lifetime dream of going to our fiftieth state! She went with a girlfriend from college. Within a few hours of getting there, they went straight to the beach. Michelle began to watch the surfers and noticed one that she thought was pretty good-looking.

To make a long story short, that surfer became the love of her life. Michelle is now married to him, Chris Librie, and they live in Hawaii. They are also the proud parents of two children. I always teased her that she must have had a thing for islands whose name begins with an *H* and ends with an *i*!

A similar love story that evolved from a trip to Pendus involved Kelly Kruekeburg. She first went with our St. Mary group to Haiti as a nursing student from Saint Elizabeth School of Nursing. She met Benedict on her trip to Pendus. She so loved her experience in

Haiti that after graduation she became a year-long Quest volunteer, living with Sister Jackie Picard in Gros Morne and working with the hospital there. A romance developed and continued even after Kelly returned to the United States.

She later made a return visit to Haiti before Benedict could get a visa to come to Indiana in early 2013. They were married later that year and are now happily living in Florida.

Had Michelle and Kelly not answered a call to go to Haiti in the first place, they would not have the opportunity to receive their respective blessings from God—finding the loves of their lives!

Talking to Peter, Jesus says, "Amen I say to you, there is no one who has given up house or brothers or sisters or mother or father or children or lands for my sake and for the gospel, who will not receive a hundred times more now in this present age...and eternal life in the age to come" (Mark 10:29–30).

We first met Benedict in Pendus when he was 11-years old. His entry into our lives was a blessing from God.

11

Sharing from Our Need

If the eagerness is there, the gift is acceptable according to what one has, not according to what one does not have.

—*2 Corinthians 8:12*

As mentioned, the last document approved just before the close of Vatican II in December 1965 was *Gaudium et spes*. The title is in Latin and means "joys and hopes." It comes from its opening line which says, "The joys and hopes, the grief and anguish of the people of our time, especially of those who are poor or afflicted, are the joys and hopes, the grief and anguish of the followers of Christ as well."

How incredible would it be if those joys and hopes, and the grief and anguish, of the poor or afflicted were shared by all! Just how would this scenario play out? *Gaudium et spes* tells us at paragraph 69: "God destined the earth and all it contains for all people and nations so that all created things would be shared fairly by all humankind under the guidance of justice tempered by charity." The really difficult part comes next as it continues by saying: "Therefore everyone has the right to possess a sufficient amount of the earth's goods for themselves and their family...People are bound to come to the aid of the poor and to do so not merely out of their superfluous goods."

That last line struck me as incredibly difficult, if not impossible, to accomplish. No matter how generous I thought I had been at any point in my life, I had *never* given from anything *but* my superfluous goods. No matter how generous I thought I had been, I always paid my mortgage payment, I always made my car payment, I always put food on the table, I always took a vacation every year. I was only giving from my leftovers. Since all my needs were being met, I was only giving from my superfluous goods! That was a crushing revelation to have to admit.

It got me thinking, *Does anyone ever give from their needs and not just from their excess?* I am sure I can come up with some people who do, but I would bet it would only happen for a loved one. Surely it wouldn't be for the poor and afflicted as directed by *Gaudium et spes!* The best examples I could think of were where a parent would scrimp and sacrifice to put a child through college or someone would spend everything in the hopes of finding a medical cure for a loved one or a child sacrifices to take care of an aging parent. The common thread in each of my scenarios was someone doing it for a loved one, someone that is the natural object of his or her bounty. Would it ever happen for a nonfamily member or better yet for a poor and afflicted stranger?

As hard as it was for me to put a name with such an example in the United States, I can easily identify three names from the relatively few people I know in Haiti! The first person was Madam Marcel Garson. She is married to Marcel Garson, and they live in Gros Morne. Their children are now all grown. However, ever since I started going to Haiti in 2000, she was the nurse who ran the small clinic in Pendus. She would take a *tap-tap*, the Haitian form of public transportation, every Monday morning from Gros Morne to Pendus. That ride takes an hour one way. She would stay in Pendus the entire week, running the clinic and seeing patients before returning by tap-tap on Friday evening. However, if there were patients who needed her continued care, she would stay the weekend in Pendus and not go home. This happened frequently, especially during the cholera outbreak a few years earlier.

She was doing this without pay, just to be able to tend to those in need of medical assistance in an area otherwise deprived of medical care. All the doctors who have gone with us on medical missions agree that she has saved many lives throughout the years of her dedicated service to the Pendus community.

One of the most important services she renders involves children. In a culture where children are frequently born at home, she has encouraged many mothers to come to her clinic to have their baby delivered under her watchful care. She has delivered hundreds over the years. Sharon has helped her on two occasions during deliveries, including one where Madam Marcel revived a baby born with its umbilical cord wrapped around its neck. Her care for the newborn is also critical in getting a healthy start to those babies' lives.

Whenever there is a medical situation that she cannot handle, she will get the patient as stable as possible and provide them transportation to the nearest hospital in Gros Morne. She is a perfect example of someone who gives her time, talent, and treasure and not merely from her superfluous supply of each! With her present in the room with us, I have told others on many of our trips that Madam Marcel is one of the inspirations that keeps me coming back to Haiti!

———>●●<———

Benedict is the second person who truly exemplifies this selfless characteristic of giving from his need and not merely from his extra. I have two stories where he did so. The first occurred when he was a young teenager. At that time, he was still living with his grandmother in Pendus. Whenever we were in Pendus, Benedict spent the entire day with us, wherever we would go, even if we hiked to Massacre or Mayombe. Since he was not officially part of our group, he would not eat with us. It was difficult enough to provide food for our group and interpreters without adding others from the community. So he would continue to have his daily meal at his grandmother's house.

One night after we had finished our dinner, we were sitting in the courtyard area behind the church. One of Benedict's friends came up to me and told me that Benedict was hungry. That surprised me because he had never said that before, and we had been coming several years by then. That day we had spent in Massacre, leaving early and returning late. Apparently, when he went home, there was no food left. Without electricity, it is difficult to save food. Whatever is fixed is eaten that same day. When it is gone, there is no more until the next day. We had no leftover food from our dinner either. However, I found some bread, peanut butter, and bananas to get him something to eat, enough to satisfy a growing teenage boy!

The next day we hiked to Mayombe, again leaving early. It was early enough that Benedict would not have eaten before he joined us to climb up that mountain. I did not want him to go all day before eating and then have the possibility of him missing his meal with his grandmother again, so I brought a granola bar with me to give to him. As we started hiking up the mountain, I discreetly gave it to him as I did not have enough for everyone.

As Benedict opened it, one of his good friends ran up to us so he could walk with us. Without anything being said between the boys, Benedict broke the small granola bar in half and handed it to his friend. Before either of them could take a bite of their meager portion, a third boy joined our group. Again, without a word being said, both boys broke off a small piece of their remaining bar and voluntarily gave it to the third teenager.

Hunger was a shared reality for those three boys, yet they could ignore their own immediate needs and think first of each other. An entire granola bar for a teenage boy probably couldn't begin to satisfy his hunger, but one-third of a bar was sufficient so no one went without at least a bite! I was certain that if I had given Benedict three granola bars to begin with, he would have shared all of them in the same manner and not save something back for himself for later. It was incredible to witness, and a lesson I will not forget.

Benedict again exemplified this marvelous selfless attribute a few years later. He was then living in Port-au-Prince and finishing up his final year of high school. It was much more expensive for us to provide for his education in PAP as it now included room and board and transportation costs. Plus, the school was more expensive than the one he went to in Gros Morne. Benedict knew this and appreciated it.

We arrived at Matthew 25 late in the afternoon on our first day in Haiti. We spent the night, planning to take off for Pendus the next morning. Benedict would be going with us that next day since he was now one of our interpreters for the trip. Eager to see us since it had been nearly a year since we were last in Haiti, Benedict came to visit us that first evening at the guesthouse. We too were ecstatic to see him. However, his first words to Sharon were, "I hope you don't get mad at me." Sharon was baffled as she could not think of any reason to ever be mad at him.

Benedict went on to tell her that he knew that it was expensive for us to provide for him to go to school in PAP. However, instead of eating two meals a day with the money we had sent to him, he was only eating one meal. The money he saved from not eating the extra meal, he was sending back to the principal at St. Joseph School in Pendus to provide tuition for three children he did not know to go to primary school there.

Of course, neither of us could possibly be mad at him. What a wonderful witness he had just given of putting his faith into action with his sharing, a sharing that absolutely was not merely from his superfluous goods!

———⇒»●«⇐———

Leonel was the third person on my list of people who gave from all he had. On Kyle's first trip to Haiti, we walked up to Massacre. We spent more time there than planned. Kyle was getting hungry. He wanted to walk back down the mountain ahead of the rest of our group. I told him he could go only if a Haitian would go with him to make sure he did not get lost. Leonel was a teenager about the same age as Kyle. He volunteered to walk back with Kyle.

We took a Polaroid camera on that trip. Getting your picture taken and getting a print of it is a much bigger deal in rural Haiti than it is in the United States. It is very much appreciated. We took many photos that we could instantly develop and give to the anxiously waiting recipient. Leonel was one of the many proud owners of his own Polaroid photo.

Later, on our last night, Kyle asked me if I had anything he could give to Leonel as a thank you for helping him earlier in the week. All I had was a T-shirt that I was wearing, so I gave it to Kyle to give to Leonel. Even a worn, dirty T-shirt would be appreciated.

The next morning as we were climbing into our vehicles to leave, Leonel came up to Kyle and gave him his Polaroid photo. Knowing how important it was to him, Kyle started to balk but I encouraged him to take it. Leonel simply wanted to reciprocate the gift exchange with Kyle. It would have hurt his pride not to accept the gift. Obviously, it was the only thing that Leonel had that he felt worthy of giving as a gift. Kyle had to accept it.

While his giving may have been on a much lesser scale than my other examples, it is not the size of the gift that matters to God. Remember in Mark 12:42 where the widow puts two small coins into church treasury. Jesus tells his disciples in 12:43–44, "Amen, I say to you, this poor widow put in more than all the other contributors to the treasury. For they have all contributed from their surplus wealth, but she, from her poverty, has contributed all she had, her whole livelihood."

I appreciate witnessing these many learning opportunities on selfless giving throughout my many trips to Haiti.

Madam Marcel has faithfully provided medical
care in Pendus for nearly two decades.

12

Pa Vini Se Pwazon

The Lord will guard your coming and going both now and forever.
—Psalm 121:8

TRANSLATED, THIS HAITIAN PROVERB MEANS, "Not to go is poison." It is like our idiom "Wild horses couldn't keep me away!" Both mean "Nothing will stop me from going!"

This saying came up on one of our earlier trips to Pendus before St. Joseph became a full-time parish with a permanent pastor assigned there. Back then, Father Cha Cha would get to the Pendus area only a couple times a month to visit with the community and to celebrate Mass. Those stays were often short stints as he had other duties to fulfill in Gros Morne and some of its many chapels. Life of a priest in rural Haiti is not easy.

However, when our group would come to Haiti, Father would get to spend more time than normal in Pendus and its six chapels as he would stay with us for our entire visit. Father would celebrate Mass every day somewhere when we were in Pendus. Sometimes it would be at St. Joseph's Church in Pendus and sometimes it would be at one of the surrounding chapels we would be visiting that day.

One day a local woman attended the morning Mass at St. Joseph. Later, she asked Father where he would be the following day and if there would be Mass. He told her he would be celebrating Mass in Massacre. He asked if she would be there too, knowing it would be a two-mile walk up the mountain. Her response was "Pa vini se pwazon." He chuckled at her answer and immediately interpreted its meaning for me. Instantly, I understood her intense desire to go to Mass no matter how inconvenient it would be for her to attend! I was impressed.

That passionate, unstoppable desire to go somewhere can also be used to describe our trips to Haiti. For most people, it would even apply to our "routine" trips from Lafayette to Pendus and not just the ones with extenuating circumstances!

A normal visit would start with getting up about 1:00 a.m. so we could all assemble at my house by 2:00 a.m. By the time we would load our luggage, usually into a Central Catholic High School bus, we would then be on the road by 2:30. We would arrive at the Indianapolis airport by 4:00 a.m. and unload our numerous bags, and there always were many! There would be four per person as we each were allowed two checked-in bags that we filled with items we were taking for use in Pendus along with one carry-on apiece and one backpack apiece for our personal needs for the trip. A small group of only ten travelers would then have forty pieces of luggage to move through the line at the airlines counter.

Once the checked-in bags were weighed, tagged, and sent on through, we each still had our carry-on and backpack to lug around with us the rest of the day. Our flights out of Indianapolis usually take off by 6:00 a.m. We then head to one of many layover cities en route ultimately to Miami. Often those layovers are less than one hour, making it difficult to make the connection even when the airlines were running on time, which isn't always the case! The short turnaround time is not only difficult for us to meet, but also for the airlines to get our massive number of bags to the connecting flight.

Once in Miami, we catch our third flight of the day on to Haiti. The turnaround time in Miami may be a few minutes longer than our first layover of the day, but we have no time to spare there either. The Miami airport is so massive and the international gate so far from our domestic arrival gate that we often do not have time to eat before boarding! Again, the luggage transfer is always a concern. We frequently deal with late or delayed luggage by the time we finally arrive in Port-au-Prince.

Once we are in Port-au-Prince and collect the luggage that made it, we proceed through customs. This can be a difficult experience at times, but one that a "tip" to the right person helps speed along! Whenever the luggage does not arrive when we do, a new set of problems arise. In the United States, the airlines will eventually deliver the luggage to you. In Haiti, you must keep coming back to the airport to check if it has arrived. The extra time necessary for this is not always a luxury that we have to spare. To make that situation even more difficult, our interpreters are never inside the secured portion of the airport to be able to help.

After exiting the airport, we meet up with Father or his drivers or with the folks from Matthew 25 Guest House, depending on what transportation arrangements had been made for that trip. Luckily, that has rarely been a problem for us. Only once has someone failed to meet us at the airport. We usually arrive at the guesthouse after dark. By the time we get settled in, eat dinner, and get to bed, we usually have been up over twenty hours.

It is easy to see why someone may think "Pa vini se pwazon" applies even to a normal trip to Haiti. However, I have four more extreme examples of our desire to reach a destination despite the obstacles in our way. Three of these stories exhibit our struggles to get from Indiana to Pendus. Two of those three incidences occurred while we were still in the United States, the third one while we traveled within Haiti. The final travel episode found us simply trying to get from Pendus to Montbayard.

<hr>

The first travel-weary story occurred during our December 2009 trip. Sharon, Kyle, and I went to Haiti six days before the rest of our group, leaving on December 20. We were meeting our friend Andre Angrand there. He was going to take us sightseeing several places throughout Haiti as well as take us to midnight Mass at his childhood church in Terre Rouge. On a normal trip, we never had time to do very much sightseeing, especially outside of Port-au-Prince. We also had never had the opportunity to celebrate the blessed Christmas holiday while in Haiti. We were anxiously awaiting these new experiences.

At that time, Kyle was in graduate school at Tufts University in Boston, so we were to meet up with both Andre and Kyle in Port-au-Prince. Kyle took the bus to New York City to spend a few days with a friend. He was then going to catch a plane that would take him directly from JFK airport to Port-au-Prince. I was a bit jealous of his travel arrangements as he would have no layovers and arrive in Haiti barely three and a half hours after takeoff! That sounded so much better than our typical itinerary!

However, the day did not go as planned. The start of our many airline problems began at the Delta counter in Indianapolis. With only one other person in line at 4:15 a.m., we were still instructed to use the kiosk to get our boarding passes instead of using the person at the counter. The kiosk wanted to charge us $25 for each of our four checked-in suitcases. I questioned the lady at the counter as our travel agent had assured us that there still was no such charge for international travel. She quickly, and rather rudely, told me that the rule was changed in September so we had to pay. I swiped my credit card, figuring I could argue later if I needed to do so. When the tags for the checked-in bags were printed, they only went to Miami and not through to Port-au-Prince. Back to the counter I went. Now we had to get in another line to address this problem, and there were about a dozen in line now.

Thirty minutes later, a different lady waited on us. She said we didn't tell them that we had an international flight, but I had told them! Besides, the kiosk did not ask if Miami was a final destination or not! She said we should have only been charged $30 for the bags (and not $25 apiece) and agreed to void the $100 charge. She said she could check our bags all the way to Port-au-Prince (PAP) for us but she could only get us our boarding passes for the two legs of the trip on Delta—Indy to Atlanta and Atlanta to Miami. She directed us to the American Air counter to get the boarding pass for the final leg to PAP.

At the American counter, the lady there discovered our bags were *not* checked through to PAP but instead to POP, which is Port-o-Plaza in Dominican Republic! Back to Delta's counter I went. This time I did not stand in line but went directly to the lady that previously mis-tagged the bags. She did apologize and said she "probably" could get this corrected. *Probably* wasn't the word I wanted to hear as getting late delivered suitcases in Haiti can be a major headache. And stuff can disappear!

Finally, we were on our way. Our Delta flight took off at 6:15 and landed in Atlanta at 7:30. While we were in the air, Kyle e-mailed us. His ordeal was just beginning. It had snowed ten inches the day before in New York City. He arrived early at JFK that morning only to find his nonstop flight to PAP had been *cancelled* and not merely postponed! His flight was a destination flight, meaning the plane was not going on further to another city, it would simply reload with passengers at some point later that day and return to JFK. There were over three hundred folks booked on this flight to Haiti and most of them were Haitians going home for the holidays. With that plane not going on to another destination, it seemed premature to cancel that flight instead of simply delaying its takeoff. Not only was his flight cancelled, but Delta had rebooked Kyle for *December 28* to fly to PAP. How could anyone assume that *eight* days later would be even remotely satisfactory travel arrangements, especially when trying to get there before Christmas!

Upon our arrival in Atlanta, I called home to warn next week's group from duplicating our Delta "kiosk" fiasco! I also called my travel agent. She always did a tremendous job for us, especially when we are having problems. Again, she stepped up to help Kyle. Both Kyle, at the Delta counter in New York, and our agent, online, tried every conceivable way to get Kyle out of New York and on some route—any route—to Haiti.

We took off for Miami at 9:12 a.m., and nothing was resolved yet. Upon our arrival in Miami at 10:50, we immediately contacted

Kyle. He was so frustrated with Delta. They would not fly him from JFK to anywhere in the United States at any time before December 28. Kyle said by 10:00 a.m., his original departure time, the tarmac was cleared and planes were taking off and landing. He decided to rent a car and head toward Miami. If he hurried, he could catch a flight the next morning from there to PAP. While trying to rent his car, he helped three Haitian nuns, who didn't speak any English, get a car rental too.

An hour after Kyle left, heading to Miami, our agent found a 9:00 a.m. flight out of Atlanta for the next day. It was the same flight we had just taken to Miami with a subsequent connection to PAP. He immediately changed directions and headed to Atlanta. He would now incur an enhanced drop-off fee from the rental company. However, this would shave at least ten-twelve hours off his driving time. That was beneficial because by then he had already been awake nearly thirty consecutive hours.

In the meantime, Kyle's cell phone was about out of charge. He had his regular charger with him but not a car charger. Therefore, he had to stop at a truck plaza to buy an AC-DC converter so he could keep his phone operative so we could stay in touch. By then Andre had already landed in PAP and was at Matthew 25 waiting for the rest of us to arrive. By text and e-mail, all of us could stay in communication with each other. Andre communicated with Matthew 25 that Kyle would not need picked up that day!

We boarded America flight No. 625 on time. However, as we started to taxi, the stewardesses realized one of the seats was empty that should have had a passenger. A young lady that was traveling with her mother was locked in the bathroom and refused to come out. The pilot made both get off, which only took about thirty minutes. However, it then took over another hour to get their checked-in luggage off the plane as well. It was a long wait sitting on the tarmac. Again, I could e-mail Andre and warn him that we would be late arriving in PAP. Thank goodness for modern technology as this communication would not have been possible a short time ago.

We landed in PAP at 5:48 p.m., almost two hours late. We would now find out if our bags made it with us or not after all the confusion earlier that morning! Once we were through immigration, Sharon watched the carry-ons and backpacks while I searched for our checked-in luggage. Almost everyone had already found their bags and left before our four suitcases finally came down the conveyor! What a wonderful sight they were to see!

We got through customs without any problems and headed outside the airport into the onslaught. We did not get too far when we saw our driver from Matthew 25. At last things seemed to be going right for us!

Sister Mary Finnick had Sharon and me staying in one of the rooftop rooms at Matthew 25 and Kyle and Andre in another. These rooms had electric fans in them this year, which is good since the temperature was in the 80s and it was humid. This was Andre's first time to stay at Matthew 25 as he and his wife Josee always previously stayed with family when in PAP.

Andre had the international package on his Blackberry, so we could e-mail and text with Kyle to monitor his progress getting to Atlanta. He was in North Carolina when we went to bed at 10:00 p.m. What a day.

I got a good night's sleep. I didn't hear any noises until after 4:00 a.m. I was up at 6:00 a.m. and took a shower. It was cold but still felt good. A shower in Haiti is not like one in the USA. It starts with much less water pressure and no warm or hot water. You get wet, shut the water off, lather up, and then rinse off. Many times you can take a shower and use less than two gallons of water!

Andre got a text from Kyle. He had made it to the apartment of his friend who lived in the Atlanta area by 3:00 a.m. to take a shower and then head on to the airport.

I exchanged some US dollars for Haitian goudes. The exchange rate was 8.2 Haitian dollars for each US dollar, which made this the highest exchange rate in my then twelve visits to Haiti. The exchange was eight-to-one the previous December and four-to-one on my first visit in 2000. Each Haitian dollar is worth five goudes, meaning each

US dollar is now worth forty two goudes. Therefore, a single goude was worth about two and half cents. Both ratios are important as some prices are in goudes and some in Haitian dollars. These math calculations will become very common over the next two weeks—and not easy to do in your head!

Andre arranged for a car rental for us to use this week, along with a driver named Leonce. He knew his way around everywhere, including many shortcuts and back roads that avoided traffic snarls. We got to see quite a bit of PAP and its surrounding sites by mid-afternoon. We then drove by the US Embassy and new St. Dameon's Children's hospital as we anticipated Kyle's arrival on the 4:00 p.m. American flight. We saw his plane fly overhead approaching its landing at PAP Toussaint International Airport. Since the embassy and hospital were close to the airport, we were there and parked before Kyle emerged with his luggage. It was good to see him. By the end of the day, he had been up over fifty-five consecutive hours! What an ordeal! But it was worth it. "Pa vini se pwazon!"

———◦———

The next extraordinary experience occurred on the December 2012 trip. I was up at 1:20 a.m. and took my last hot shower for a while! When I went downstairs, there were already several vehicles in my driveway and on the street in front of my house. We were to meet here at 2:00 a.m. but most were here early, a very good sign for this group!

Our drivers had the Lafayette Central Catholic High School bus there ready to take us to the Indianapolis Airport. Even Deacon John Jezierski, who did not go on this trip, came to give the group a final travel blessing and pass out crosses to each of us. Once everyone said their final good-bye to those not going, we were on the road by 2:20 a.m. Little did we know that would be the last time that day we would be ahead of schedule!

Blizzard conditions were forecast in Indianapolis that morning. Luckily, we made it to the airport by 3:45 a.m. before it began snowing! We checked in at the United Airlines counter. Each of our bags weighed just under the fifty-pound limit. However, United charges $25 for the *first* bag and $40 for the second. Good thing I had a charge card with me! As we were finished checking in the departure board still had our flight listed as on time. That was good as we only had a scheduled ninety-minute layover in Newark, New Jersey. It was also good as many of the later flights for the day had already been canceled in anticipation of the bad weather predicted for the day!

However, by the time we reached the gate at 5:00 a.m., our takeoff was pushed back an hour to 7:15. We were told that the head pilots scheduled at both our gate and the adjoining gate were both sick. Because the adjoining gate's departure was slightly before ours, that flight took our assistant pilot and took off nearly on time. We were assured that two backup pilots were on the way and would man our flight. Unfortunately, now it was snowing!

By 7:00 our takeoff was pushed to 7:30 and then to 7:45. Our window of opportunity to make connections in Newark was quickly dwindling to mere minutes. Our arrival gate was only four numbers from our gate of departure in Newark. That might be our saving grace. I talked with the lady at our gate. She said they could not guarantee our connecting flight would wait for us even though we have eleven in our group. This was disappointing to me since that flight is a destination flight to Port-au-Prince. It did not have to go on to a further stop.

Finally, we boarded. I was already seated when the lady from the gate came to me. She said that our estimated arrival time in Newark was now 10:30, a full thirty minutes past the scheduled departure of our connecting flight. If we go and miss the connection, we will be stuck in Newark and the best she could do for us was find a flight to Port-au-Prince on December 31! To make matters worse, we would not get a refund for that portion of the flight even if we returned to Indianapolis! It was a quick decision, but we decided to get off. It took about thirty minutes to get our bags off the plane and returned to us at the baggage claim area. The blizzard conditions were now here in full force. Soon all flights were canceled for the rest of the day at Indianapolis, and the plane that we were on did not ever takeoff. The lady did, however, issue each one of us a full refund from the gate area!

As the others in our group gathered our twenty-two suitcases and duffels, I got on my phone. First I called Western Union to add more minutes to my phone card to make anticipated calls to Haiti this morning! Next, I contacted our new travel agent, who was based in Colorado. It was a two-hour difference in time, meaning it was only 7:00 a.m. in Colorado. He was off work this week but put me in touch with his partner. My first question to him was, "Can we get to Port-au-Prince today or tomorrow?" We had a place to stay at Matthew 25 Guest House that night but not the next one. If we could arrive in PAP early enough the next day, say before 3:00 p.m., we could simply get picked up at the airport and drive straight to either Gros Morne or Pendus. We have never attempted that before, mainly because it wasn't always safe to drive at night. But the roads, at least to Gonaives, are in much better condition than in the past. We could potentially get to Gros Morne in about four hours as opposed to six to eight hours in years past.

It was obvious that we would not fly out of Indianapolis at all today. I went downstairs to check rates and availability of vehicles at all six car-rental places at the airport. Only one had two minivans that would accommodate eleven people and thirty-three pieces of luggage, twenty-two for our check-ins plus eleven personal carry-ons, plus backpacks for everyone. I found out the price for one-way rentals to both Atlanta and Miami. The lady at National promised to hold both for me until we could find out about possible flights.

Back upstairs I went. I tried to call Matthew 25 but no one answered. I knew there was a new volunteer starting today at Matthew 25, so I wanted to let her know we were not coming and ask about possibly staying tomorrow.

I e-mailed everyone in Gros Morne to let them know of our situation—Father Joseph; Father Wilner; Sister Jackie; Sister Pat; and Aileen Reed, the year-round Quest volunteer at Sister Jackie's house in Gros Morne. I did not know who would be the first to see the e-mail about our predicament and respond. Aileen answered first. She said she would try to contact Matthew 25 for me. She also would notify Father Joseph of our logistical problems and see if they could get us from Port-au-Prince whenever we would arrive.

After many e-mails and phone calls, our travel agent said he could get us all on a flight from Atlanta (on Delta) in the morning to Ft. Lauderdale. We would have to shuttle all our stuff to the Miami airport. Thankfully, we would have a four-hour layover to do it in! He then could get all of us on the mid-afternoon American flight to PAP. At least this was doable and the pieces of this puzzle were starting to fit together. I still did not have a place to stay in PAP the next night.

We decided to go ahead and rent the two vehicles. Even with blizzard conditions in southern Indiana, I estimated we could be in Atlanta between 11:00 p.m. and midnight. I went to rent the vehicles. However, we'd need someone with a driver's license and credit card for each vehicle. Unfortunately, I did not bring my driver's license this year. I have never needed it in the past as my passport was sufficient for any ID purposes. Therefore, I could not be a driver or the one to rent the vehicle. Luckily, others in our group had their licenses. We paid for two drivers for both vehicles and for insurance on the vehicles as we did not know how bad the wintery conditions would be that we may encounter. We had Mickey Rigdon and Tamara Shields rent the first vehicle and Jim Morris and Paula Max the second.

At 12:20 p.m., we loaded up and left the airport. Jim drove the vehicle that I was in along with Paula, Allison, and Danielle. Mickey drove the other vehicle with Tamara, Heather, Sydney, Jennifer, and Kaitlyn. The road conditions were not good, but the road was still passable, and there was some traffic. We drove between twenty-five and thirty miles per hour all the way to Louisville, Kentucky, taking over three hours to go that first one hundred miles. Slow as that was, it was still faster than traveling the mountains in Haiti!

I rode shotgun and worked my phone the entire time as I was still trying to get everything worked out with plane arrangements,

Matthew 25, the interpreters, and the two drivers who were going to be picking us up in PAP. I guess it was a good thing I could not drive. In anticipation of the drive, Danielle and Paula bought a couple plugs for the car cigarette lighter that would allow our phones to be charged by our electrical chargers. That too was a good thing as we all took turns keeping our phones charged.

About an hour into our drive, our agent called with wonderful news. He found a flight that would accommodate all eleven of us to take us from Ft. Lauderdale to Port-au-Prince, meaning we would not have to man-handle luggage from Ft. Lauderdale to Miami! I quickly called the folks in the other car and told them the good news. It was about time we had some that day!

When we got past Louisville, the snow stopped and we drove in a mist. Eventually it dried up, and we could drive at the posted speed limit, which was 75 mph in some parts and 70 mph in others. Our vehicle stopped at a Ryan's Restaurant in Bowling Green, Kentucky, for dinner. It was a welcome respite. Instead the other group made a stop at the Bowling Green Kmart before meeting us to get enough gas to reach Atlanta. I guess they had enough snacks to satisfy themselves without stopping to eat.

Our drive took us through Nashville, Tennessee; Chattanooga, Tennessee; and eventually to Atlanta. Mickey and Jim wound up doing all the driving. By the time we reached the airport in Atlanta at 10:45 p.m., I figured we nearly drove the same distance as from Miami to PAP, having just driven from Lafayette to Atlanta! We discussed getting a hotel for the night but decided against the extra expense, especially since we would only be there about four hours before returning to the terminal to get checked in.

Unfortunately, our ordeal was not yet over. Mickey and Jim let the rest of us off at the departure area for Delta while they returned the rentals. This is a huge area as Atlanta is Delta's main hub. We amassed the luggage along a wall, and I went to look for an open desk. At this hour, there was only one open clear at the other end of the terminal. I asked a lady at the desk how early we could check the luggage. She said any time up to twelve hours before our flight left. That was great news as we could now rid ourselves of lugging those bags everywhere! I got in line for that desk as there were about a dozen folks ahead of us. The others began to bring the bags close to this counter. Soon Mickey, Tamara, Jim, and Paula were back to help. However, when I got to the counter, the lady said the twelve-hour rule applied only on the day of travel and it wasn't yet December 27. The check-in counter did not open for the next day's flights until 4:30 a.m. So we hauled the luggage back toward where we started.

Once spread out along the wall, we all began to get ready to sleep on the floor around all those bags. We had all been up for at least twenty-four hours by the time we laid down! Most of us had brought a lightweight blanket for use in Pendus, which we used as we tried to rest on the hard tile floor. Many of us also used our backpacks for a pillow. I had a Tilly hat which I laid over my face to block out the light of the airport. It was difficult to sleep, between the lights and the noise of cleaning crew and few passengers walking past us, but we were exhausted.

The floor was hard, and I did get chilly by the time I got up. I know I managed to get a couple hours of sleep before getting up at 3:30. A trip to the closest bathroom allowed me to brush my teeth and wash my face.

The lady at the Delta counter was still there. Apparently, she worked the graveyard shift. She told me she would open the check in counter at 4:15 just so we could be first in line and give them our twenty-two check-in bags. Delta did not charge for the first bag and because four of our group now had first class tickets, they did not have to pay for their second bag either. That did save a bit considering everything else has turned out to be more expensive thus far.

By the time we got all our bags to her check in station, there was a line forming for the normal 4:30 a.m. start. They must have wondered why we were getting to cut to the front and begin checking in before the posted opening time!

We went through security and headed toward the gate. About 6:20 a.m., I got a call from Duane Sellers. His St. Thomas Aquinas group (from West Lafayette) was attempting to do the same United

Airlines flights from Indianapolis that we were scheduled to take the day before. They were already delayed enough due to mechanical problems to make missing connections in Newark a real possibility. He said between his group and another, there were forty-five people heading to Haiti from the Indy airport today! I later learned that they indeed missed the connection and had to spend the night at a hotel in Newark at the expense of United.

We all boarded Delta flight No. 2352, and it took off on time at 6:55 a.m. We were finally on our way! We landed in Ft. Lauderdale about 8:30. It was fifty-five degrees outside.

We had plenty of time to eat. I also e-mailed Fritzner. Since we were not staying at Matthew 25, I wanted to know if he could help me exchange some US dollars for Haitian goudes. He said we could stop along the way to Gros Morne and make the exchange. He said the current exchange rate was almost 8.5 Haitian dollars for each US dollar. From a Haitian's perspective, the exchange rate keeps getting worse.

Kyle e-mailed me and said he had friends who lived in St. Marc and had worked for him at the plastic recycling plant in PAP that he ran earlier in 2012. He said he had contacted them and they could make food for us and sell it to us as we passed through St. Marc as we headed north. It was a gracious offer, but Father's e-mail to me said that Madam Marcel Garson would have dinner ready and waiting on us when we arrived no matter how late that would be! She is such a good cook that you don't want to miss one of her meals.

Many of us also made final phone calls home before leaving the United States.

We finally boarded American flight No. 2285 and took off for Haiti about 1:15 p.m. As usual, the flight took about two hours as we landed in PAP at 3:15. It was eighty-seven degrees and sunny! We deplaned and walked across the tarmac to get inside the airport. Since the earthquake in 2010, the normal part of the airport for baggage claim, immigration, and customs had been closed for repair (using temporary quarters at the end of the building). However, it was now open again and was very nice. It now had air conditioning.

It only took about an hour to get through immigration and collect our luggage. Every bag made it! We piled the bags on six carts and walked our caravan of luggage to customs. The official stationed there asked if we had any medicines. We didn't, and I told them that. He did not seem to believe me as he saw all those full bags. Finally, he waved us through and we were quickly outside. We quickly spied our drivers and interpreters and got loaded up for the long drive north to Pendus. It was a snug fit in both vehicles for this ride. With the interpreters, we now had fourteen people plus two drivers and the luggage, some of which was tied down on top!

Our travels had us in St. Marc at 7:30 p.m. We stopped long enough for Fritzner to get me some money exchanged and for a couple of the girls to experience going to the bathroom alongside the road (in the middle of town)! At least it was dark outside. Welcome to Haiti! We continued to make good time heading north as we reached Gonaives at 8:00 and Gros Morne at 8:45. There to meet us at the rectory was Father Joseph Telcin, Father Wilner Donecia, Sister Jackie Picard, Sister Pat Dillon, Aileen Reed, and Fessen. We all had a chance to use real restrooms and then transfer our bags from this vehicle to one more suited to traverse the rougher terrain awaiting us over the last ten miles to Pendus.

At 9:30, we took off for the final leg of our journey. Father Joseph was riding his motorcycle with us to Pendus, so I hopped on for a ride. It was a beautiful full-moon evening, which allowed more of the terrain to be seen at such a late hour! There was much jostling in the vehicle on this leg, bringing home the point that we were truly in a country lacking in modern infrastructure available to us in the USA.

I was disappointed that everyone was not able to see much of the surroundings on the ride north from PAP because it was dark most of the way but grateful to be able to arrive in Pendus that day. When you think about it, we usually reach Pendus sometime in late afternoon or early evening on our second day of travel. On this trip, we arrived in Pendus at 10:30 p.m. on our second day, not that much later than usual! We somehow were back on schedule.

The third prime example of our dogged determination to get to Pendus, and possibly the most difficult trek of all, occurred on our December 2004 trip. It took us three days and two nights to get from Port-au-Prince to Pendus! Fortunately, our travel from the United States to Haiti went smoothly that year.

We landed in Port-au-Prince airport at 3:00 p.m. on December 27. It was sunny and a pleasant eighty-four degrees. We had a doctor and three nurses on this trip, so we had a lot of medicines with us to be used for clinics during our stay. All the suitcases arrived, and we made it through customs without any problems. Things seemed to be going our way!

While we were gathering our luggage the word *probably* became the word of the trip! I asked Domond, our driver, how many pieces of luggage he had already taken out to the truck. He answered, "Probably nine!" I didn't want *probably*. I wanted *exactly*!

We were scheduled to take our eighteen checked-in bags directly to the domestic airport in PAP, located about a half mile west of the main terminal. Instead of driving to Pendus, we were flying from PAP north in the morning to Port-de-Paix (PAX). The planes that we would use were very small and had severe weight limitations. We needed the luggage at the domestic airport then so it could be flown to PAX on both the last flight of that day and the first flight the next. Hopefully, the luggage would then be in PAX airport when we finally arrived. When I asked Domond if the luggage would be safe in PAX until we got there, he again answered, "Probably!" Again, not the "exact" answer I was looking for!

While the others waited at the airport parking lot with the carry-on luggage, Domond, Michelle Ray, and I took the checked-in pieces to the domestic airport. We got them scanned through security and then weighed. However, since we were so late leaving Miami and arriving in PAP, we missed putting them on the last flight of the day. We were told that they would go on both the 6:30 a.m. and 8:30 a.m. flight in the morning. Each person on the Tropical Air flight was then allowed sixty-pounds of luggage. All extra weight was charged at fifty-cents per pound.

We drove back and picked up the rest of our crew and luggage. They had been by themselves with their carry-on luggage for over an hour in the parking lot, enough time to make even a veteran to Haiti a little uneasy. We quickly loaded up and headed to Visitation House. We arrived shortly after 4:00 p.m. Our rooms were the ones on the upstairs balcony area. It was too late to try and go anywhere in PAP, so we had plenty of time to relax, look at the arts and crafts for sale at VH, and to simply talk.

I had several letters to deliver to different people in Haiti upon my arrival. They were in the top outside zipper compartment of my carry-on. However, American Air made both me and Roy check them at the last moment before boarding in Miami. All the envelopes in that compartment were opened. If any money or checks were in them before, they were now gone. So were two music CDs I brought. Roy checked his bag and found his cell phone, which he stored in the same compartment on his carry-on, was also missing. We did not know whether the items were tampered with in Miami or Port-au-Prince. Maybe we would find out when we got home.

We all settled up with Visitation House which had prepaid our Tropical Air flight that we'd be taking the next day. Many of us got our first Haitian shower that night. There was a near full moon out that night and the temperatures were very comfortable both for sitting outside as well as for sleeping. We were all in bed by 10:30 p.m.

I slept very well despite a few night noises, such as dogs barking, roosters crowing, and some traffic driving by VH. I was up at 5:45 a.m. and took a morning shower.

Breakfast was at 6:30 a.m. Our flight with Tropical Air was on a twelve-seater. We had twelve people, the nine of us plus three interpreters. We took off at 8:45 a.m. The skies were clear and the view spectacular as we took off.

Our thirty-five-minute flight to Port-de-Paix turned cloudy before we could fly over Gonaives (about halfway). By the time we landed at PAX it was raining and had been for about twenty-four hours. The gravel runway that we landed on had many puddles of standing water.

Once we landed, we learned that only one of our checked-in bags was in PAX and the other seventeen were still back in PAP. We were told they should be up on the next flight, which was at 11:00 a.m. We stood around for about a half an hour before Sister Jackie arrived with our two drivers, Tidan and Barak. The muddy roads from Gros Morne had slowed their travel time to come meet us.

We decided to leave Tidan and Fritzner (with our carry-on bags and the one checked-in suitcase we already had) to wait on the arrival of the other checked-in pieces. The rest of us, thirteen in all, headed in one van for Pendus shortly after 10:00 a.m.

The approximate twenty-four-mile trip usually takes about two and a half hours to complete. There was intermittent rain the whole way and lots of mud to maneuver through. There was lots of jostling in the back of the vehicle. We stopped for a stretch break in Basson Bleu, where we could buy some snacks such as Pringles, cookies, and drinks.

By 1:30 we arrived at the Pendus River crossing. It was raining hard, and the river was high, about belt high. It was too deep and flowing too fast for us to drive across. The "miracle" of this trip is that there were now cell phones that were operable in these remote mountains. Madam Marcel had one in Pendus while Sister Pat, Father Wilner, Tidan, and Sister Jackie all also had one! We called Madam Marcel and told her of our predicament. She said she had food ready for us and would walk it down to us via another route through the mountain that had an easier pedestrian crossing over the river.

Since we were cramped and muggy inside the car, we told her we'd backtrack about a half mile to the chapel at Berard and wait for her there. Several of the locals were at Berard soon after we arrived, including Simeon Pericles, a young man who I knew. He could speak some English, so it helped in our conversation. Before long we saw Tidan pass by the muddy road in front of Berard. We got his attention, and he stopped. Only eight more suitcases had arrived on the 11:00 a.m. flight. They assured us the rest would come on the 4:00 p.m. flight. However, Tidan couldn't stay that late in PAX as traveling in the dark is not safe even with good weather conditions.

A couple of the neighboring ladies brought hot chocolate and bread over for us. About the same time, Madam Marcel and ten others arrived carrying our dinner on their heads, walking through the mud and the rain! We shared the hot chocolate with those who carried the food since they were wet and cold. Some of us even shared our jackets with them to help them warm up.

What a feast Madam Marcel brought! We had chicken, rice and beans, french fries, bread, peanut butter, pop (Coke; Sprite; and Corroune, a Haitian cream soda), and beer (Prestige). When we finished eating, we decided to try and make it to Gros Morne for the night and then try again to reach Pendus the next day.

We made it to the next-to-last river to cross heading east when we realized we wouldn't be able to cross that river either. It was much too deep, even deeper than the Pendus River was! Now we couldn't go north (to Pendus), east (to Gros Morne), or south (because the Twa Riveria paralleled much of the road from PAX to Gros Morne.) We could not go west all the way back to Port-de-Paix either. It was too far. Our only choice was to head back west toward PAX to stay at the chapel at Kayimit or sleep in the cars!

Therefore, we headed to Kayimit, not arriving until after dark about 6:30 p.m. In a matter of minutes someone heard our horn and came to let us inside. Seemingly minutes later, someone else brought us enough pillows for each of us and some sheets to use as covers. We had no lights, electricity, or water at Kayimit. We simply turned some pews around to face another pew and make a "bed" out of it. It was 7:30 p.m., and we were all tired and had no lights but our flashlights, so we all went to bed.

There was no bathroom there either, but there was an outhouse, a short muddy walk outside the side chapel door. It did get used several times during the evening and night.

It rained periodically throughout the night, and the temperatures cooled off. I was sleeping without a sheet, and I had loaned Onvile my jacket back at Berard. I started the night in shorts and T-shirt. Before the night was over, I put on a pair of socks, long underwear (both top and bottom), and a pair of pants, and another shirt to try and stay warm. Once I was warm, it was amazing how well I did sleep on wooden pews!

We all were roused at 5:45 a.m. when Tidan and Barak turned on the hazard lights on their vehicles. They both thought we could cross the Lacul River if we left immediately, so we packed up quickly and headed for Gros Morne. By 7:30 we arrived for a brief stop at Father Wilner's rectory called Kay Pe.

We met Father Wilner there for the first time. Father Nestley and Fessen were also there to greet us. We then headed to Sister Jackie's house called Kay Se. Sister Pat Dillon was there to greet us and assign us our rooms. Madam Marcel had called already that morning and said the Pendus River was still too high and that we'd be better off trying again the next day.

Kay Se is a wonderful three-story concrete building, housing the nuns living quarters and gathering rooms, a kitchen, a dining room, a computer room, several guest rooms, and two shower-bathroom areas. This is where Kyle lived when he spent the summer in 2002. There are three pets there: two dogs named Tigger and Timmy and a cat named DC, which stands for Darn Cat or Dear Cat depending on the situation! They had decided to get the cat when a mouse ate through part of a recipe book they had.

After breakfast, Sister Jackie opened the artists' room at Kay Se so we could make any purchase we wanted. There were many hand-woven baskets and hot pads, small hand-painted crosses, and some Haitian embroidered clothing. Roy and I also went to the artists' building just outside the Kay Se compound. We met a couple of the local artists there, and Roy even bought one of their paintings.

Several of us then went down to the high school, John XXIII, which is located just down the mountain from Kay Se and the artists' building. The ground floor of the school housed a cyber café and a phone center, both of which were funded by the group that Lafayette businessman Jerry Brand headed up on our May 2004 trip.

Outside the high school is a soccer field. The basketball court was still not completed. It still needed a fence around it for safety since it is ground level at the north end and a nine-foot drop-off at the south end of the court! Father Nestley said he was still working to finish that project.

We drove down to Kay Pe for a late lunch about 1:45 p.m. Father Wilner, Father Sylvio, Father Nestley, and his brother Gabe Jean Jacques (who is an engineer) joined us for lunch. This was our first real chance to get to know Father Wilner. He told us that he was fifty-four years old and had been a priest for twenty-two years. His birthday is December 28, so we sang a belated "Happy Birthday" to him. He said he felt like "a child walking among us" since he was so new to Pendus and Gros Morne, having been there only six months. He had previously been the director of Caritas in PAX for ten years and was at St. Louis de Nordand Jean Rabel before that.

We went back to Kay Se for the evening. We shared our reflections on the day and the trip so far after we ate. The evening was cooler than the previous night, and there were a few stars peeking through the clouds. However there also seemed to be an intermittent spit of rain too! We were all in bed by 9:45 p.m.

I was up at 5:45 and got shaved and showered before anyone else was up and about. We had planned on getting an early start on our trek to Pendus. However, Madam Marcel called again and said we should wait another two hours to give the river more time to recede. We had a light breakfast of oranges, bread, jelly, and peanut butter before loading up and heading for Pendus at 9:30 a.m.

Our two vehicles were full, one with luggage and one with people. To make room to add Father Wilner to our vehicle, I offered to ride in the back of the luggage vehicle. There was a small space in the back corner for one person. I couldn't see the driver or Roy or Fritzner in the front seat because the luggage was stacked so high. The luggage also shifted with nearly every bump in the road. It wasn't long before I was fighting just to keep the small space I had!

We stopped for nearly a half an hour at the first river outside Gros Morne. There was a truck stuck on the opposite side. Hundreds of others waited with us for another truck to come along and help pull it out on the other side. Once the truck was moved, Tidan had us ready to roll so we could be the first ones through before anyone else could get stuck.

Despite all the mud, we were at the Pendus River at 11:00 a.m. The flow of the current would help us get across but would work against us coming back. Tidan said he could possibly get across the river but fearful he could not come back across. Since he still had to go back to PAX airport, he didn't want to be stuck on the other side of the river. Therefore, we emptied all the suitcases, carry-ons, and backpacks and prepared to walk across the river! Onvil, Serge, Vincent, Jean Claude, Johnny, and Benedict were there to meet us and help get us and our stuff across safely. Once everything was unloaded from the vehicles, Tidan and Fritzner headed for the airport in PAX while Barak headed back to Gros Morne.

Sharon, Michelle, and I went first so we could get across and take video and photos of the others coming after us. Two Haitians took Sharon's and Michelle's hands and helped them across the river. It was only about belt deep, but the current was quite swift.

While we were trying to get all our stuff across, there was a funeral marching down the hill, with about fifty people following the casket procession. They needed to cross the river as well. The casket was carried across by four or five men. At one point, they nearly stumbled due to the current. Dave Schmidt stepped in and helped keep the casket from falling into the river.

It took less than thirty minutes for us to unload the vehicle and for all of us to get across with the luggage! Once across, the Haitians each took a suitcase and headed the last ten kilometers for Pendus. As usual we were strung out as we hiked that last bit.

Father Wilner and I brought up the rear. We talked with each other the best we could. His English is much better than my Creole, but not proficient enough to make conversation easy. I did learn that his favorite Bible verse is Luke 4:16–21, so we did communicate somewhat! I knew I would have to look that verse up when I got there.

By 1:00 p.m. we were all finally at Pendus! Despite our long ordeal, each one of us would wholeheartedly agree that not to have gone would have been poison!

The fourth story found our December 2006 group trying to get from Pendus to the chapel at Montbayard. We had twelve people on that St. Mary team plus two interpreters and Father Wilner that needed to travel that eight-mile trek and then back again at the end of day. Thankfully, the first five miles were traversable by vehicle. It was the last three miles that were difficult.

Our two vehicles drove us to the Twa Riviere (translated as "Three Rivers") area. From there, we had to walk the final three miles up the mountain to Montbayard. Tidan, one of our trusted drivers from Gros Morne, rode a four-wheeler to meet us there. He used it to drive us across the river, three or four at a time. Once all were across, Sharon took off with several of the group. She wanted to be in front on the way up as the lead group can rest periodically while the others catch up to them. This hike was longer than those to Massacre and Mayombe but not as steep. However, the exposure to the sun would be harsher as there is almost no shade along the entire way.

Unbeknownst to me, Tidan left the four-wheeler for us to use. He asked if any of us ever driven one before! I said I had. At least two people would be able to ride on it as well as some of our gear. We had three suitcases of medical supplies, one bag of children's benediction gifts, and a five-gallon Culligan water bottle to take with us.

The people of Montbayard were also supposed to meet us and help transport our bags. Unfortunately, only one man on a donkey came to meet us. He could only carry two of the suitcases. I only had one small strap to hold the remaining bag and the five-gallon water container. Since Sharon had already left, I asked one of the interpreters to ride with me and help secure our cargo. To make room for me and my passenger, I had given my backpack to Alex Angrand to carry for me.

Frank Donaldson, Mollie Hanlon, and Emily Hilycord took turns carrying the last suitcase, often on top of their heads, Haitian-style.

Our group was well strung out in our caravan to Montbayard. Although I was riding, it was almost easier to hike than to drive as the terrain was so uneven that it was not conducive to any vehicular travel. I did not catch up to Sharon until about halfway up. I offered to give her a ride where the interpreter was sitting, so she hopped on behind me. I only went a few feet when the trail narrowed with a large drop-off to the left. With the cargo not secure, it all shifted, causing Sharon and the two items to fall off the back end. Sharon was okay but had a nice bruise on her arm. She declined to ride any further and continued walking.

Several of us tried to get the four-wheeler restarted after that incident, but no one had any luck. We even tried turning it around and jump starting it as it rolled down hill. Even that did not work. We did not want to simply abandon it, so we kept pushing it uphill. As is typical in Haiti, several Haitians, most of them children, came out to help push. Eventually, Father Wilner joined us and helped us find a home where we could safely leave it temporarily. The remaining walk instantly became much easier for me but not Alex. He volunteered to carry the five-gallon water bottle the rest of the way.

The walk down the mountain at the end of the day was much easier. Since the sun was down, the temperature was much more comfortable. It was also quite beautiful as there was a full moon in the cloudless starry sky. The moon was so bright that it did not matter that everyone did not have a flashlight.

Despite the hardships of getting to and from Montbayard, that day was one of the highlights of the trip for our group. None of us would have wanted to miss it. It would have been poison not to go!

⸺⸰⸺

I have one more example of "pa vini se pwason" to share. For the first decade of our trips we made to Haiti, there was a United

States State Department travel advisory against travel to Haiti. We went anyway.

As the leader of those trips I always was concerned about whether I was taking others into harm's way. "Should we go or not go?" was forever weighing on my mind. I would share these concerns with the rest of the group as we planned for our trip. While the end of the Duvalier reign was long over by the time we started going in 2000, there still was plenty of civil unrest through some of the Aristide and Lavalas Party years.

Thankfully, most of the hot spots were in Port-au-Prince. We would minimize our exposure to potential problem areas by spending as little time as possible in PAP at each end of the trip. However, there were a couple years where potential trouble existed in St. Marc and Gonaives, both of which were on our way if we drove from PAP to Pendus. It was during those two years that Father Cha Cha had us fly from PAP to Port-de-Paix and then drive south to Pendus, thereby flying over any possible danger areas.

We never have come face-to-face with any trouble on any of our trips. We always encountered the best of mankind and of Haiti when we were in the northern mountains! When we would finally arrive back in Miami on our way home to Indiana, I would always ask the rest of the group if they would go back again. Would a travel advisory affect them differently the next time? Without fail, the response was unanimous that everyone would immediately get on a plane and return to Pendus. We were worried for nothing!

It truly would have been poison to let a mere threat keep us from where we were being called to be.

Since the Pendus River was too deep to drive through,
Serge and Johnny help Dr. Don Clayton walk across.

13

Avoid the Sin of Omission

In his mind a man plans his course, but the Lord directs his steps.
—Proverbs 16:9

"DON'T FORGET TO AVOID THE sin of omission." This is a favorite expression of Father Bob Klemme. He used it most often when we would be hiking in the mountains in Haiti, especially when we were going up. We often heard him say this to whoever happened to be walking with him. It was his code that he needed to pause and rest. So we would stop with him! Usually we needed a break just as much as he did. He just wasn't afraid to say it first. However, he also did not want us to miss absorbing the beauty of our surroundings.

For anyone not familiar with hiking in general, and more specifically in a mountain terrain, your focus as you walk is, or should be, on the ground immediately in front of you. It is important to make sure of the soundness of the footing for each step you take. It seems obvious when you say that, but you can't be looking around without greatly enhancing the opportunity for a misstep to occur. The more uneven the grade is, the greater the chances for an accident.

Mud, rain, and rocks also increase those risks; so do majestic panoramas that tend to divert your attention. When you are hiking carefully, you often don't see much more than your shoes and the area immediately around your next step. So if you don't frequently stop and pause to soak in the beauty all around you, you will miss some incredible views. This is especially true when the terrain you are hiking is so different from what you are accustomed to back home.

The beauty that exists in Haiti is readily apparent in the rural areas, with the streams, rivers, valleys, vegetation, and mountains providing the backdrop for wonderful vistas everywhere you look. Even a deforested side of a mountain becomes a thing of beauty to a flatlander from northern Indiana! Frequent heeding of the call to avoid the sin of omission provides wonderful opportunities to absorb the scenery sweeping all around you.

Avoiding the sin of omission also has a greater significance. Often we go through life the same way that we hike—so focused on the next step that we fail to pay attention to all that surrounds us. The "steps" we take in life keep us focused on the next bill to pay, the next task to complete at work, the next chore to finish at home, the next item on our to-do list. The list is nearly endless that keeps us preoccupied. Instead we need to stop and think about the "what," and more importantly the "who," that we are failing to notice as we trudge through our daily grinds.

As important as those frequent stops to avoid the sin of omission are in Haiti, they are equally impactful when utilized back home, if we just take the time to do so.

Being careful and watching your next step is important when hiking in the mountains. However, one must also take time to notice the beautiful scenery that surrounds you.

14

Do What You Can, God Will Do What You Can't

For human beings it is impossible, but not for God. All things are possible for God.

—*Mark 10:27*

ONE OF THE BEST KNOWN biblical stories is the multiplication of the fish and loaves. At the end of the day, the disciples wanted Jesus to disperse the crowds so they could find something to eat for themselves. Instead Jesus instructed the disciples to feed them. They replied that they only had a few loaves of bread and a few fish. The obvious implication was that it wasn't enough. Offering those meager rations in prayer, Jesus was able to do what they could not—feed the multitude with plenty of leftovers.

He could have easily performed that miracle without any help at all, but Jesus wanted them to do what they could before he did what they could not! I love that message. Jesus expects us to be vested ourselves before he acts. He is not to be simply at our beck and call to fulfill our needs. He is not the genie in the bottle! As St. Augustine once said, "God provides the wind, but man must raise the sails."

There have been many times when this has come to pass in our Haiti ministry. I will share the two best, dare I say miraculous, stories. The first occurred early in our twinning relationship.

Microlending has always been a keen area of interest in promoting economic development. In 2004, Fonkoze was a fairly new banking institution in Haiti. Its focus is on lending to the poor. There were just a few Fonkoze branches scattered throughout Haiti and none located in Gros Morne or anywhere close to Pendus. Its lending practice is based on the Grameen Bank model in Bangladesh. It makes small loans, or microloans, to the poor without requiring typical collateral. The name *Fonkoze* is a blend of three Haitian words *Fondasyon Kole Zepol*. They translate into "shoulder to shoulder foundation." It clearly has more of a mission of solidarity with the poor than one of a business relationship. Fonkoze also provides literacy training for many of its women customers to enhance their life skills as well as their business skills.

I invited Anne Hastings, the executive director for Fonkoze, to come and speak at the second annual Central Indiana Churches for Haiti (CINCH) Haiti Gathering in Lafayette. She was the first widely known speaker to come to our event. She spent the entire weekend with Sharon and me at our house. We had lots of time to talk about microfinance and its ramifications for a community. We wanted to have one close enough for the people in Pendus to be able to utilize. We realized that Pendus was much too small for such a branch, but Gros Morne would be ideal.

However, Anne said that it would take $30,000 to start a new branch in Gros Morne. She said it was so expensive because a building would need to be rented and adapted to being a bank. It would need a safe, a computer or two, teller areas, and several motorcycles called *motos* in Creole. Since there are no "Brinks trucks" in Haiti, the bank itself was responsible for getting currency from one branch to another as needed daily thus the need for the motos. I was very disappointed. I had thought that a smaller number, say more like $5,000, could have been raised without harming the other projects St. Mary was working on in Pendus. But I could not see us ever having $30,000 extra to spend, especially since its focus would be much broader than the Pendus area.

The Haiti Gathering was on a Sunday in early October at St. Mary Cathedral. The local newspaper, the *Journal & Courier*, covered the event, the only time ever that they did. An article appeared in Monday's edition. The story only focused on the positive impact Fonkoze was having for the working women in Haiti and not on the rest of the Gathering's agenda. It also did not mention where in Haiti the various branches were located or that there was a need for one in Gros Morne.

I got home late that Monday. Sharon said a local lady who we did not know saw the article and called. I was to call her back whenever I got home, so I called. She said she had always wanted to help women in a third world country somehow and knew that St. Mary was doing wonderful things in Haiti. I remember vividly her saying, "I want to help." I was always excited to get new people involved in helping Haiti, so I said, "What do you have in mind?" Her response nearly floored me. She said, "$30,000." That number was never mentioned in the newspaper story.

I told her I had to sit down! I then proceeded to tell her the rest of the story, about Anne Hastings spending the weekend with us and how much it cost to establish a new Fonkoze branch and how that was miraculously the same number she mentioned to me earlier! She then told me she was leaving for a few weeks and instructed me to call when she got back.

I called her early in November. She started the conversation with, "I've been thinking." My heart sank a bit as I figured that she had changed her mind. And she *had changed* her mind, only now she wanted to give us $35,000. She wanted to give more so Fonkoze could not only start a new branch in Gros Morne but also have money to lend out when it opened. Talk about God doing what you can't! I did what I could by bringing Anne Hastings to town and getting the newspaper to cover the event! God did the rest.

I received her money by Thanksgiving and took it with me when we went to Haiti on December 26. We met with Anne Hastings that evening at Matthew 25 Guest House and delivered the check to her. She did not wait long to get started establishing this new branch as the dedication for the opening of the Gros Morne Fonkoze was barely two months later, March 2! Kyle was able to attend and speak as the representative from St. Mary.

The second wonderful story of this nature occurred many years later. Through the early years of twinning, St. Mary's goal was to provide some basic needs for Pendus and its six chapel areas. So we focused our early efforts on improving infrastructure for the entire community, such as building new chapels, new schools, and even a dispensary. By this time in our twinning relationship, we had raised the money to rebuild four of Pendus's five chapels that needed to be replaced. The only one still unattended to was the chapel at Montbayard.

Montbayard has a bigger population than Pendus, and it is much poorer. It also is very remotely located with terrain that often makes it very difficult to reach. The first obstacle in getting there is crossing the Twa Riviere. This is one of the biggest rivers in Haiti. It is an hour drive from Pendus just to reach the river crossing. For much of the year the water is only a couple feet deep, in part due to the breadth of the river. Local drivers all know where the shallow portions of the river are located. They never drive straight across from one side to the other. Instead they drive into the water and traverse along one of the longer sandbar areas before finally crossing to the other bank. During the rainy season, the river becomes much deeper and a vehicle would not be able to cross at all. This further isolates Montbayard.

The roadway on the other side is extremely poor and was for many years impassable when we wanted to visit. The steep grades at various parts of the ascent cause a lot of the problem when driving. One year we had to walk nearly three hours from the river up to Montbayard. The lack of a good transportation route greatly increased the estimated cost of getting materials that would be needed to Montbayard.

Because of the population of the community, the chapel there was larger than any of the structures in any of our other chapels. However, it was structurally not very sound. There were visible cracks in the walls. Father Wilner Donecia obtained estimates to build a new chapel on the same site. The cost was very high, much more than we could raise in several years.

Despite its shortcomings, the chapel was still being used. The concrete block building somehow survived the massive earthquake of January 2010 but did not survive a hurricane in August of 2011. After the earthquake, the cost of construction in Haiti went way up. It now was going to cost approximately $110,000 to rebuild Montbayard's chapel. With the ongoing support of teacher salaries and other projects, we were not able to amass the extra funds needed to start building a new chapel in Montbayard. Even if St. Mary could set aside $10,000 a year, it would take over a decade to gather the $110,000 needed for this project.

In the meantime, the people of Montbayard removed a wall between two of the classrooms at their school to create a bigger worship space. However, these two rooms combined were less than twenty percent of the area of the destroyed chapel. I am not sure how they survived without adequate space to gather as a church community.

Finally, in April 2014, a miracle occurred. God provided what we could not do ourselves. An anonymous donor in Lafayette knew of our plight and prayerfully stepped forward to contribute a gift of $100,000 specifically to rebuild this chapel. The donor was especially happy to learn that the Montbayard community had already collected over $5,000 toward this endeavor, with much of it coming from community relatives who lived near Miami, Florida.

Money was sent in three installments beginning in late April 2014 and construction began in May. Father Sylvio sent photos back to me periodically showing the progress of the construction. It was amazing to watch this project from afar. It was even more amazing that it was completed in less than eight months! When our December 2014 group went to Haiti, we celebrated Mass on New Year's Day in the new Montbayard chapel.

The road entering Montbayard approaches the new chapel from behind. Even from that vantage you could tell this was a fabulous structure, especially for rural Haiti. Once we parked and got out, I immediately began to take pictures. There was still some scaffolding standing at the two front corners of the building, but the steps and main entry were complete. The only noticeable task still to be completed was painting the chapel.

The open space once inside was magnificent. There were a limited number of pillars to hold the massive vaulted tin roof up. The pillars that were there had open arches above them, giving the worship space a very wide-open look. I could not tell exactly how high the ceiling was. I estimated that it had to be over twenty-five feet high along the walls and more in the middle where the highest point of the roof peak ran the entire length of the church. You could see the metal trusses that spanned the width of the room. There were fifteen of them in all. There were doors on both sides of the church, and the altar at the far end was elevated.

What surprised me the most were the four-plug electrical outlets that lined both sides of the church about eighteen inches off the floor as well as the florescent lights that also lined both sides of the church about eighteen feet above the floor! There was even an electrical fuse box near the left front of the church. What makes this so surprising to me is the fact that there is no electricity in Montbayard. I know a generator, along with batteries and an inverter, will soon be on their wish list!

There were windows along both sides of the church. They are simply cement blocks with open spaces in them and not glass windows. There was one exception. There were no windows in the corner nearest where traffic came into town. Since the road was so dusty, it would help keep the church cleaner inside with no windows in that area.

The cement floor was not finished yet. A final top coating was still needed. I was not sure whether it would be another layer of cement or tile. There were four steps up to the altar. Both the steps and the entire altar were covered in a white tile, giving it a nice finished look.

Along the back wall, the altar had another raised area with two steps. The first step had a wooden chair on both sides for an altar server to sit. The second step, which was recessed back from the first, held a wooden chair in the middle for the presiding priest to sit. In the middle of that top step was a small concrete structure that was also covered in matching tiles. On top of it was a smaller concrete structure that resembled an open-faced manger. Most likely it would eventually become a built-in tabernacle.

The altar itself was made of concrete and was draped by a white cloth that fit perfectly for the top with a sufficient amount hanging over the two ends. There was a long electrical cord hanging down toward the center of the altar. Father said that a light fixture would eventually hang over the altar.

After Mass, I stepped off the measurements for the dimensions of the church. I did this both on the inside and outside of the church. In both instances, I found the length of the church was eighty feet and the width was forty-five feet. The altar area comprised one-fourth of the inside of the church as it was the last twenty-feet of the inside space. There were seventeen rows of new pews on each side of the main aisle. They had backrests but no kneelers. There were another ten older wooden benches without backrests on either side of the back portion of the church. I estimated the seating capacity to be about four hundred.

When we came back in 2015, the final touches had all been completed. The church was painted a beautiful sky-blue color with white trim. The rest of the floor inside the church was now tiled to match the altar area. It was absolutely beautiful, the prettiest church I had ever seen anywhere in Haiti! There was only one thing missing: there was still no generator. Someday, God will provide for that as well.

This magnificent worship space is my best example of our doing what we can and God doing what we can't! Thank God for both of our wonderfully generous donors!

This beautiful chapel at Montbayard was built in 2014
as a result of the generosity of an anonymous donor.

15

Benedict Remy

The Lord bless you and keep you. The Lord let his face shine on you.
—Numbers 6:24–25

I KNEW BENEDICT REMY FOR several years before I found out his given name was actually Rubenn Remy. Benedict was simply his nickname, but that was the only name I heard anyone ever use for him. The first time I met him he was wearing a green T-shirt that said "Yes I Can" across the front. That slogan would be a great precursor for his life!

He had just turned eleven when Sharon and I first went together to Pendus in December 2000. Father Ronel Charelus introduced him to Sharon by saying that Benedict's mother had died and his father was now remarried and currently was out of the picture. Benedict was living with his grandmother in Pendus. I remember Father's exact words to us, "Benedict is not going to school at St. Joseph, but he has a lot of potential."

Sharon and I looked at each other. Without needing to converse with each other, we immediately said we would love to sponsor Benedict. Turning to face Benedict, Father Cha Cha then surprised us by saying, "Benedict, this is your new mother!" A new and strong relationship began at that instant.

From that moment forward, Benedict spent every day he could with us when we were in Haiti. If we hiked to a chapel, he hiked with us. Most often he would be at Sharon's side giving any assistance she may need on the mountain paths. If he wasn't with her, he would be with me carrying my backpack! The only time he did not go with us was when there would absolutely be no room left in a vehicle when we were driving somewhere instead of walking. We met his grandmother shortly after that meeting with Father Cha Cha. She told us, "Benedict only wants to stay at the church when you are here!"

Our last night in Pendus that first year was New Year's Eve. Father Cha Cha held a midnight Mass to begin the New Year! Benedict came with us to Mass but sat in the pew directly behind us. About halfway through Mass I noticed him asleep on the pew, but by the end of Mass he was awake again. We both gave him a huge hug and fought back our tears as we thought of having to leave him the next morning as we headed back home. The harder we tried to hold back the tears, the more it made both of us cry.

As we left the next day, Benedict cried as he ran after the truck as we drove away. He wasn't the only one with tears in his eyes. We thought long and hard about adopting him, but when we came back the next year, we saw him with his friends, always with a smile on his face. He was so proud to be in school. He was doing quite well at St. Joseph. He seemed happy in his own country and culture with his friends and extended family. He was thriving well in the only environment that he knew. It did not seem appropriate to take him away from that situation. In addition, adoption would have also been difficult to accomplish because his father was still alive at that time.

In the early years, he still had to eat and sleep at his grandmother's house because there was no extra room in our compound area and he was not yet officially part of our St. Mary team.

Benedict is very gifted musically. When he was young, he loved to play the tambou, the handmade drum made from the upper portion of a coconut tree with a goat skin stretched across the top. He was very talented in playing this instrument. Not only would he play for me and our group, but also as an accompanist for Mass at St. Joseph Church.

Once he completed primary school at St. Joseph School in Pendus, he attended secondary school at Jean XXIII in Gros Morne. There are no secondary schools closer to Pendus. It was run by the Montfort priests, the same order that Father Cha Cha and Father Wilner Donecia belong. By then, Father Wilner was our twinning priest.

It is reality for rural children to leave home and family to attend secondary schools in bigger cities, often located some distance away. Father Wilner told us that can be beneficial in the long run as "children need to learn to be on their own at an early age in Haiti." It broke Sharon's heart when he acknowledged that truth about life in Haiti. Because Gros Morne was too far to commute from Pendus, Father secured a place for Benedict to live at his rectory at Our Lady of the Light Church in Gros Morne. It would then be an easy walk for him to get to and from school.

On our visit in 2006, Benedict expressed a growing interest in music. He was then in the equivalent of middle school at Jean XXIII and was learning to play the saxophone. The school only had one saxophone for the six grades of the combined middle and high school. Since the one instrument had to be shared, he could not practice as much as he wanted.

Upon hearing his plight, my assistant, Linda Prage, had one her children used to play. She wanted Benedict to have it. When we came back in December of 2007, we surprised him with a saxophone of his very own. The smile and excitement he displayed upon opening that gift was priceless! He immediately assembled the instrument and began to play. Not only did he have a passion for playing the saxophone, he had an extraordinary talent for it as well.

While Benedict was at Jean XXIII, Father Wilner became his local father figure, overseeing his studies, his grades, his involvement in the church, and his obsession for playing the saxophone. Living in the convent across the street from the rectory was Sister Marianne

Sultan. She became a mother figure who Benedict came to rely upon for consolation and advice when we were not around.

———⊰●⊱———

Benedict's musical talent continued to grow. He learned to play the guitar and began to write his own music and songs. On the 2010 trip, Benedict sang a thank-you song to Sharon and me in church as we lingered after a children's benediction. It was heartfelt and had me teary-eyed before he finished! I had to concentrate simply to hold my camera steady as I videoed him singing!

———⊰●⊱———

In 2011 Benedict wanted to finish both his twelfth year of high school and the following year of philosophy in Port-au-Prince. Both were part of a typical Haitian educational timeline. The philosophy year is an extra year of schooling, similar in nature to much of the course work of first year of college in the USA. To do this, Benedict had to move to PAP. Madam Marcel had a connection for someone he could live with. However, they did not live very close to his school. He told us he needed two tap-tap rides to get to school each morning and two for the ride home.

By the year 2011, he had learned enough English at school that he began working as an additional interpreter for our group. He would then get to eat, sleep, and travel with our team. When he met us at the Matthew 25 Guest House in PAP before we headed for Pendus that December, he was wearing a blue soccer shirt with "Remy de Pendus" written across the back. It means "Remy from Pendus." He liked to use that as his stage name when he played music for others. Father Wilner later suggested that he use "Remy de Haiti." Father knew that Benedict was talented enough that he would eventually be more widely known as his career progressed!

———⊰●⊱———

Benedict played his saxophone so much he needed a new one by 2012. Again, we surprised him with another on that trip.

He had written a new song he called "Open Your Eyes." At several of the children's benedictions, he would teach the refrain of the song to the eager children. He would then sing each verse and have them chime in for the refrain, which they gleefully would do! The words to the refrain basically say, "Open your eyes, there are others worse off than you." It then encouraged everyone to get involved and help in any way. It was a powerful song. I only wish I understood Creole better to truly appreciate the impact of the tune and the words.

That year a Christmas Gala was held in the courtyard area of the rectory in Gros Morne on December 30. Benedict was scheduled to perform at this event so Father Joseph Telcin arranged a ride for our whole group to attend. There was a stage with lights and a sound system. It was quite a production. At least five hundred people found their way to that courtyard area to watch.

None of us knew what to expect at this gala. The talent ranged from very young children dressed in white shirts, dark pants, and red Santa hats to several choral groups of older men and women. There were also a couple young band groups that played lively music and got the crowd fully involved. Since it was Christmastime I thought I would recognize some of the tunes (such as "Silent Night") even if I did not understand the words in Creole. However, most of the songs were new tunes to me. In fact, not many were Christmas songs.

The audience clearly loved watching their children and friends perform. Many proud fathers stepped to the front to take pictures at the appropriate time. Many of the female nursing students in our group had young Haitian children watching the show while sitting on their laps, which helped keep them warm as it got chilly as the evening wore on.

Benedict performed about ninety minutes into the show. We thought he was only going to play "Circle of Life" on his new saxophone. However, he opened by singing his song "Open Your Eyes" while playing his guitar. As usual, he had the crowd joining in for the refrain with him. He then picked up the sax and played Disney's hit song from *Lion King*. As a proud father, I too marched to the front and took photos and videos of Benedict performing. I took so much video that my chip in my camera was full. I had to borrow a camera to finish recording his performance. Not only was it a special evening for Benedict, our entire group loved it too.

—————⟫●⟪—————

Kelly Krueckeberg was a nursing student on our December 2010 team from St. Mary. She and Benedict met for the first time during that trip. After her graduation from St. Elizabeth School of Nursing in August 2011, she took a year-long volunteer Quest position with Sister Jackie and Sister Pat in Gros Morne. The nuns try to utilize the talents of the various Quest volunteers each year. Because of her background, she would work in the hospital in Gros Morne that year.

Despite Benedict being in PAP for school, Benedict and Kelly kept in touch with each other throughout her year's stay in Haiti. A budding romance rapidly developed between the two. The connection was strong enough to endure the hardships of a long-distance relationship that continued even after she moved back to Lafayette at the end of her year in Gros Morne.

Kelly returned once to spend an extended vacation with Benedict. Together they applied for and finally obtained a visa for Benedict to come to the United States in early 2013. He was not quite finished with his year of philosophy. However, visas of any type are very difficult for most Haitians to ever obtain. He simply could not take a chance on missing his opportunity to come to the USA, so he immediately left Haiti and came to Lafayette in February 2013.

Both Kelly and he lived with Kelly's mother upon his arrival to Indiana. Immediately upon his arrival to Indiana, Benedict experienced winter and snow for his first time!

—————⟫●⟪—————

Never in my wildest imagination would I have ever thought Benedict would someday get married at St. Mary Cathedral in Lafayette, Indiana! But he did. He and Kelly went through the marriage prep classes with Father Bob Klemme and set a wedding date of September 7, 2013.

I was honored when he asked me to be his best man. I felt bad that none of his aged friends from Haiti and none of his extended family could get visas to attend the wedding. However, Father Wilner, Father Sylvio, and Sister Marianne were able to come to Lafayette and help celebrate that special day with Benedict and Kelly. In addition, many of the St. Mary parishioners who had been to Pendus were there and shared in the joy of the day.

There were several memorable moments for me at the reception that followed in the Bishop's Memorial Hall at St. Mary, including my delivering the toast as best man and Sharon and Benedict in the groom-mother dance. However, the true highlight was Benedict serenading Kelly. He sat her on a chair beside him as he sang a song he wrote especially for the occasion. He even accompanied himself on the guitar. When he finished, he had all the ladies in the hall teary-eyed—and probably a little envious!

———⟫●⟪———

Benedict and Kelly lived in Lafayette for a short while before moving to a warmer Tampa, Florida, area. While there, he continued to write and produce songs. He sent two of them to me before our 2015 trip to Haiti. One was called "Mesi" and the other "Traditions Lost."

This first was a thank-you song for the many people who have impacted his life. The second one was a heartfelt Christmas song recalling the traditions of the season he remembered as a child. Not only did he write the songs and sing them, he played the instrumental parts as well. He then mixed them together for the final product. They were both beautiful pieces of work, not only in the quality of the music but also the message being delivered.

I downloaded them to my phone and took them with me to Pendus. I played them for Madam Marcel, Father Sylvio, and many of Benedict's friends. Even his uncle Walter Remy heard them both and had to wipe away some tears before they finished playing. Again, I wished I understood Creole better to appreciate the full impact of both songs on those listening. Even without knowing all the words, it was very easy to feel the rhythm and uplifting nature of the songs.

Benedict and Kelly moved again in 2016, this time to Jacksonville, Florida. Benedict was accepted into the University of North Florida to study international business.

Remember that green T-shirt Benedict initially wore that said "Yes I Can." It sure was prophetic!

After being in the USA for nearly three years, Benedict joined our December 2016 group that visited Pendus. Since he was living in Jacksonville, Florida, we simply planned to meet up with him at the airport in PAP.

He did not tell anyone else that he was coming so he could surprise them. He told his best friend Romeo (Madam Marcel's son) that he needed to meet me at the PAP airport when I came as I had something to give him. Originally, Benedict's flight was to land shortly after ours, but due to travel delays we incurred, he landed well before we arrived. Therefore, I missed seeing this reunion. However, I did see Romeo as we exited the airport and he was still ecstatic.

It was wonderful to watch Benedict interact with others during the week, both with folks that he already knew but had not seen for several years as well as with the youth in Pendus. Most of them were either not yet born or too young to remember him when he was living in Pendus over a decade ago! He spoke at the Benedictions for both St. Joseph and Massacre schools. His words of inspiration and encouragement were well received and very much appreciated by Father Sylvio.

Benedict is a gifted musician and song-writer. The saxophone
is one of many instruments he is adept at playing.

16

Fritzner Guerrier

You have been told, O man, what is good, and what the
Lord requires of you: Only to do the right and to love
goodness, and to walk humbly with your God.
—Micah 6:8

"Hello, Father." That simple greeting changed Fritzner Guerrier's life.

Fritzner was fourteen years old when he first met Father Bob Klemme in 1996. Father Bob was in Haiti with a group from St. Elizabeth Ann Seton visiting their sister church in Duval, Haiti. He was walking on a hilltop where the parishioners were planning to build a new church in the rural mountains of Haiti. Fritzner suddenly came up beside Father Bob and began talking to him—in English! Those first words caught Father off guard, hearing English where he least expected it to be spoken.

Father Bob stopped and introduced himself and asked Fritzner where he learned to speak English. Fritzner said that he learned it while living at an American orphanage and going to school there. However, because of his age, he was too old to continue residing there. He told Father that he was living with an aunt and was no longer in school because "no one can afford to pay" for him. He was totally unsure of what his bleak future held in store for him.

Before continuing with his walk, Father asked Fritzner what was his greatest wish for his future. Without hesitation, Fritzner responded "to finish my education!" Father Bob said he immediately felt it "would be a sin" for him not to help this young Haitian boy. So Father began to pay for Fritzner's schooling and living expenses. He became Fritzner's surrogate father!

Fritzner was born October 3, 1981, in a village just outside of Port-au-Prince. His mother died when he was eight years old. Because his father had very little to do with him since then, he wound up living at the orphanage. He was the third of five siblings, having two brothers and two sisters. Once Father Bob began to sponsor his education, Fritzner began to live during the week with a cousin closer to Port-au-Prince and closer to his new school.

His typical day during those school years had him getting up at 5:00 a.m. He would take a tap-tap to school, arriving just before class began at 7:20 a.m. His day at school would only last until early afternoon. Another long tap-tap ride got him home in time to finally get something to eat. He would do his daily homework before it got dark each night.

On Fridays Fritzner would walk two hours back to his home village to be with the rest of his family. He would make the return two-hour walk to his cousin's house on Sunday afternoon to begin the weekly cycle all over again. It took several more years for Fritzner to finally graduate high school.

When St. Mary's took its first trip to Haiti in March 2000, Fritzner was one of our interpreters. His English not only caught Father Bob's attention, it now could begin to earn him a living. Being an interpreter was educational for Fritzner in many ways. One of the most important was he began to see parts of Haiti he never had a chance to visit before. Another was the opportunity to meet many new people. Through Father Bob's connections he would interpret for Indiana groups from Anderson, Carmel, Indianapolis, and Lafayette, as well as many others.

By the end of our first visit, Fritzner drew a picture for me. He described it as his vision of an ideal homestead in Haiti. This dream home was built of concrete blocks with a tin roof, so it was a sturdy and safe shelter. It was located by a river, making water readily accessible. It had palm trees in the yard, granting precious shade for the home. It also had chickens running around in the yard, providing a source of food. Most importantly, it had a family in it. Quite a profound statement from a simple pencil drawing!

Over the years Fritzner became much more than an interpreter for us, he was a trusted friend. He was always looking out for our well-being, often suggesting that we walk a different route or avoid a certain situation just to keep us as safe as possible. We could give him money to exchange for us or to buy something needed for the trip, and he always got what we wanted.

Fritzner always met us at the airport on our arrival. While he could not get inside to help us gather our luggage or make our way through customs, he was usually the first person we saw once we stepped outside the airport. He would already know who was there to pick us up and where they were parked. He would then help us get our bags to the waiting vehicles.

Fritzner loved to tease and was a great sport about getting teased. His smile and laugh were captivating. I often teased him simply by telling each new member of our group that they were required to tease Fritzner at least one time every day during the trip!

He grew to be much more than an interpreter and confidant; he was an integral part of every mission team too. He understood what we were trying to accomplish and would pitch in and help in any way he could. He was always so gentle and caring when dealing with children. He could get their attention and direct them to do whatever was needed in a way that was also enjoyable for the youngsters. He also had an eye for someone who was in true need, often asking us for extra soap or clothes or food. He would then discreetly give it to that person without anyone else even knowing what he was doing.

Our son Kyle went to spend the summer in Gros Morne after he had graduated high school. His luggage did not arrive with him in Port-au-Prince. This was before cell phone and Internet use in Haiti, so communication was much more difficult than it is today. Sharon and I knew he made it safely to PAP but did not know if he ever got his suitcase. We finally reached Fritzner by phone. He promptly got on a bus and went from PAP to Gros Morne to find Kyle. He managed to get word back to us that Kyle finally got his suitcase before leaving PAP and made it to Gros Morne.

Often we would have a sharing session after our final meal of each day. He would freely join in the conversation, adding something that he noticed that was important during the day. He also would genuinely thank every group near the end of the week, professing how important it was that we came, we visited, we shared, and we loved those that we encountered during our stay.

He particularly enjoyed when we held a children's benediction, passing out gifts to the school children as they received their semester report card. The gifts typically were a pair of underwear, a toothbrush, a bar of soap, and either a Matchbox car for the boys or some hair barrettes for the girls. That may not sound like significant gifts but Fritzner would always put things in perspective for us. Growing up in an orphanage, Fritzner knew what it was like to never receive a gift from anyone. I distinctly remember him telling us one night, "Those children will be so excited when they get home, they won't be able to go to sleep!" All because of a Matchbox car or baggie of hair barrettes!

Fritzner was so proud when his dream of his own family began. His son, also called Fritzner, was born on Christmas Day in 2004. Still, Fritzner was dedicated to helping our mission too. So on December 26, he met us at the airport to spend the next eight days at our service. Granted he needed the work and the income it generated, but he knew he was now building something bigger and more enduring than just for himself!

Four years later his daughter Stacey was born. Again, Fritzner was a very proud and dedicated father, something not always seen throughout Haiti! He attended to both of his children's needs, including having them enrolled in school.

Fritzner's English skills finally earned him a job with the United Nations in 2009. He would travel all over the country, helping interpret in many situations. On January 12, 2010, he was called away from his main UN building in PAP shortly before 5:00 p.m. Within minutes the catastrophic earthquake devastated the Haiti capital. The building he had just left collapsed, killing many of the occupants.

With cell phone signal knocked out, he could not check on his family and friends. He frantically made his way back to his apartment. It was a three-story building with his unit on the top floor. The building had collapsed, but the top floor was not completely destroyed as the building pancaked downward. Stacey was there with her maternal grandmother. She was trapped within a bubble of space among the concrete rubble from the third floor. It took two days of digging by hand for them to reach her. She was fine, just scared and hungry. Fritzner and his children lived in a small tent for many months thereafter.

Through his connections in the United Nations, Fritzner finally got a visa to travel to the United States. He came in May 2010, just four months after the earthquake. The trip was a dream come true for him to travel to the United States and visit his many friends in Indiana. Adel and Lulu Yaacoub and Sharon and I picked him up near midnight at the airport in Indianapolis. He brought a small bag with him, but it had nothing in it. He was still wearing the clothes he had on the day the earthquake hit. He did, however, have a small camera with him to record the many things he would see and experience on this trip. Without photos, it would be difficult for him to accurately explain to others what he was experiencing.

Despite it being nearly 1:00 a.m., we stopped at a Walmart when we got back to Lafayette. I teased him that the inside of the Walmart would be bigger than all Pendus. I was exaggerating, but it was the biggest building he had ever been inside! Instantly he began taking several pictures inside the store! We got him enough clothes to get him through his visit.

During his stay, he told us that he was going to get married the following January and that Father Bob would perform the ceremony. By then Father Bob had moved from St. Mary Cathedral to pastor two small churches in neighboring Benton County. That week, we took Fritzner out and helped him buy simple wedding rings and dress shoes for the occasion.

Fritzner visited each of the classrooms at St. Mary School when he was here. He was an instant hit with the children. He always looked directly at a child when talking with him or her, even bending down to get on the child's own level. His smile and joyful personality prevailed even when he was talking about enduring hardships such as the earthquake. The schoolchildren did not hold back from asking him tough questions, yet they were also curious about such things as his favorite food.

During his visit to Indiana he spent time with all the communities he had previously helped: Lafayette, Anderson, and Carmel. Each group made sure to further enhance his experience in the United States, taking him to the Indianapolis zoo, an ice skating rink, the museum, to Chicago, and many more places!

Fritzner did get married on January 2, 2011. He planned the wedding day so it would be the last day of our mission week and the first day of Father Bob's week so both groups could all already be in Haiti and attend the wedding. In all, there were twenty-seven Americans in our combined groups at his wedding. His timing of the wedding between the two groups also meant he could work both weeks as our interpreter, allowing him to earn two good paychecks!

A couple years later his third child was born, a son named Marven Klemme Guerrier. Fritzner was so proud of his children. He was also proud of the new home he was able to build for his family. In Haiti, you don't borrow money and build your house; you pay for it as you go. The combination of continued help from Father Bob along with gifts he received from his wedding as well as his own earnings allowed Fritzner to purchase the land and start to build. He could then add on as needed when more money was available. He so wanted his house to be perfect, I remember buying him a bag of grass seed to take back with him after his first visit to the USA.

Fritzner was one of the interpreters for all twenty-three of St. Mary trips through December 2013. Then on Easter Sunday, April 20, 2014, I received an e-mail with news you never want to get and never are prepared for. Fritzner died earlier that day in a hospital in Port-au-Prince. He went to St. Joseph Hospital in PAP a week earlier. He picked that hospital because it was run by his good friend and confidant Father Hilaire Calixte. Fritzner had complained of stomach pains and possible internal bleeding. No one was ever quite sure what he suffered from and not sure what caused his untimely death. He was thirty-two years old and survived by his wife Marlene, Fritzner (then age nine), Stacey (then age five) and Marven Klemme (then age two).

We were all in shock. Short of sending money to help his family there was nothing we could do. We organized a memorial service for Fritzner at St. Mary Cathedral on Monday, April 28, 2014. Father Bob Klemme, Father Jeff Martin, Father Ambrose Ziegler, Father Patrick Baikauskas, Deacon John Jezierski, and Deacon Jim Rush all helped celebrate Mass. That was quite an array of clergy on the altar for the Mass!

Father Bob gave a touching, heartfelt homily recounting Fritzner's life and his impact on all who attended. Through the years, Father Bob either enhanced or initiated Haiti ministries at four Indiana parishes: St. Mary in Anderson, St. Elizabeth Ann Seton in Carmel, St. Mary Cathedral in Lafayette, and at the combined parish assignment in the Benton County parishes of St. Patrick in Oxford and St. Charles in Otterbein. Many people from all those parishes knew Fritzner as their friend and attended the memorial service. Over 120 people were in attendance. It was quite a testament that a poor Haitian orphan could rise to such heights as to impact so many people from this far away!

After the memorial service, we held a reception in the social hall. In addition to food and drinks, we displayed many photos of Fritzner as well as a power point presentation of him. Many in attendance shared their memories of Fritzner. There were some laughs as well as some tears. It was a wonderful, heartfelt session, helping us all to come to grips with our shared profound loss.

On our next trip to Pendus in December 2014, we invited Fritzner's son to join us for our week. By then he was ten years old. Little Fritz sat next to Kyle on the bus ride from PAP to Pendus. Kyle's ability to speak Creole helped create an immediate bond between the two, almost as if they had always known each other. About two hours into the drive, little Fritz laid his head on Kyle's lap and took a nap. Everyone in our group felt a continued connection with Fritzner through spending that week with his son.

Fritzner Guerrier was a loving father to his three children. Here he holds his oldest son also named Fritzner. He was invaluable as a friend and an interpreter for every mission trip by St. Mary Cathedral until his death in 2014.

17

Men Anpil Chay Pa Lou

Be doers of the word and not hearers only.
—James 1:22

THE CONCEPT OF THIS PROVERB is not unique to Haiti. In fact, it is universal. It means "many hands make light work." This really is a mathematical idea. If many people cooperate, the work that would otherwise be onerous for one person becomes lighter to each participant. Culturally, it is a reality in Haiti. Families and communities often unite for the common good of all. *Konbit* is the Creole word for this phenomenon. It means working together to complete a common task. Many either share their small living spaces with others or live near each other. They assist each other in raising their children. They often share manual labor, especially when it comes to planting and harvesting crops. When a task is shared, and done together, it truly makes each person's work lighter. The underlying thought of helping one another is set forth in Ecclesiastes 4:10 when it says, "Woe to him who is alone; when he falls, he has no one to lift him up." Even Jesus had Simon of Cyrene to help carry his cross!

Likewise, this proverb applies to St. Mary's Haiti ministry. Many hands do make light work, yet many of those helping hands have never actually been to Haiti. The number of people who have traveled to Pendus is relatively small when compared to the multitude of people who have supported this endeavor throughout the years.

I am always amazed at how many people who have never been to Haiti, so readily offer their time, talent, and treasure to help this ministry along the way. This applies to both parishioners and non-parishioners of St. Mary Cathedral. This reality has given me a greater appreciation of how Christianity spread in its early years, starting with the few apostles with first-hand encounters who spread their good news "to all the ends of the earth." Like the first disciples, those that have gone to Haiti have come home and infused others with stories of their experiences, prompting them to also become involved.

Two wonderful examples of such modern-day "eyewitness" disciples who have spread an enthusiasm for ministry in Haiti are Father Bob Klemme and Theresa Patterson. Father Bob has had an enormous ripple effect on the several central Indiana parishes from his passion for ministry in Haiti. Theresa Patterson has been the only executive director of the Parish Twinning Program of the Americas. Under her tireless dedication and leadership, the PTPA has grown from the initial Tennessee parish working in Haiti to over 350 twinning parishes worldwide.

However, my admiration also goes out to those who have never physically been to Haiti yet are still dedicated to the ministry. The words of Jesus to the apostle Thomas after the resurrection are equally applicable to this situation. Jesus tells him at John 20:29, "Because you have seen me, you have believed; blessed are those who have not seen and yet have believed." I believe I am the fortunate one to have gone and experienced many blessings from Haiti. However, the fervor and commitment of those who have not gone are a continual inspiration to me because they "have not seen and yet have believed."

⸺⸺•◆•⸺⸺

While every project and fundraiser St. Mary has accomplished over the years is a prime example of the "many hands make light work" principle, our desk-and-pew endeavor of 2002 sits at the top of the list. I put it there because of the vast number of people who contributed to the success of this project at both ends of the relationship, in Indiana and in Haiti.

Early in the twinning relationship, the church at St. Joseph had been remodeled and a new chapel and school were built in Massacre. There was a need for new desks and pews for each of these sites. Because wood is scarce in Haiti, St. Mary decided to make them in Lafayette and ship them on a sea container to Haiti.

Doug Granlund stepped up to lead this project. First, he designed the desks and pews and then supervised a summer-long endeavor of cutting, sanding, planing, routing, and staining all the wood needed for 120 four-foot desks and 120 eight-foot pews. All the holes for the nuts and bolts were also predrilled in Lafayette. The pews that were being replaced at St. Joseph Church were simple benches with no backrests. Not only did Doug design backrests into these new pews, he added an attached kneeler so the St. Joseph parishioners would no longer have to kneel on the concrete floor. They would now be kneeling on a two-by-four piece of wood. To them that was a major improvement!

Each desk and pew was then individually packaged to contain all the pieces necessary to assemble that desk or pew, including the nuts and bolts. We wrapped each package in cardboard and bound them with banding wire. He designed it that way in case a package was lost in route to Pendus, only that one desk or pew would be affected and no more. We did not want a package of "left legs" of the pew to go missing causing us to not be able to complete the project.

Nearly three dozen parishioners from St. Mary provided the labor for this endeavor. Most of them had not been to Haiti; they simply had a passion to help in this ministry. Henry Chua and Aloha Auto provided us with both the space and much of the machinery needed to complete these tasks. It was an epic example of many hands making light work. When completed, we loaded the equivalent of an entire sea container into a semitrailer to be hauled to our shipper in Ft. Lauderdale, Florida. Included in that cargo were several extension cords and electric drills needed to assemble each piece once it reached its destination. It was then shipped to Port-de-Paix, a port much closer to Pendus than PAP, thereby helping logistically in getting that massive load to St. Joseph Church.

Alan Banning and I teamed up with Doug on the next December trip to Pendus to assemble each of these desks and pews. We figured we would spend our week working on the assembly process in Pendus by ourselves. What we did not expect was the overwhelming number of hands in Pendus that wanted to help us put each of these desks and pews together. Everyone, including the men, women, and children, as well as the priest and nuns, was fascinated with the assembly process we set up in two of the school's classrooms. They all wanted a chance to use the electric tools. Unfortunately, only a couple of the Haitian men had any previous experience or mechanical skills, so we spent a lot of time teaching each person how to use the jigs and drills. The constant training slowed our process, but the multitude of smiles of satisfaction on the Haitians faces helping was our reward.

What surprised us the most was how frugal the Haitians were. We were simply going to throw away the cardboard that wrapped each pew and desk. It was trash to us. Not so to the Haitians. Everyone wanted to take the cardboard home with them. Each piece would be used as a mat to sleep on the dirt floors of their homes, at least until they got too wet to be of any further use.

The desks and pews that were destined for Massacre had to be carried two hours up the mountain to that destination. It only took one Haitian to carry a four-foot desk balanced on his head up that rugged terrain. Two boys would share the load of toting the eight-foot pews. Our group hiked up to Massacre near the end of that visit. We took off ahead of the folks, toting the desks and pews. I was shocked when they passed us well before we reached Massacre! They were sitting in the chapel upon our arrival!

⟫●⟪

A few years into our twinning relationship, Father Cha Cha asked if we could bring some gifts for the children in Pendus and each of the chapels. We always come right after Christmas, so he thought it would be nice for the children to receive something at that time of the year. Many would not otherwise get anything. He called this a children's benediction!

Because we wanted enough gifts for one thousand children, we had to be careful selecting the items to take. We decided to give a Matchbox car for each of the boys and a baggie of hair barrettes for the girls. Both were small enough and lightweight enough to be able to take the massive number of each that we would need, plus they would be durable enough not to get broken along the way. In addition, we would take a toothbrush, small hotel-sized bar of soap, and a pair of underwear for each child.

We found the most efficient way to distribute these gifts in Haiti was to combine the children's benediction with the students getting their report cards from school. This worked out quite well since their semester break, and report-card time, coincided with our annual Christmas-New Year trip.

Collecting all that we needed for these children's benedictions is another wonderful example of many hands making light work.

The St. Mary School helps to collect a substantial portion of these items. This creates a meaningful connection between the St. Mary school children and the Pendus school children. St. Mary School is kindergarten through third grade, so the ages of the children at both schools are very similar. Before they would collect each year, Sharon and I would share pictures, videos, and stories with the St. Mary classes about Haiti and our sister parish in Pendus.

Many parishioners from St. Mary also donate these items for us to take as well. In addition, Ginny Windler and the EDGE middle school youth group have conducted several Undy 500 events for us each May to help gather much of the underwear needed for the benedictions.

In addition, the Greater Lafayette community also contributes many of the targeted items to each mission trip. Many of the ladies from my office, the courthouse, and several downtown businesses as well from Sharon's office at Purdue University donate on a regular basis. Over the years, Carolyn Rigdon, Allison Claypool, and Janelle

Fleming have taken turns making colorful bracelets to be included in the gifts for the Haitian schoolgirls.

Motel 6, Homewood Suites, and Jonathan Ricketts have donated multiple cases of the small hotel-sized soaps we give away. Soap is a critical gift in light of the cholera outbreak after the 2010 earthquake. The smaller sized soaps are important because we can take enough, within our weight limitations, to give one to each student at each school. The Athlete also donates several soccer balls each year. I try to take at least seven every year, one for St. Joseph School and one to each of the six chapel areas. All ages enjoy playing soccer!

Dr. Jim Bayley, DDS, has provided toothbrushes for over half of our trips to Pendus. Several other Greater Lafayette dentists have also contributed over the years, including Dr. Fred Sputh, Dr. Trevor Murray, Dr. Christian Mazur, and Dr. Robert Bouggy.

We also take medicines when we go. If we have doctors or a nurse practitioner, we can take prescriptive medicines to use in our clinics and then leave for Madam Marcel to disburse in the dispensary in Pendus. If we don't have a medical team going, we can still take many over-the-counter items that are critically needed, such as aspirin, ibuprofen (both pill and liquid), antiseptic wipes, gauze, Band-Aids, antidiarrheal meds, and hydrocortisone. Some trips we will take over ten thousand vitamins, including children's and prenatal varieties. Randy Gerhart, owner of Parkside Pharmacy, has been a generous supporter of this aspect of our ministry over the years. Even though we buy some of these supplies from him, he also donates a portion, allowing us to better resupply the dispensary each year.

My assistant Linda Prage leads the Friendship Bible class at Thorntown United Methodist Church. They purchase and assemble seventeen top-student bags for us to take for the schools at St. Joseph and Massacre. These bags contain many useful school supplies such as paper, pens, pencils, erasers, rulers, and scissors. A small toy or two are also packed in each. We use these at the schools' children's benedictions. Both the priest and the teachers recognize the top student in each class as the report cards are distributed. We then present these extra gifts to each top student. I once asked Father Joseph if doing this created any jealousy. His response was that he hoped it did as he wanted every student to strive for that little extra reward!

Finally, Von Tobel Lumber & Hardware supports our ministry by giving us such items as tarps, rope, duct tape, zip ties, electrical tape, small tools, surge protectors, and extension cords to take each year. One year, we were to do some repair work on the roof of the dispensary, so they donated some trowels and cement repair supplies.

It is obvious that our Haiti ministry is bolstered by broad community support from many people, both parishioners and non-parishioners. Again, the adage of "Many hands make light work" is clearly evident.

We always have a packing party a couple weeks before we go to Haiti. As many as a dozen or more folks lend a hand, joining our group to help with each of these packing parties. Doug Granlund and Roy Dejoie, who have both been to Haiti, always help at each of these sessions as well.

Each person who travels with us to Haiti takes two fifty-pound suitcases packed with a multitude of items that we take to Pendus. Originally, we could take those two bags apiece without additional costs. Depending on the airline we use now, we often have to pay for both checked-in pieces of luggage. Our personal effects are in our carry-on suitcases and backpacks.

It takes several hours to do this packing. We do not want to waste any available space, so we carefully weigh each bag, making sure each one weighs as close to fifty pounds as possible. We get some incredulous looks at the airlines counters when every bag is between 49.5 and 50 pounds! It would be much easier for the group if all the Matchbox cars were in one or two suitcases, the underwear in another and the medicines in yet another. However, the heavier items would not fill up the space available in most suitcases so we mix things up to maximize the capacity of each bag.

We also do not want to take trash that would need to be disposed of in Haiti, so we take the Matchbox cars and underwear out of their packaging. That also frees up some precious extra ounces for each suitcase. We do the same for the medicines, taking each item out of the box that usually surrounds the bottle of actual vitamins, ibuprofen, etc.

We put colored strands of yard on each bag and number each one, recording a master list of each bag and its contents. The yarn helps our group identify our bags as they come off the baggage carousel. The master list is critical when luggage is missing upon our arrival in PAP. We can accurately identify each misplaced bag as the airlines search for them in their system.

Doug Granlund also plays a critical role by being our point person while our group is in Haiti. He will have a list of phone numbers and e-mails for a contact person for each member of our mission team. When we arrive in PAP, Matthew 25 Guest House, and then later in Pendus, I text or e-mail Doug and he passes that information along to everyone's family at home. Because cell service is often sporadic in Haiti, especially in the mountains, this is beneficial as I only have to make contact once, with Doug, and not have to try myself multiple times to reach everyone on the list.

His job as the conduit of information becomes even more important when things change and don't process as originally planned for the trip. Whether we have delays or weather issues on our way to Haiti or missed connections on our way home, Doug keeps everyone up-to-date on what is going on with the trip.

Coordinating these trip details is also critical as Doug is responsible for getting our group picked up from the airport in Indianapolis at the end of the trip. There have been many trips where we got home much later than expected, even as late as the next day. He would take care of the logistics of getting our group picked up at the airport. Sometimes that would mean finding different drivers and vehicles available for the new estimated arrival time.

For the last dozen trips or so, Dan Korty has simplified the logistics of getting our group to and from the airport. Instead of needing multiple vehicles and drivers, he has arranged the use of the Lafayette Central Catholic High School bus. Dan's dedication to this part of the ministry is appreciated, especially since we are always driving to the airport between 2:00 and 4:00 a.m. Since the Indianapolis airport is only seventy miles south of Lafayette, Doug and Dan don't have to leave Lafayette to come pick us up until we have notified them we are taking off for our last leg home.

Doug and Dan have truly lightened the load with their dedication. Without their efforts, the logistics of our trips would be much more difficult for those traveling.

Shortly after we got home from our December 2011 trip, Sister Pat e-mailed me. She needed help getting parts to make some hinges for a gate. The RJM nuns oversee Fonebo, a school for the poor in Gros Morne. As part of the curriculum, the nuns implemented a program to teach the children how to grow their own food, items such as spinach and other nutritional vegetables. However, the goats in the neighborhood kept getting into the schoolyard and eating everything they tried to grow. The nuns wanted to build a gate to keep the goats out.

As a bit of background, there is no "fence" around the school yard as we Americans would think of it. No chain-link, wood-planked, or other type of fence. Instead the area is encompassed by a cactus hedge. The only metal part of the entire enclosure would be the gate that completes the fence for the school.

Sister Pat could not find the parts she needed, either in Gros Morne or online. She knew that Chloe Harshman, a St. Mary parishioner and a nurse, was scheduled to be in Gros Morne with a medical team the following week. Chloe could bring the items if we could find them quickly enough.

I did not know anything about gates and the hardware needed, but it only took two contacts to solve Sister Pat's problem. First, I called a friend, Gene Hurt. He owns a local fence company. He said he could get the hinge parts by the next day from his supplier. Once he learned what they were to be used for, he refused payment and donated them. However, he did not have any of the thirty-two sets of washers, nuts, and bolts that were also needed.

After picking up the parts from Gene the next day, I visited Von Tobel Lumber and Hardware and explained what I needed and why. Tom Shorter, the company's president, immediately donated all we needed. What a wonderful testament to our local community and their support of a mission that is so far away.

On my way home, I dropped everything off to Chloe. She said she would find room in her luggage for the approximate eight pounds of metal to take to Haiti. About two weeks later, I got an e-mail from Sister Pat with a photo of a completed gate at the school!

Sometimes the help involved in this ministry isn't provided by "hands" at all. St. Elizabeth Hospital has allowed us a storage room in a warehouse for us to house many items used in this ministry. We collect used suitcases to take and leave for each trip. We also collect many of the things needed for the children's benediction and other aspects of the twinning relationship. We also use this space to conduct our packing parties in preparation for each trip.

Without this essential space, it would be very difficult to conduct our ministry as efficiently and effectively.

Over the years our core Haiti committee at St. Mary consisted of Helen Hession, Dave Schmidt, Andre Angrand, Tony Behr, Roy Dejoie, Chris Siener, Sharon, and me. There have been others who have joined and served along the way as well. The leadership and guidance of this committee has been critical in nurturing the twinning relationship between St. Mary and St. Joseph. However, the entire parish community supports this ministry with a multitude of donations of time, talent, and treasure.

Those "many hands" are most evident in our many fund raisers we have conducted over the past decade and a half. We have been creative in the number of ways utilized to raise money and awareness of this ministry.

The most successful fund raisers, and the ones we have conducted several times each over the years, are a golf outing, garage sales, Taste of Haiti, and the Purdue Glee Club dinner and concert. In the background of those events were the many hands of those helping to set up tables and chairs, serve food, sell tickets after Mass, pick up a multitude of items for the garage sales, wash dishes for the dinners, and clean up after each one. Those many unsung heroes have impacted many lives in Pendus, Haiti, by their selfless acts of love in each endeavor.

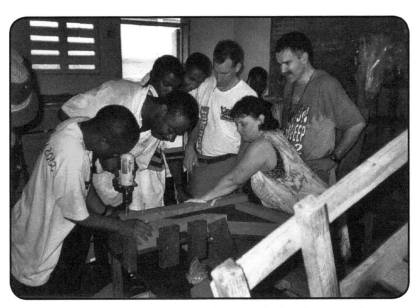

Doug Granlund oversees Father Ronel Charelus's use of a power drill as he assembles a new school desk. Fritzner and Sharon lend a helping hand as Jeff watches.

18

Andre and Josee Angrand

A faithful friend is a sturdy shelter; he who finds one finds a treasure.
—Sirach 6:14

MUCH OF MY KNOWLEDGE AND understanding of Haiti I learned from Andre and Josee Angrand. Those learning opportunities arose both in Indiana and in Haiti. They greatly expanded my comprehension of Haitian culture, history, language, and cuisine.

Andre and Josee were both born and educated in Haiti but have lived in the United States since the 1980s. Andre is a chemical engineer; and Josee, a nurse. They were living in North Carolina when Andre took a job with Eli Lilly and Company in Lafayette, Indiana, early in 2005. Andre moved to the Lafayette area to begin working. The rest of the family followed at the end of their two sons' school year.

There are six Catholic churches in the Greater Lafayette area. Andre had been to several of them as he searched for a new church home. He happened to be at St. Mary for a Sunday Mass late in February 2005. He noticed one of the priests appeared to be Haitian, a fact he confirmed once he heard Father Wilner Donecia speak. Before Mass ended, he heard there would be a Haiti presentation later that evening in the social hall.

Andre was not expecting Indiana to have any connection to Haiti. His curiosity was roused, so he attended that presentation.

While Father Wilner can speak and understand English, Andre volunteered to interpret for Father Wilner even though Andre knew no one else at the gathering! These connections to Haiti helped Andre to pick St. Mary as his new church home. Little did either of us know what a great relationship would begin that evening!

A Haitian proverb that comes to mind says, "Yon bon zanmi pi bon pase fre." That simply means "A good friend is better than a brother."

⟫•⟪

Once Andre and Josee were settled in Lafayette and at St. Mary Cathedral, they both became active in our Haiti ministry. Still they were both apprehensive to go to Haiti on our next mission trip. However, after encouragement from Sharon and me, they decided to take their nineteen-year old son Joandy with them on our December 2005 trip to Pendus. They traveled to Haiti several days before the rest of our group so they could spend the Christmas holiday with family who they had not seen in many years. On our ride north from PAP to Pendus, Josee thanked me because she said without our mission trip they would never have traveled to Haiti at that time. In fact, her family had told them not to come to Haiti due to recent civil unrest, especially in the Port-au-Prince area. Had it not been for their desire to be part of St. Mary's mission in Pendus, they would have missed out on their quality family time over Christmas!

During that week Josee spent a lot of time with Madam Marcel at the dispensary, helping her tend to the patients there. Josee said many times that she was amazed at all Madam Marcel did for her patients, how knowledgeable she was in the medical field, and how much she cared for the whole Pendus community.

Andre spent a lot of time that week helping to interpret. He also spent a lot of time talking with many people from Pendus, including Father Wilner Donecia. Understanding both cultures and languages, he could communicate in a much more effective way than I ever did on any prior trips.

Josee and Andre also lead in-home interviews of many Pendus residents in preparation for starting a Gift of Water project in the area. The questions asked involved family health history, income, nutrition history, and other personal information necessary to properly implement the new water endeavor in Pendus.

After we got home, Josee wrote the following to me to share at a presentation about our trip:

> I want to thank you for giving me the opportunity to be part of something so big. Besides helping a few financially and sending money for diverse charities...I have always wanted to do more. But knowing the unsafe conditions of the country has always been a barrier for years. Seeing your determination and dedication has lifted the load and opened new doors.
>
> Being from Haiti, I know firsthand the misery and hopelessness of the country, the face of hunger and suffering. I say it could have been me or my child. This trip has reopened my eyes and also Joandy's to the daily struggle of certain families to survive. Listening to some of them at the clinic or during the Gift of Water survey was a hard hit and made you want to help them in any way possible. They don't dream of big things; they dream that their situation will get better so their children could have a better future. By going there to help and share the ministry of God, you are giving them that hope and touched them in many ways.
>
> I have experienced many exciting moments and also some sad times. However, the part of my trip that will forever be engraved in my mind and heart was seeing the smiling little faces of the kids when we arrived at the different parishes and the gratitude and hope on the teachers and parents

faces. My heart-breaking moment was leaving friends behind.

Thank you guys so much for your generosity, your ministry, your love and your gift of hope to the country I am from and love. I am forever in it with you.

———————

The next year Andre and Josee brought their other son Alex with them to Pendus. That year we also had a doctor, a nurse practitioner, and a nursing student with us so we could have several medical clinics that week. Josee was invaluable, both with her medical knowledge but also with her Creole. There was no chance of something being lost in translation with her ability to speak the native tongue! Both Andre and Alex also helped to translate during those clinics.

Andre invited Haiti's minister of education Gabriel Bien-Amie to come talk with the teachers from St. Joseph School and several of the surrounding chapels that week. Gabriel's position is analogous to the secretary of education in the United States. Not only was Gabriel a great personal friend of Andre and Josee, he was the best man at their wedding!

Andre also brought a laptop and projector with him on this second trip. Several evenings that week he set up a "movie night" in the courtyard area. We hung a white sheet on one wall of the cistern and showed the movie on it. Once word got out the entire courtyard area was full of children watching what I presumed was their first "full screen" movie! Madam Marcel even made some popcorn for everyone to share!

———————

Three years later Andre invited Sharon, Kyle, and me to come to Haiti six days ahead of the rest of our St. Mary team. He wanted to show us some historical and cultural parts of Haiti that we never had time to experience during a normal mission week in Pendus.

Among the many places he took us in and around Port-au-Prince that year was Fort Jacques, located up the mountain beyond Petionville in the village of Kenskoff. Located 1,300 feet above sea level, the fort strategically sat on a ridge that overlooked PAP and the harbor below. Fort Jacques was named for Gen. Jean Jacques Dessalines, a leader in the Haitian fight for independence and the first president of Haiti in 1804.

Built in the early 1800s by Alexander Petion, the fort still contained several original cannons on the premises. The fort also had a sixteen-foot-deep cistern to hold water as well as an escape tunnel. There is a second fort, Fort Alexander, which is located a short distance away. However, this fort was never finished after the death of Petion, so we did not visit it.

It was extremely foggy during our morning at Fort Jacques. Our visibility was limited, and we could not see the valley and water below. Despite the fog, the setting was still magnificent. After visiting the fort, we drove back to Petionville and had lunch at a restaurant called Harry's. It was a new experience to go out to eat at a restaurant in Haiti. However, the typical Haitian meal of pork called *grio* and plantains was not better than Madam Marcel's back in Pendus!

Other stops that day included College Canado where Andre once taught; the National Palace; the Legislative Palace; Champ-De-Mars Park; and the Bicentennial Tower, a monument built by former President Aristide for the 2004 bicentennial celebration. We also visited *Neg Mawon*. That translates in English to "Unknown Slave." It is a statue of a slave who has broken free from his ankle shackle and is blowing on a conch shell announcing his freedom. It is located near the Palace and Champ-De-Mars. It is very inspiring. (The National Palace and Legislative Palace were destroyed in the 2010 earthquake. Neg Mawon survived.)

We also drove along Harry Truman Boulevard and saw some of the poorest sections of housing outside the confines of City Soleil. Many of the "homes" were not much more than ten-foot-by-ten-foot lean-to structures stacked right next to each other for several blocks.

The next day we drove to Cap Haitien. Andre's intent was for us to then travel the short distance to Labadee, Haiti's resort on the northern coast, and spend a couple nights there. However, our rental car had some issues arise about an hour's drive north out of PAP. By the time the rental company sent a replacement vehicle for us we had lost over three hours. That extra delay caused it to be dark when we reached the highest points of the mountain range between PAP and Cap Haitien. Unfortunately, it was also raining. That combination greatly slowed our travel time. We wound up spending the night at the house of Curdy Angrand, Andre's father, in Cap Haitien.

Because of the change in plans, Andre and his father took us out to eat at a Cap Haitien restaurant located right on the water's edge called Deco Plage. It happened to be its first night open for business. Both owners were there to warmly welcome us. We had plates of pork and chicken with french fries and plantains. The food was good.

We did get to Labadee the following day, but would only have one night there now. It was a good thing we waited and not tried to go in the dark. Even in the daylight, it took us forty-five minutes to go five miles from Curdy's house on a muddy road that ended at the water's edge where Andre and Curdy dropped us off. There is no way to drive all the way into Labadee. Our destination was so secluded it took a ten-minute water taxi ride around a point of land into a sheltered harbor to finally reach Labadee.

We stayed at Norm's Place, which was an old French outpost in the late 1700s. It was a very picturesque setting along the water's edge in the comfort of the shade of many huge trees. It had its own private beach area. There were five separate rooms available and a sleeping capacity for fifteen people. The lobby was an open stone structure that also served as our dining room and a reading room that overlooked the water. Our room had three beds in it, each with a mosquito net hanging above it.

We were told we had to put our order in for dinner by 3:00 p.m. if we wanted to eat there that evening. Where else would we eat in this remote region of Haiti? There was no menu. We simply were told our choices were fish, beef, or pork. So I chose fish, and Sharon and Kyle picked beef. We had no idea what that would turn out to be!

Sharon and I went out to sit on the beach. While it wasn't threatening to rain, the sky was cloudy. I decided I was not coming this far and not getting in the water. I know that surprised Sharon! I was afraid tomorrow's weather could be worse. The water was not warm but wasn't cold either. Both of us got all the way in after wading out about fifty yards. There was no one else swimming anywhere close to us.

We took turns getting cleaned up and found a book to read as we waited for dinner to be prepared. The lobby was a peaceful, serene place to relax, listening to the constant lapping of the waves on the shore just a few yards from where we sat.

I was informed that the fish I was served was called *Sad*. It was bigger than the plate it was served upon! It was very tasty. The beef served to Sharon and Kyle was not steaks that they were expecting but rather bite-sized pieces served family style along with bowls of rice, sauce, lettuce, tomatoes, and plantains. It was good too. While we ate, the sun was setting, not over the water since we were facing north but the sky was colorful nonetheless.

That night we all slept very well, tucked under our mosquito nets. The sound of the waves helped lull us to sleep. The temperature was very comfortable for sleeping, yet the sheet and quilt on our beds felt good by morning.

We were in no hurry the next morning. I woke up to the sound of someone sweeping the ground outside our room. They did take very good care of the property at Norm's Place. Kyle was already up and out by 7:00 a.m. He went exploring, hiking a trail clear back to the point we came around on the water taxi yesterday. The trail involved actual rock climbing for parts of it.

The newest addition to our neighborhood was the Royal Caribbean cruise ship named *Jewel of the Seas*, anchored about a mile north and east from Norm's Place. All the beaches belonging to the cruise ship line were located close to where the water taxis picked us up. However, throughout the day, there were folks parasailing, Jet Skiing, and kayaking in the bay in front of Norm's Place.

I tried out one of the hammocks behind our room. I could get used to that every day, relaxing in the shade and listening to the water in the distance. Breakfast was not until nearly 9:00 a.m. Sharon and I ordered omelets and Kyle scrambled eggs. We also had toast, apricot jelly, peanut butter, and gernadia juice (made from a local fruit).

It was a beautiful sunny day. Sharon, Kyle and I spent the rest of our time at Norm's Place either on the beach or in the water. At one point, there were five young Haitian boys, probably six-eight years old, skinny dipping in the water near us. They were laughing, splashing, and having a great time.

Sharon swam out over fifty yards from shore and surprised several of the cruise ship kayakers. They were not expecting to see a white person, let alone an American, coming out toward them. Sharon told them that there was much more to experience in Haiti than the isolated area the cruise lines allowed them to visit.

We could have been on any island in the Caribbean and not had any better conditions than we had that day.

Unlike anywhere else I have ever stayed, we did not pay for our room and meals until it was time to check out. Norm's Place was very reasonable as it only cost $40 per person per night for the room and breakfast plus twelve dollars apiece for our dinner the night before. That was a grand total of only $156. I would come back here again if it wasn't so remote!

Andre and his dad picked us up after our water taxi ride back. They were in suits as they had both been to a wedding before coming to get us. On the return ride, Andre took us to his old school, College Notre Dame. Dinner that night was at Curdy's house. He fixed us chicken, rice and beans, lettuce, tomatoes, avocados, and plantains. I told Curdy that he spoiled Kyle by also having cake. He kept referring to Kyle as his new grandson!

After supper, we got ready for Midnight Mass with Andre at a church in Terre Rouge where Andre attended as a child. Details of that wonderful experience are set forth in the next chapter on universality of the church.

We thoroughly enjoyed these new experiences in Haiti. We are forever grateful to Andre for providing these opportunities to see

Haiti from a perspective different than mission mode. During those few days, we felt like tourists enjoying vacation, sightseeing, eating out at nice restaurants, staying at the beach. We could not have had a better time anywhere else in the Caribbean! That is a side of Haiti few ever get to see or enjoy.

———⊰●⊱———

After taking Sharon, Kyle and me on a whirlwind tour through Haiti, Andre had one more surprise planned for our whole group the next night. The rest of the group was scheduled to arrive in PAP about 4:00 p.m. on December 26. Once everyone got checked into Matthew 25, he was going to take us all out for an evening of music and dancing.

However, those plans got waylaid when their plane was delayed leaving Indianapolis, causing them to miss their connection in Atlanta. They would not arrive in PAP until the next day on December 27; so only Sharon, Kyle, and I joined Andre for this cultural excursion.

Andre took us to a nightclub called Djoumbala to see the iconic Haitian band Tropicana. This beloved group consisted of ten musicians, several of whom Andre knew from Cap Haitien. The band has been extremely popular in Haiti for over forty years. I described them as the Beach Boys of Haiti.

The venue was packed and the music was great. They played a style of music called *kompa*. The atmosphere was electric. Unlike in America, everyone got up to dance for every song! The rhythm of Haitian music almost compels you to want to dance, so we joined in the fun as well. We stayed until they wrapped up at 3:00 a.m.! It was a wonderful evening and a far different cultural emersion than we had ever had before in Haiti. It was exactly what Andre wanted us to experience.

———⊰●⊱———

Both Andre and Josee were very active on St. Mary's Haiti committee as well. For several years Josee was head chef for our Taste of Haiti fundraiser. Because we knew that most parishioners would never be able to go to Haiti, we decided to bring some of Haiti to St. Mary. Throughout the evening, we would attempt to assail all five senses for those who came. Smell, taste, and touch were the three obvious senses to be satisfied. We included a slide-show presentation depicting life in Haiti. We also began the evening by singing a Haitian prayer before the meal as well and played a variety of Haitian music throughout the entire evening.

Josee and Sharon took several days preparing all the food necessary to feed nearly two hundred attendees. Several others helped them cook and serve a dozen different foods and desserts buffet style. We even created recipe cards showing the many ingredients that went into each of the dishes available to sample.

⸻▸●◂⸻

For me, the most beneficial contribution Andre made to our twinning relationship was teaching me how to speak Creole. What surprised me was the fact that he first had to learn the Creole language himself before he could instruct us! Growing up, French was all that was taught to Andre in school. He was discouraged from speaking Creole as it was perceived to be only for the uneducated. Remember, Creole was not officially recognized as a co-official language of Haiti and taught in Haitian schools until many years after he had moved to the United States. However, it was similar enough to French that it did not take him long to be proficient himself.

Over a four-year period, he taught more than twenty of us the elementary Creole grammar lessons. Four students were there for most of his classes: Sharon and me from St. Mary Cathedral and Duane Sellers and John Ginda from St. Thomas Aquinas in West Lafayette. The four of us benefited from new members who would periodically join our weekly class. Each time a new student would join, we reviewed all the earlier lessons as they were brought up to speed with us. That continual review made those early lessons routine for us. We got to where we could even teach "Creole 101"!

While Creole is a fairly easy language to learn, Andre liked to tease us that we often stumbled on our Creole because we did not remember our English grammar lessons from long ago. That was especially true the further we progressed in our proficiency. I hate to admit it to Andre, but he was right! He would even bring his own English textbook with him each week just to prove his point! Whatever topic we were trying to learn in Creole always made more sense after he gave us a refresher on the English equivalent.

I am so grateful for all I have learned about Haiti from Andre and Josee. They expanded my comprehension of the culture, history, and daily life in ways that were not possible on a typical mission trip.

Andre Angrand demonstrates how to use a laptop to many teachers, students and community members in Pendus.

19

The Universality of the Church

So we, though many, are one body in Christ.
—*Romans 12:5*

THE REVELATION OF THE UNIVERSALITY of the Catholic Church is another great lesson I have learned from my trips to Haiti. While I knew intellectually that the church existed throughout the entire world, I did not appreciate precisely how identical a Mass in another country was to what I was familiar with in Indiana.

Before I went to Haiti the first time, I had rarely been outside the United States and those trips were short one-day jaunts just across the border into Canada and Mexico. So I had not encountered anything even remotely close to an immersive experience. The only Masses that I had ever heard not in English were in Latin when I was a child!

One of the first masses I attended in Haiti was celebrating the feast day of St. Joseph at St. Joseph Church in Pendus. The church was packed, so much so that folks were standing along the walls on the sides and in the back of the church. Each pew, which is nothing more than a wooden bench, was crowded beyond what would be comfortable in the United States! There were no windows, at least not windows as we know them. Instead there were concrete blocks with openings that allowed light, as well as wind and rain, into the interior of the church. Kids were lined up outside the church, peeking into those slots, trying to get a glimpse of what was happening inside.

There was no permanent electricity at the church. However, because of the huge feast day celebration, there was a generator running outside the church. Someone had an electric guitar and a PA system that was on loan for Mass that day. Music and singing were an integral part of the Mass. While there were no songbooks available, every verse of every song was sung from memory by the entire congregation—and with a joy and passion that was contagious! A procession of young girls danced and sashayed as they led the priests into the church. The atmosphere was truly one of great celebration.

I instantly fell in love with the beat provided by the men playing the two tambous. Even without any other accompaniment, the tambous provided a festive atmosphere unlike any I was used to hearing. Watching the tambou players was entertaining as well. They would use their entire hand—fingertips, palms, base of their hand—as well as their elbows in playing. I never had any trouble picking up the beat when listening to the music with tambous. It was hard not to start dancing in church! The music sure had a way to lift your spirit too.

I did not understand any of the words being spoken or sung throughout the two-and-a-half-hour Mass, so I could only observe and marvel. It occurred to me that the Word of God could still be effective in me even without me understanding any of the actual words!

Somehow at every critical part of the Mass, I knew exactly what the appropriate response in English was to the prompt that was said in Creole! Simple responses such as "And with your spirit" and "Amen" flowed naturally from my lips. What surprised me was I was saying the Penitential Act; the Creed; the Holy, Holy, Holy; and Lord's Prayer in English at the correct time they were being recited in Creole. I had never thought about what a foreign country's church service would be like, but for some reason I did not expect it to be so identical to what I was accustomed to back home. Having grown up Catholic, I instinctively knew what was next. It was amazing to me how much a part of the Mass I felt even though I had no idea what was specifically being said!

A surprisingly special part of Mass was at the sign of peace. I suppose it may have been that I was a guest; but it seemed that I greeted, and was greeted by, nearly everyone at the Mass and not just by the people sitting immediately around me. It did make me feel welcome. Even the priest came down from the altar for a heartfelt embrace!

Over the years there have been other outstanding examples of the universality of the Catholic Church at St. Joseph. One year there was a Creole banner that stretched clear across the back of the altar that read "The Year of Faith" as proclaimed by then Pope Benedict XVI. On a subsequent trip, there was another banner proclaiming "The Year of Mercy" as established by Pope Francis. It is great to be sharing our faith, not just in our own parish and diocese, but clear around the entire globe. Often it is easy to lose sight of the magnitude of the church.

———◦———

Thomas Siener was twenty-years old when he went with his father Chris on our December 2014 trip to Pendus. While in high school he was a member of the Knights of the Holy Temple at St. Mary Cathedral. It is an elite group of older altar servers at our parish. I told that fact to Father Sylvio Jean before our first Mass at St. Joseph, so Father gave him an alb and had Thomas assist him at Mass.

For those unfamiliar with what an altar server does at Mass, his or her primary role is to assist the priest in any manner needed. That help can be simply holding the book for the priest to read or pray from, carry candles or incense, help in the presentation of the gifts brought to the altar from the congregation, assist the priest in washing his hands, or perform any other task. While a priest may have individual preferences in some of these specific tasks, the order and content of the Mass is consistent throughout the entire Catholic Church.

Even though Mass was celebrated in Creole, a language that Thomas did not understand, he had no trouble following what to do and when to do it as an altar server. That is a great testament to the universality of our Catholic Church. Thomas did a great job learning exactly how Father Sylvio wanted everything done during Mass and continued to do so at every Mass we had that week.

———⟫●⟪———

Because our visits to Haiti were usually right after Christmas each year, we never got to celebrate that blessed day in Haiti. It is easy to understand that most people want to spend that holiday with family at home before leaving for another country. However, it was a bit different for me as my family, Sharon and Kyle, was coming with me to Haiti. We could still celebrate Christmas together wherever we happened to be. Father Wilner Donecia invited us to come a few days ahead of the rest of our group in 2006 so he could take us to the Citadel in northern Haiti and then have us spend Christmas with him before meeting up with our team.

We flew to Haiti on December 23, taking the entire day to get to PAP. We then flew in a puddle jumper from PAP to Cap Haitien the next morning and met up with Father and his nephew. They drove us about an hour south to Milot to visit both the Citadel and King Henri Christophe's palace called Sans Souci.

We did not get back to Gros Morne until well after dark that night. Father had us stay at Kay Se, the nun's house, with Sister Pat Dillon while we were in Gros Morne. Sister Jackie Picard, a mainstay on all our prior trips to Haiti, was not there but rather was back in the USA visiting her ailing father.

Later that night, there would be a huge Midnight Mass at Our Lady of the Light, Father Wilner's main church in Gros Morne. However, he would not be there as he was celebrating Midnight Mass in a remote chapel about an hour's drive away. That chapel was not part of Pendus, and all the driving in the mountain to get there and back would be in the dark, not making it the safest of trips to take. So

Father told us that we could go with him for his 4:00 p.m. Christmas Day Mass at a different chapel. Again, it was not a chapel associated with Pendus, but we could enjoy the travel to and from it in the safety of daylight the next day.

After a leisurely morning visiting friends, we were dressed and ready to go to Christmas Mass when Father Javier arrived to pick us up. We assumed he simply was taking us to meet Father Wilner, who had gone on ahead to prepare for Mass. We didn't know for sure as Father Javier did not speak much English and we did not have an interpreter. So we took off with him.

A short distance outside Gros Morne, we took a left at the first river and followed it several hundred yards to the Twa Riveier. This river was fairly low, about knee high at its deepest. Father Javier slowed down as he prepared to cross through the river. Barely halfway across he got stuck.

Several Haitians were washing their motos, small motorcycles that are a common form of "taxi" in Haiti, along the edge of the river. They stopped and came over to try to help us. Kyle and Benedict both had dress shoes on, so they took them off and went barefoot. I had on waterproof sandals that I always wear in Haiti, so I was good in the water. All three of us rolled up our pants and got out to help push and dig out for traction. Once we were sure that we were not going to get out easily, I sent Benedict on a moto back to Gros Morne to find Barak, a mechanic and often our driver, to come help us. I had tried to reach him by cell phone but service was not good in Gros Morne.

Sharon had gotten out of the vehicle and was standing on a nearby sandbar. It was now dusk, and she was worried both about mosquitoes and our general safety standing in the middle of a major river at dark. After about ninety minutes of trying to get the vehicle unstuck, I asked Father Javier, in the best Creole I could, if Mass was already started since we were so late. I was still under the impression that Father Wilner was already there. He looked up at me, smiled, and said, "No I the priest!" Kyle simply looked at me and said, "Are you going to tell Mom or me?" as he looked over at his mother on the sandbar.

Once I realized Father Wilner was not going to be there and it was not a chapel we were familiar with and it was now nearly dark, we decided to get three other motos and go back to Gros Morne ourselves. The fifteen-minute ride back got us to the rectory at about the same time that Father Wilner was pulling into the church parking area too.

He had been detained earlier. When he realized that he wasn't going to be back in time for the 4:00 p.m. Mass, he had asked Father Javier to cover it for him. Because we did not have good cell service, he could not call us to tell us of the new plans. I guess that is life in Haiti. You just have to get used to it and go with the flow! Father did get a big laugh out of the fact that the three of us rode separate motos back from the river, instead of doubling or tripling up on one moto like most Haitians would have done.

So much for us experiencing Christmas Mass in Haiti!

Finally, Benedict and Barak showed up at Kay Pe. Benedict had searched all over Gros Morne before he located Barak. Once we explained the situation to him, Barak took off to go help Father Javier.

On the bright side, Sharon had heard of a Christmas meal being planned for that evening at Kay Se. We thought we would miss it because of being at Mass so far away. However, we were back in time for dinner with everyone. We had a huge ham with pineapples, green beans, scalloped potatoes, sweet potatoes, rolls, and cold water. The sisters also had bit of wine to go with the meal. It was quite a feast! By the end of the meal, Barak showed up. He had been successful in the dark in freeing Father Javier's vehicle from the river. Exhausted, he too sat down to eat.

Sister Pat and the other nuns that were there held a communion service for us later that night. Their chapel room had a Nativity set and was lit by candlelight. The mood was very calming. We took turns reading the readings for Christmas day. We each then gave a reflection on those readings and how they applied in our lives. At the end, we each shared in communion. Although there was no priest present to celebrate Mass with us, they had a small tabernacle in their chapel, which had some consecrated Eucharist. It was unique and wonderful end to a unique and wonderful day.

———⟫●⟪———

Three years later we tried again. This time Andre Angrand invited Sharon, Kyle, and me to spend some time with him for a few days before the rest of our group arrived. He wanted to show us some historically significant places in and around Port-au-Prince and Cap Haitien as well as celebrate Midnight Mass at his childhood church in Terrier Rouge in northern Haiti.

After supper with Andre's father, Curdy, in Cap Haitien, we all got ready to drive to Terrier Rouge. Located about twenty miles east of Cap Haitien, it would take us about thirty minutes to get there. How is that possible? It had the best stretch of highway I had ever seen in Haiti in the ten years I had been going to Haiti! If had closed my eyes I would have thought I was driving on a good Indiana two-lane highway. It helped that the road was completely straight and level, but there were yellow lines down the middle of the road. Some of them were dotted and some were solid lines indicating no passing. There also were white lines on the edges of both sides of the road. There were also street signs! I particularly recall seeing two signs for animal crossing and children crossing as well as a speed limit sign. It was amazing to me. Andre said the government had hired a Dominican company to construct this road. I had not realized just how close we were to the Dominican Republic as it was only about ten miles further east.

We arrived at Terrier Rouge about 10:00 p.m. Andre introduced us to his good friend and one-time fellow seminarian, Father Leclerc Eyma. The church was celebrating its three hundredth anniversary and was already packed. The children were already singing and could be heard even outside the building. Apparently, they were waiting just for us to arrive so they could start Mass, which then began at 10:45.

The atmosphere was spectacular. The music was great. There were two tambou players plus an entire drum set, and electric keyboard, and a bass guitar. As usual, every song was sung through every verse with no one using a songbook. The celebratory nature of the night was obvious and contagious.

It took twelve minutes for the opening procession to enter the church down the main aisle from the front door. There were three servers, nine young girl dancers, and the priest in this procession. This aisle was no more than fifty feet long. The girls would dance to the front a couple steps, then to the side and back, and repeat this movement to the music many times as they ambled toward the sanctuary. They truly were only concerned with the celebration of the moment and not with how long it was taking! No one was in a hurry all night. Music even erupted during Father's homily. Several times he would break out into "Gloria" to emphasize the point he was making and the entire congregation would join in singing!

When Mass was over, Father Eyma reintroduced Andre to the church. Andre had been there several times in the past few years to help in various ways. Father then introduced Sharon, Kyle, and me and had each of us speak.

Afterwards, Father took us back to his rectory for cake and drinks. He tried to get us to spend the night too, but we had not brought anything with us to do so.

The ride back on the wonderful road was interesting. Not only were there speed bumps about every mile or so, but there were animals of all kinds simply sleeping on the road. There were cows and calves, donkeys, dogs, and goats. They were sleeping in groups on the road as it was still warm for them from the day's exposure to the Caribbean sun. We would have to stop each time we came upon them scattered across the road and watch as they would slowly get up, give us a look of inconvenience, and then finally mosey out of our way so we could proceed.

We also enjoyed a beautiful star-filled sky on the drive back to Cap Haitien. It was after 3:00 a.m. before were arrived back at Curdy's house that night. Finally, we experienced Christmas Mass in

Haiti. It was a wonderful experience and another great example of the universality of the Catholic Church.

———————

A common thread woven through all the above universality of the church examples is the location of the Mass does not matter. The core components of the Mass itself are the same wherever you celebrate it. Mass can even be held in nontraditional venues such as your own living room, which we did one year.

On one of the early trips, my travel agent came across an opportunity for our group to be bumped in exchange for a free ticket for each from that airline. The agent had an e-mail waiting for me with this option when I got back to PAP at the end of our visit to Pendus. Therefore, this opportunity was very last minute, changing how we got home, when we got home, and potentially who would be able to pick us up at the airport. It also got us home very late, and many of our group had to be at work the next day. We would have to scramble to make it work.

Our group liked the chance for a free ticket. However, we were about to reject the offer because the new timing would force us to miss going to Mass on that day of travel, which happened to be a Sunday. Father Bob came up with a solution that was satisfactory to everyone. He offered to celebrate Mass in my living room when we are got back to Lafayette. To keep the length of the Mass short, allowing more time for everyone to still drive to their homes and get some sleep, he promised to keep his homily to only one sentence. With that assurance, we all accepted the new arrangements and the free ticket that came along with it.

The intimacy of the Mass in my living room was wonderful. Our group grew very close during our week's journey to Pendus. We had celebrated Mass nearly every day while there, but this Mass seemed the most impactful to me, probably because it would be our last time together. Father Bob kept his promise too. It is funny that I cannot remember what he said, only the fact that it was one short sentence in length!

The banner depicting The Year of Faith declared
by Pope Benedict XVI spans across the altar
of St. Joseph Church in Pendus.

20

Gift of Life

Then the angel showed me the river of the water of life.
—Revelation 22:1

WATER IS ESSENTIAL TO SUSTAIN all life on earth, whether it is human, animal, or plant life. While water covers over 70 percent of the earth's surface, there are many water-vulnerable areas in the world, especially in underdeveloped areas such as Haiti.

Imagine how much time and effort it would take if you had to go outside your home every time you needed to get water for cooking, drinking, or cleaning. This would be extremely inconvenient even if you only had to go a few feet from your dwelling. How time-consuming would it be if you had to go to the end of the block to fetch the water and carry it back inside? Take it a step further and make the water source a mile or two away from where you live. An inordinate amount of time and energy would be spent simply in providing water for you and your family's daily needs.

When we first arrived in Pendus, the main source of water for the community was the Pendus River. There was an old well near the river, but it had not been operable for quite some time. It always amazed me that the predominate source of water for drinking and cooking was drawn from the same water that humans and animals walked through, people bathed in, and clothes were cleaned. Even vehicles and motorcycles simply pulled into the river to be cleaned when needed. Nothing was done to treat the water before consumption.

This scenario repeats itself throughout most of Haiti, especially rural areas. It is no wonder that Haiti has one of the highest mortality rates for children age five and under. That age bracket is the most susceptible to the multitude of problems that unsafe drinking water can cause.

Dr. Dave Schmidt has been to Pendus twice on medical missions with St. Mary. I have heard him say many times that the best preventive medicine we could provide to the country would be safe, clean drinking water for everyone. Clean water alone would get rid of, or at least minimize, many of the routine health problems Haitians face daily.

When our groups are in Pendus, we always have access to purified water. In Haiti, it is often referred to as Culligan water even if Culligan wasn't the manufacturer. (That is like all tissues being called Kleenex. It simply shows how powerful the brand name is for that product!) It would come in five-gallon bottles that could be purchased in Gros Morne. Our groups would each pay for the good water. We use it both to drink and to have our food cleaned and cooked with it.

While the cost is not exorbitant for us, it would be prohibitive for local Haitians to utilize this source of safe drinking water for several reasons. First, the actual cost would be a burden on a population that earns less than $2 per day. Second, the time, energy, and expense of traveling ten miles each way to Gros Morne and back to buy it would be high. Even if a local entrepreneur set up a way for it to be available in Pendus, the cost for the convenience would only increase the price of the water.

Third, good water works only if a person drinks it exclusively. It is not effective to drink good water some of the time and contaminated drinking water at other times. The problems associated with the poor water prevail. Therefore, any ultimate water solution for the area needs to provide potable water to the community all the times—at home, at school, at neighbors' homes, or while working. To provide that much infrastructure requires a massive undertaking.

Having safe, clean drinking water readily available to us is a blessing we in America frequently take for granted, or worse, completely overlook! I know that I am thankful for this benefit much more now that I have traveled to Haiti so many times. Often, I hear from others who have gone that they appreciate this fact as well. This newfound consciousness now leads them to do simple things such as taking much shorter showers or turning the water faucet off while brushing their teeth instead of letting the water continually run. For us, it is now much easier to understand how truly precious water really is.

⸺∞∞⸺

There are many different nongovernment organizations (NGOs) that help provide clean drinking water in Haiti. There have been two that we have utilized in the Pendus area.

Gift of Water was founded by Phil Warwick, an engineering graduate from Purdue University. He developed a two-bucket system that purifies water so well that it is safe for Americans to drink! Simplifying the process, five gallons of water are put in the top bucket along with a bleach tablet. The water is then filtered as it passes through to the bottom bucket, where another tablet is added. It is ready for consumption in an hour. The real beauty of this system was it is portable. The buckets can be taken to and used easily in the most remote areas of Haiti. Once the buckets are obtained, the only ongoing expense for the user is for the tablets needed and a new filter periodically, depending on usage.

The trip before we began using Gift of Water, we had to do a series of in-home interviews with as many local residents as we could. The responses would allow Gift of Water to assess the need in the area. Andre and Josee Angrand were on that team and acted as extra interpreters for us as we visited homes in the Pendus area. The questions were quite personal, such as asking what illnesses and diseases the family encountered over the prior twelve months as well as how often the family ate a meal and how often meat was part of their meal.

St. Mary purchased the first four hundred units soon thereafter, and they were quickly distributed within the Pendus community. Families with young children were given a priority in the process. Subsequently, more units were bought and donated throughout the community.

We revisited many of the same homes the following year to see how well the Gift of Water systems were working. We were very pleased with the responses we received. The best one was from a mother of several young children. She simply said, "We have not been sick at all this past year!" Dr. Schmidt was right!

Unfortunately, Gift of Water ceased operating about two years later and remained closed for nearly two years. Luckily, Pete Murphy and Laura Moehling, both of Carmel, Indiana, spearheaded an effort thereafter to resurrect its operations in Haiti. While Gift of Water was closed, we turned to Deep Springs International for our in-home water systems for the Pendus area. The main difference between the two companies was Deep Springs utilized a one bucket system; therefore, there was no filter, just bleach was used in the process. Having only a single bucket, this system also was extremely portable and easy to take into the remote mountain homes in Pendus. Michael Ritter heads up Deep Springs. He made several visits to the Pendus area in preparation for our switch to Deep Springs.

The key to the success of either of these two systems is regular follow-up visits by technicians to ensure the users were fully benefiting from the process. There is an educational element to these visits as well. Not only do the technicians test to make sure the people are correctly purifying the water, they also make sure the people know and understand that good, clean containers are needed after the water is purified so the benefit of clean water is not immediately lost.

Under both companies' business model, the technicians' salaries were to be eventually covered by their selling the bleach and other related items to the end users. Thus, both had potential to become self-sustaining projects. However, the cholera epidemic in Haiti hit about this same time. With all good intentions of helping the people, bleach was given away by other not-for-profits throughout Haiti. This undermined the ability of technicians to sell their products, leaving them little or no income. In turn, this led to fewer and fewer home visits. Without regular follow-up by the technicians, the efficiency of both systems dropped dramatically. This is an example of unintended negative consequences resulting from initially good intentions!

Father Wilner had a vision for another way to provide safe drinking water to the Pendus area. He found a natural spring near the top of the mountain in the Mayombe area. It was another forty-five-minute hike further up beyond the Mayombe chapel. He had the spring monitored for an entire year, through all four seasons. It never went dry, even in the non-rainy months. It proved to be ideal for his project.

Before starting this endeavor, he took several of us up to see this spring. It drained from an opening in a rock. The flow was constant and was about the size of my little finger. It was sheltered on three sides by other rocks. While I did not try to drink any of it, I knew from my backpacking experience that this water was safe enough for me to drink if I really needed it for consumption. We were high enough on the mountain that the only water coming into this spring was from rainfall that had been filtered through the ground. It amazed me that being this close to the top of the mountain, such a steady flow was possible.

Father built a captage that engulfed the spring. The concrete structure was four feet high by four feet wide and six feet long. It gathered enough water to create sufficient pressure to send the water through a pipe approximately three hundred feet to the edge of the plateau of the mountain. There he built a bigger captage to hold additional water. This concrete catch basin was about eight feet high by ten feet wide and ten feet long. It could hold much more water than the first one, thereby creating sufficient pressure, when combined with gravity, to send water nearly three miles down to Pendus.

The topography between these two catch basins was basically level. That initial pipe was metal for greater protection. From the larger captage, PVC pipe was used to transport the water downhill the rest of the way. About every five hundred feet or so, a water station was built. At each station, a *T* was inserted in the PVC to direct water to the nearby outlet. A five-foot-by-five-foot concrete pad was constructed with a four-foot concrete post in the middle. The PVC was directed up both sides of the post to respective faucets for easy access by everyone. Eventually, the PVC between each of the water stations was buried for further protection.

Several hundred yards downhill from the Mayombe chapel another captage was built. It was similar in size to the other larger one closer to the source. It allowed more water to once again be accumulated to keep pressure constant the second half of the way down to the valley where Pendus is nestled. The two big captages keep sufficient water pressure in the entire system even if multiple faucets are opened at the same time. The two captages also have overflow outlets to release excess water for the times when none of the faucets are being used.

The beauty of this water system is there is no need for electricity as no pumps are necessary. It simply utilizes gravity and the pressure created by collecting the water in three captages along the way. Because of the design of the water stations, people could now get water close to the main walkway instead of having to climb down to lower points wherever the water would have otherwise naturally been flowing. Often access to those spots was difficult to get to and usually muddy. In addition, at each station along the way downhill, people were getting as clean of water as they would have at the top without any of it having been contaminated by humans, animals, or nature. Before, the lower down the mountain one was, the more contaminated the water for them to use became.

I know the people could tell a difference in the quality of the water they were getting from these stations. I have often heard residents refer to the stations as where they get their "cholera free" water!

Water is also critical to the agricultural needs of the community. Many of the people in the area are subsistence farmers, trying to grow enough to feed their immediate family with possibly some leftover to sell or trade.

Irrigation is not utilized in the Pendus area of Haiti. It is very mountainous, and access to water is often very difficult. The people simply rely on rainfall for their crops. Father Cha Cha says that rain can be both a blessing and a curse. It is an obvious blessing when the rain comes at regular intervals in normal amounts to help the various crops to grow. However, there are many times during the year, particularly during hurricane season, when the deluge simply washes out whatever is being grown in the area. Therefore, rain can also be a curse!

With the deforestation that has occurred over the years, the soil often gets swept away by these heavy rains as well. After the rain has ended and the river receded, I have actually witnessed men with five-gallon buckets and shovels going to the bends in the river and retrieving the fertile top soil that once was on their property!

The rainfall is not always constant for comparable times of the year. My first trip to Haiti was in the month of December. The Pendus River was only ankle deep where we crossed it to enter into Pendus. Since then, there have been two Decembers where the Pendus River at this same location was chest deep and flowing too fast to risk driving a vehicle through it. Those were the times we had to wade across with the help of the local Haitians.

A woman does her laundry along the Pendus River, which
is the source for drinking water for many in Pendus.

21

Lost in Translation

Let us then go down there and confuse their language,
so that one will not understand what another says.

—Genesis 11:7

I NEVER TRULY UNDERSTOOD THE expression that something was lost in translation until I went to Haiti and began to learn to speak some Creole and needed to translate something. Speaking a foreign language was no longer simply an academic exercise, it now was a necessity!

From the first moment I set foot in Haiti, I wished I was fluent in Creole. I wanted to carry on a conversation without needing an interpreter. I regretted not being able to speak confidently many times over the years. I always needed an interpreter for any serious conversation beyond the perfunctory "hello" and "how are you?" Because Haiti was my first immersive experience, I did not realize just how many times the interpreter and I did not even understand each other and how that may have snowballed misunderstandings of which neither side was ever aware.

Hopefully none of the misunderstandings we encountered caused any harm to anyone. I guess I may never know! However, I do know that some of language episodes I have encountered throughout the years were quite humorous.

One of the first phrases of Creole that I learned on my initial trip to Haiti was "Kouman ou rele?" Literally, it translates "How are you called?" but really means "What is your name?" I must have asked one young man five times "Kouman ou rele?" Not only did I not understand his answer, I did not know how to ask it any other way. Finally, I tried to apologize for repeating myself, in English of course! He responded back to me with his limited English, "No Danger!" I must have had a look of not understanding because Sister Jackie promptly told him, "No, you mean 'no problem'!" Of course, she said it to him in Creole.

I can easily understand how "problem" and "danger" have overlapping definitions but they are not interchangeable words. I wondered just how many times my limited knowledge of Creole had me saying the equivalent of "no danger" when I should have been saying "no problem!" If someone was not around to catch it like Sister Jackie did in the above scenario, I would have simply gone on with the conversation with the misguided assumption that we both understood each other! Just because it was said aloud, heard by someone, and even acknowledged by them does not mean it was truly understood. There is a Haitian proverb directly on point: "Tande pa di konprann pou sa" means "To hear does not mean to understand." That was a huge lesson to learn! Needless to say, "no danger" became a hit phrase for the rest of our stay that year and a reminder to me that the first response may not always be accurate.

<hr />

Another misunderstanding occurred on the trip that Jim Rush and Jim Weiss were on together. The two of them were introducing themselves to some of the local people without using an interpreter. That meant the locals were trying to understand their English. Jim Rush went first and simply said, "My name is Jim." They responded, "Ah, Jim," using the soft *J* French sound, as they took turns shaking his hand.

Jim Weiss followed by saying, "My name is Jim as well." They responded, "Ah, Jim as well," again using the soft French *J* sound as they slurred it all together as if it was one word! Needless to say, he was called Jimaswell by our entire group the rest of the trip and frequently after he got home! Laughter never failed to follow the recounting of this story. Sadly, Jim died several years later. This story was retold as his life was remembered—and still brought smiles to all who heard it.

———>●<———

One of the funniest language encounters came on the very first St. Mary trip to Pendus. Brian Roark had such a big heart. He was always trying to help everyone he met the entire week. He also was fascinated by the machetes and wanted to buy one to take home for himself and his son. He had an interpreter go with him into the market to buy them. They found out that he could buy three of them for $10. Brian felt that price was too low, that he was somehow taking advantage of the seller, so he insisted on paying $15 for the three machetes instead of the ten. Of course, we all teased him unmercifully. We were never going to have him barter for us!

Later, I told this story to Sister Jackie and asked her what you called someone who paid fifteen dollars for something that cost only ten dollars. Her response sounded like "farouche." Sometime thereafter, I was talking with an American Quest volunteer who was also acting as one of our interpreters. I asked her what *farouche* meant. She did not know. So I had her ask two of the nearby local men, Jean Claude and his nephew, what *farouche* meant. They discussed among themselves for a bit before saying it was someone who bid up the price, as in an auction.

I immediately said that *farouche* was not the word I was looking for. Could they help us find the right one? So we began to tell them what Brian had done. As soon the volunteer finished saying that Brian actually paid $15 instead of the ten, Jean Claude's nephew emphatically blurted out, "Em-Be-Sill!" I did not need an interpreter's help understanding his response! I guess some words such as imbecile are universal. Therefore, they can't get lost in translation.

We all laughed so loud at the nephew's answer that within moments, Brian walked into the room to see what was so funny. It was even more hilarious when we retold the scenario to him. We were laughing so hard we all had tears in our eyes, including Brian! Brian took the name as a badge of honor and promised to put "Imbecile" on the front of a T-shirt and wear it the next time he came to Haiti.

———⟫●⟪———

Words that are the same in both languages rarely get misunderstood, as do some gestures. John Condreay is a professional photographer who went on one of our trips. The large lens on his camera was never inconspicuous. However, John could shoot from so far away most people did not even know he was taking a picture. He was always snapping photos. He brought back some wonderful candid shots of both people and scenery in Haiti.

We were sitting in a bus at a gas station. In Haiti, there always is an armed guard somewhere near the pumps with his weapon in open view for all to see. While still sitting inside the bus, John aimed his camera toward the guard. The guard caught sight of what John was about to do and turned to face John. The guard said nothing, but he did hold up his right hand and wiggle his index finger back and forth indicating not to do that! It was the same gesture that the NBA's Dikembe Mutombo would do after blocking a shot! So John complied.

John chose not to focus on the finger wagging but rather the gun when he said, "The man spoke no English, but his assault rifle was multilingual!"

———⟫●⟪———

My biggest communication problem is that I tend to overthink what I want to say. I usually overcomplicate how and what words I want to use. One day we were in the courtyard in Pendus watching Jean Claude fill the water tank on the roof of the guesthouse.

Usually, he would be the only person up there. However, one of the young boys, named Fagant, climbed up there with him without his knowledge.

The generator room is located behind the guesthouse. There was an electrical wire that ran from the generator room, up over the roof of the guesthouse, and on across the courtyard into the church. It was resting on top of a concrete block on the roof of the guesthouse. I saw Fagant start to touch that wire. I wanted to tell him that it was dangerous, that he could get electrocuted, that he shouldn't even be up there to begin with. Of course, I did not know any of those words in Creole, and there was no interpreter around to help me.

Luckily, Kyle came by at that time. I promptly explained to Kyle what Fagant was doing, what I wanted said to him, how urgent the situation was, and that I did not know the words to say any of it! Kyle simply turned to the boy and sternly said, "*Fagant!*" Startled, the boy jerked around to face Kyle. Kyle then said, "Uh-uh!" as he wiggled his right index finger back and forth. Fagant immediately stopped and got down from the roof.

I told Kyle that I could have done that! But I didn't think of it. I wanted to use the more complicated words to fully express myself, instead of simply communicating as Kyle did! That was a lesson well learned.

———⟫●⟪———

As much as I want to practice my Creole when I am in Haiti, most Haitians love to practice their English with us even more whenever they get a chance. You never know when such an opportunity will arise.

We were at Matthew 25 Guest House one evening at the start of our trip. There is a nice soccer field adjoining the guesthouse, and a game was being played that evening on it. There were some huge speakers blaring out upbeat music as they played. It was a festive atmosphere that beckoned us all to come and participate! When the game was over, the music continued. Frank Donaldson, Dave Schmidt, and

Sharon were the first to join in the on-field dancing. Most of the dancers were young children simply having a moment of fun.

Finally, the music ended and everyone was beginning to leave. One young boy, probably only seven or eight years old, smiled at Sharon and waved, as he said, "Bye, bitch!" Startled, Sharon asked him to repeat what he had just said. So he did, and it came out the same. She began to shake her finger at him, scolding him. She said the look on his face was that he was both surprised at her reaction and very sorry! Overhearing all of this, Kyle was nearby, laughing. He said the young boy had no idea what it was that he had just said but that he had probably heard it in some song and was simply repeating what he thought was an appropriate greeting. He was practicing his limited English!

———⇒❖⇐———

Another example of a Haitian wanting to practice his limited English occurred on our three-mile hike from Montbayard down to the river near where a vehicle would be waiting for us. We had just finished conducting a medical clinic at that remote site.

We got a late start walking down the mountain, so we were in a hurry to finish before dark. The last of our group to leave were Father Wilner, Dr. Dave Schmidt, Frank Donaldson, and me. There was one young Haitian boy who eagerly ran up to tag along. He clearly wanted to practice his very limited English.

He did not know much English at all, but he would mimic anything that Frank would say. It became a bit of a game for Frank and the boy. Finally, Frank taught him to say "Thank you, Doctor Schmidt." Once he got it down, we sent him on up to where Father Wilner and Dave were walking several yards ahead of us. He repeated the phrase so often that it seemed like we were listening to a parrot. "Thank you, Doctor Schmidt. Thank you, Doctor Schmidt." Even Dave got a laugh out of it.

———⇒❖⇐———

One of my best intended attempts at speaking my limited Creole that could have ended disastrously occurred several trips after I had begun to learn some Creole. I knew enough to get by most situations, but obviously not enough!

Sharon and I were entertaining several children in the courtyard area. Sharon wanted to go across the school yard into a classroom and do some arts and crafts with them. Instead of instantly looking for an interpreter, I tried to communicate with them myself. I knew all the words needed to say, "Do you want to go to the classroom with us to make something?" Or so I thought. I asked them, "Eske nou vle ale avek nou nan klas la fe bagay?" I was proud of myself for completing this rather long sentence!

Sister Jackie broke out laughing, which was unusual. I did not understand, especially since two of our other interpreters were there and had no reaction at all. What I did not know was that I should have said *fe yon bagay* at the end of my sentence. I used the words *fe bagay* because I thought *fe* meant "to do" or "to make" and *bagay* meant "thing." It was logical to me to put them together to mean "to make something." Instead, when used together the words *fe bagay* become a slang expression meaning to have sex. *Fe yon bagay* is the word combination that means to make something.

No wonder Sister Jackie was laughing at me. I guess the Haitian expression is similar to our understanding of "sleeping with someone." It has nothing to do with sleeping, but is an expression that is understood by all.

You can bet that lesson is one I will never forget!

———◈———

My Creole gets a little better each time I go. The problem is I don't use it for almost a year between annual visits. Therefore, much of my vocabulary and sentence structure is relearned each time I go. It does, however, come back to me quicker after all these years.

I must understand more Creole than I give myself credit. On one of my recent trips, I was sitting in the courtyard talking with several of the teachers from Massacre with Serge Fortune acting as my interpreter. We were talking about the new chapel that was built in Montbayard. Since the Massacre teachers rarely get to that distant chapel, I was describing it to them. As I do with most stories I started at the beginning, telling them about the structure surviving the 2010 earthquake but not the 2011 hurricane.

It takes a certain skill to properly use an interpreter. Too often the speaker will say so much that the interpreter essentially begins to paraphrase instead of actually interpreting. I have been guilty of being too long-winded many times. The solution is to break your thoughts into short sentences, pausing so the interpreter can repeat exactly what you just said. There is an added benefit of speaking that way. It gives me a better chance of understanding what the interpreter is saying in Creole since only one short thought at a time is being translated.

Serge was repeating my story in Creole to the teachers when he got stuck on the Creole word for *hurricane*. He paused long enough for me to comprehend he was stuck on a word. Because I had been using short sentences between translations, I knew exactly what word he needed so I blurted out, "Cyclone," which was correct! Everyone got a great laugh out of me having to help Serge interpret the English into Creole!

───⟫◆⟪───

Sometimes we have to interpret English colloquialisms for our bilingual friends in Haiti to comprehend. One year early in our twinning relationship, I positively responded to Father Cha Cha's question with "You betcha!" He did not understand me. Even the interpreters, who knew what I meant, were having a difficult time trying to translate my use of slang. With lots of feeling, I finally said, "It means *oui, oui, oui!*" He then understood me and began to use that phrase whenever possible.

Another such occurrence arose while we were at the domestic airport. Another mission team from southern Indiana happened to be there at the same time as us. One lady from that group warmly greeted us, "Hi y'all. How are all y'all!" None of our interpreters had a clue what she had just said to us! We got a big laugh from both hearing the southern drawl greeting in Haiti and their reaction. We had to explain the difference between the singular *y'all* and the plural *all y'all*.

<hr />

Often communication occurs despite neither side knowing much of the other's language and only a few words being spoken aloud.

Sharon was initially disappointed when she learned the custom in Haiti is to call a married woman "Madam so-and-so" and not by her first name. She would often introduce herself as "Sharon" only to have them reply to her "Madam Jeff." It was meant as a sign of respect and not as a slight to her independence!

One day Sharon was not sure where I had wandered off to, so she tried to find me. She walked out of the church compound and headed down the dirt road that leads out of Pendus. She had guessed right that I had gone that direction. However, I had gone further down the road than where she was looking and had gone into the house of a family we both knew, so I was out of sight.

As she was walking, a small pickup truck, a tap-tap in Haiti, pulled up beside her and began to creep along at the same rate she was walking. There were several teenage boys riding in the bed of the vehicle. They were talking and looking at her. Sharon stopped, so they stopped. She started walking, and they began to move slowly. Sharon had no idea what they were saying but for an instant felt uncomfortable. Neither of us ever had any reason to be frightened in Pendus; this was simply an involuntary reaction to seeing the boys and the vehicle mimic her pace. Sharon did not speak Creole, so she could not chat with them, and she did not know anyone else who lived in the immediate stretch of that road.

Almost simultaneously as her moment of panic set in, a gentleman came out of the house closest to where she was walking. She did not know him, but he obviously recognized her. He greeted her warmly with "Madam Jeff." He put his arm around her and pointed her toward the house that he must have seen me visiting, directing her in my direction. Nothing else was said, nor needed to be said. He had sensed she needed some help and came to her rescue! He thought she only needed to know where I was, which she did. But more importantly, she was ecstatic to have a helping hand appear at that precise moment.

From that point on, Sharon did not mind being called Madam Jeff.

Sometimes you have to be creative to be able to communicate. On Kyle's first trip to Haiti, we were all at the rectory in Gros Morne. There was a pickup basketball game going on that Kyle was watching. He wanted to stay while the rest of the group went to tour the nearby hospital.

When we came back I noticed Kyle standing near the court speaking with a Haitian boy about his own age. I asked Kyle if the boy knew English. Kyle said the he did not. Since Kyle could not yet speak Creole, I was curious how they were talking, so I asked him. Kyle had taken Spanish in high school as did the young Haitian. They were using Spanish as a common link to be able to communicate. Neither was fluent in Spanish, but they spoke enough of the language to understand each other.

That was not only creative, it was very effective!

Some words simply do not have a good translation from one language to the next. Sister Jackie Picard told us *awesome* was one such word. She also gave us a few others that needed more than one word to get the meaning across during translation.

Father Bob gave a homily in one of the early visits at the chapel in Massacre with Sister Jackie translating for him. During his reflection, he intentionally used *awesome* and one of the other words in one sentence. As he spoke those words, he smiled and looked directly at Sister Jackie. The look he got back from her was priceless! She knew he selected those words on purpose. Not to be outdone, she immediately began to translate what he said. However, it took about three times as many words to get the same message across. We always teased her that we got her homily and not the priest's version when she translated anyway!

We all knew what he was doing and got a good chuckle out of both his attempt to tease her by using those words and her quick-witted response!

My many linguistic experiences in Haiti have greatly enhanced my newfound appreciation for learning a foreign language, for those who are bilingual, and for avoiding potential miscommunication situations.

Our translators play a vital role in our mission trips.
Here Sister Jackie Picard translates the homily of
Father Bob Klemme during a Mass in Massacre.

22

New Year's Tradition

For I know well the plans I have in mind for
you, says the Lord, plans for your
welfare, not for woe, plans to give you a future full of hope.
—*Jeremiah 29:11*

FOR THE PAST SEVENTEEN YEARS, I have ushered in the New Year in Pendus, Haiti. I have missed all typical festivities associated with that holiday in the United States, including the parties, hoopla, and bowl games. I even missed seeing my alma mater Purdue play in the 2001 Rose Bowl. I would not trade those times in Haiti for any of the things that I may have missed. Pendus is where I am content to be and to bring others with me to share in the experience.

January 1 not only is New Year's Day, it is Independence Day in Haiti. It is the holiday during the year that everyone tries to go home to be with family, much like we do for Thanksgiving in the USA. The traditional food for the day is *Soup Joumou*, a squash or pumpkin soup with meat in it. It also has vegetables such as cabbage, potatoes, carrots, and whatever else is available. This soup is as significant in Haiti as turkey is for our Thanksgiving Day.

Before Haiti gained its independence in 1804, only the slave owners and slave masters ever had soup with meat in it. The slaves would rarely, if ever, get to eat meat. To celebrate their independence, they chose to eat what the slave masters would eat—Soup Joumou! Thus, the tradition was started!

Because January 1 is such a big holiday, the day before often becomes a big market day in the community. Since no one in Pendus has electricity, no one has a refrigerator. All foods need to be purchased as close to time of consumption as possible to avoid spoilage. This particularly applies to the purchase of meat. If you have never been to a market in a developing country, the "meat department" may surprise you.

All types of meat to be sold at market—beef, pork, chicken, and goat—arrive alive at the start of the day. The chicken and goats are sold alive and taken home to be slaughtered later. However, cows and pigs provide so much more meat than a typical family can consume that they are slaughtered on-site. Using machetes, smaller quantities of beef and pork are parceled off and then sold to individual consumers. My curiosity in watching this procedure has gotten me too close that I have found myself in the splatter zone! Once all parts of a cow or pig are completely sold, another animal would be slaughtered, beginning the process all over again. Great care is taken to avoid wasting any part of the animal or to have any unsold quantities left over to spoil when the market day is done.

Many other edible items are also available: vegetables such as lettuce, cabbage, potatoes, carrots, yams, sweet potatoes, tomatoes, beans, beets and onions as well as staples such as rice, corn meal, flour, sugar, salt, and various other spices. Common fruits are bananas, plantains, grapefruit, mangos, oranges, citrons, and avocados. Sugarcane, pwa congo, coconuts, okra, malanga, and mayok are some of the local items not typically available in the United States. In rural settings such as Pendus, nearly everything is sold in small quantities and not in bulk as in the USA.

Much more than food is sold at market as well. In fact, many of the things available at a Target or Walmart can be found in a rural Haitian market. While the selection choices may be very limited and the quantities on hand small, clothing items such as pants, shirts, shoes, sandals, belts, and hats are available to purchase as well as household items such as soaps, cooking oil, batteries, flashlights, rope, brooms, cooking utensils, toothbrushes and toothpaste, and shampoo.

In Pendus, most of the items being sold are displayed on a blanket on the ground. Potential customers walk through the narrow pathways between the multitudes of merchants sitting next to their wares. The interior part of the village is packed with people and products.

As in the United States, where there is a crowd, there will also be food sold for immediate consumption. One of my favorite things to buy at market is cassava. It is an edible starch made from ground-up mayok root and cooked on an open fire. When finished, it looks like cooked bread the size of a medium or large pizza. Serge taught me a long time ago to have some sugar added for a sweeter taste. While it is best when eaten warm, the cassava will last all week without need of refrigeration.

During the year, every village has its regular market day so merchants can sell their wares nearly every day of the week by traveling to where the market will be each day. This helps the locals in each area from having to travel so far to buy the products they need. The merchants often will have a regular spot where they set up to sell in each village, making it easier for their customers to find them each week. In the bigger villages or towns, there will be open air buildings with individual stalls for each merchant to set up within. Often the commerce spills out into sidewalks and streets in the bigger cities. These types of markets embody the self-employed merchant economy that is so prevalent in Haiti.

———✦———

It took us a few years to get started, but we soon established a tradition of having our own New Year's Eve party in the church compound area every year. Because the church has a generator, we would have at least minimal lighting in the compound, making it a natural gathering spot in the village. The first few years we simply had the church's two tambous brought outside. Jean Claude, Hebert, Serge, and Benedict would take turns playing those drums as we gathered around and listened to the rhythm they created. That by itself was enjoyable for me! Often Jean Claude would also play the church's battery-powered keyboard as accompaniment to the tambous. Father Wilner would also play the *graj*, which is a metal instrument that looks like a cheese grater. He would use a metal rod and strike it to the appropriate beat.

However, these parties really caught fire once Benedict got his saxophone. Now we officially had a band! Benedict's proficiency elevated the entertainment level several notches. Soon we would have a crowd of locals joining us in the festivities of the evening. Fritzer, Sergo, Octa, and Serge often lead singing of various Haitian songs, which all the Haitians quickly joined in on. Of course, we did not understand the lyrics, but we could easily feel the joy and passion generated by vocals mixed with the music. One song could easily last over fifteen minutes.

Most everyone would also dance to the music, creating a nice finishing touch to our impromptu New Year's Eve party. To top off the atmosphere, we usually had a beautiful star-filled sky above us. In addition, Madam Marcel often made popcorn for everyone to share.

The consummate entertainer, Benedict always had the timing of "Auld Lang Syne" to begin promptly at midnight. The only thing different from a New Year's Eve party back home came next. Our Haitian parties always shut down immediately. Usually we are in bed by 12:15 as we almost always have to be up and going again by 6:00 a.m.

We have continued these New Year's Eve celebrations for three years after Benedict moved to the United States. However, they are not the same without him and his saxophone.

⸺⸻►●◄⸻⸺

Benedict returned home to Pendus for the first time with our 2016 group. Because he could not bring his saxophone with him, he planned something different for New Year's Eve: a party for his generation, the post-teens through young thirty-year-old young adults. He arranged for someone with a sound system and speakers to come to our compound area. He also arranged for the cooks to make rice, beans, and chicken for everyone to eat as well as have drinks available.

We all joined in the fun and danced as well. However, my greatest pleasure was watching Benedict interacting with his friends.

Playing his saxophone, Benedict was the leader of the
impromptu band on New Year's Eve for many years.
Other instruments include the graj, two tambous, a guitar,
and a battery operated keyboard. Great fun was shared
by many as a new year was ushered in with music.

23

Concept of Time

Teach us to count our days aright, that we may gain wisdom of heart.
—Psalm 90:12

ISLAND TIME DEFINITELY PREVAILS IN Haiti, as it does throughout the Caribbean. This is especially true in the rural mountain areas. There never is a sense of urgency to "be on time!" However, Haitians also have an innate ability to live in the moment. I think I could learn to relish such a lifestyle if I had a longer opportunity to be in Haiti and thus have a better chance for it to rub off on me! Unfortunately, my type A personality continues to prevail, driving me to always have a schedule and to be on time!

My first experience in this laid-back attitude came on my initial trip to Haiti. There was a quadruple wedding scheduled for 8:00 a.m. on Saturday during our stay. Two of the couples had to walk over ninety minutes down the mountain just to get to St. Joseph Church. It was incredible watching people dressed in their finest clothes, which would be suits for the men and nice dresses for the women, walking down a mountain path heading to Pendus. Even some of the bridesmaids wore their gowns as they hiked to church. They were easy to spot as the pastel colors of their dresses stood out against the drab mountain background, which was brown from a lack of recent rain.

It was obvious that the ceremony was not going to start at 8:00 a.m. as all four of the wedding parties were not even there. Even the church was not yet full. I could not imagine the anxiety that one bride would have in the United States if her wedding was not going according to a carefully planned schedule. Now we had four brides that would be running behind on their wedding day. Apparently I was the only one concerned!

The wedding Mass finally started shortly before 9:00 a.m. and was a beautiful ceremony with a packed church. It lasted nearly two hours. I don't think any of the Haitians even realized that it started late!

Another example of a different style of time management comes with the ringing of the church bells. Because St. Joseph was not a stand-alone parish at the beginning of our twinning relationship, it did not have a full-time priest stationed in Pendus. People did not always know when a priest would be there to celebrate Mass. Even if they knew the priest was in the area, there was no preset Mass schedule like every church in America strictly adheres to!

Whenever the priest would decide to have Mass, he would have someone ring the church bells. Usually that was Jean Claude's job. The ringing of the bells would indicate to anyone within earshot of the church that a Mass would be forthcoming soon. Father said that it usually meant it would start thirty minutes later but even that was just an estimate. No one complained if they came and Mass was not yet ready to begin.

Arriving at Mass late is not frowned upon in Haiti either. Often the folks would need more than the half hour notice given by the bells to get cleaned up and walk to church. No one took offense by the late arrivals to Mass!

Time never seems to be a factor at any Mass in Haiti, especially the ones I have attended at St. Joseph in Pendus. No one gets antsy when the celebration lasts more than an hour. In fact, I have been to many Masses in Pendus that went longer than two hours.

It makes perfect sense to me that time is not so important. First, the religious celebration is vitally important to those in attendance. They truly desire to be there. I am not saying that we Americans don't, just that our days are so packed with activities that we usually have another activity to attend next!

Second, the church in Pendus is the only place where people can gather. It truly is the focal point of the community. There is no store, there is no mall, there is no movie theater, and there is no gymnasium. Most people's homes are barely big enough to hold the family living there, let alone host any guests. Nowhere else in the village can people gather inside together at the same time. It does not matter why they are gathered; it is simply important to have an opportunity to be together. If they weren't in church, where else would they go?

I also got a chuckle out of the fact that there was a clock on the wall behind the altar in St. Joseph Church. You could easily keep track of how long a service or homily was lasting simply by looking over the priest's shoulder! That would never happen in America! If there was even a clock inside a church here, it would be on the back wall where only the priest could see it.

———❖———

Another great example of how "time" affects daily lives in Haiti differently than here at home came on my second and third trips to Haiti, my first visits to include New Year's Eve during my stay.

During my second visit to Pendus, Father Cha Cha held a Midnight Mass to begin the New Year. People began gathering well before 11:00 p.m. on New Year's Eve. The church was almost full an hour early. While we waited, a rosary service was held. It was neat to hear the Our Father and Hail Mary prayed aloud in Creole. About

11:40, everyone in the church knelt on the concrete floor and stayed there in prayer until midnight when Mass began. I know it was the first time I had ever ushered in a New Year on my knees! It was a humbling experience.

Our next trip to Pendus was also over New Years the following December. I told everyone about the wonderful celebration we had to ring in the New Year on our previous trip. However, we did not do it that year. I was curious so I asked Father Cha Cha why the change. His reply was, "There was no full moon this year!"

I had not thought at all about that fact. The prior year I remembered the beautiful full moon. I could walk around outside safely without a flashlight. That also meant the people could safely walk down the mountain paths to and from the midnight celebration as well. I would say without a flashlight too, but most of them would not have even owned a flashlight! That second year there was no full moon and precious few flashlights. So it would not have been prudent for people to come to such a celebration. I could not ever think of a church service back home that was dependent on whether there was a full moon or not!

———◆———

The only time I ever saw a strict adherence to time was by Jean Claude when he would ring the bells for the Prayer of the Angelus. *Angelus* is Latin for "angel." The prayer commemorates the angel Gabriel revealing to Mary that she would conceive a son. Historically, this devotion is recited in many Roman Catholic churches, convents, and monasteries three times daily: at 6:00 a.m., noon, and 6:00 p.m. This ritual began over seven hundred years ago at a time before electricity and common usage of clocks. Therefore, it was usually accompanied by the ringing of the Angelus bell, which was a call to prayer to everyone within earshot.

Growing up Catholic, I remember stories of older men that got to ring the church bells at their churches. I never got that opportunity, mainly because by then our bells were automated and not manually rung at St. Mary. I loved to watch Jean Claude ring the bells. One day he even let me pull on the rope to ring them instead of him. He could tell that I was excited to do that. Many times thereafter when we were in Pendus, he would track me down to come assist him with the bells. It did not matter whether it was the early morning, midday, or evening ringing of the church bells, he would come find me to help.

What struck me as odd, in a culture devoid of any perceived attention to being on time, was Jean Claude's insistence on the accuracy of ringing those bells at exactly the precise time. He would hold his wristwatch in his hand, carefully watching the second-hand approach the appropriate hour. He would hold out his other hand indicating for me to wait. Not until the exact second occurred would he then signal for me to begin ringing the bells! It reminded me of a producer signaling the start of a broadcast after a commercial! At no time else in all my travels in Haiti did anything ever seem to be so exactly on time except the tolling of the bells in Pendus three times each day!

One quality that I greatly admire in most Haitians is their ability to live in the moment. To me that is related to my other stories regarding their sense of time. While they may not care if they are on time, they do make the utmost use of the present time. If you have an opportunity to have fun, even for just a few moments, you seize the chance to do so.

Often we will be at one of the chapels preparing for a children's benediction. The school children will sing for us, accompanied by someone on the tambou. The whole atmosphere is uplifting and the beat contagious. I can't help but feel the rhythm. However, I don't get up and dance. Invariably there are some adults in attendance in addition to the schoolchildren. Those adults don't have any hesitation in grabbing a few brief moments of fun, standing to dance in place, always with a big grin on their face.

To me that moment was not planned to be a time to dance, so I would not do so. It was supposed to be a time for the children to be celebrated. Thankfully, the Haitians don't share that sentiment and do grab the moment, even if it lasts only a few seconds. After all, it may be a long time before another such opportunity presents itself.

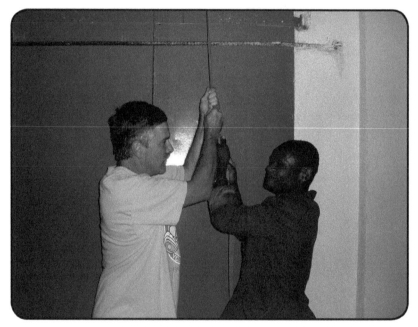

Being "on time" only seems to matter for the ringing of the bells for the Prayer of the Angels at 6 a.m., noon, and 6 p.m.

24

Humorous Anecdotes

A joyful heart is the health of the body.
—Proverbs 17:22

THERE MUST BE A HAITIAN proverb on humor, maybe something like "Laughter is the best medicine." I just have not been able to find it. That doesn't mean Haitians don't have a sense of humor. They do have a great sense of humor. All the Haitians I know love to laugh and love to tease each other, just like we do in America. I have many humorous stories from Haiti to share, ones that aren't necessarily related to language mix-ups.

———◆———

My favorite funny story occurred in Haiti, but it was an American, Sister Mary Finnick, at Matthew 25 Guest House who provided the humor. A Gray Nun of the Sacred Heart, she ran the guesthouse for the Parish Twinning Program for many years. Most groups that twinned somewhere outside of Port-au-Prince would stay there on their first night in Haiti before leaving early the next day for their destination. Part of the fee to stay there included transportation to and from the airport, as well as dinner and breakfast. It was a very good deal, especially for first-time travelers. The guesthouse also sells a variety of Haitian art work, which is another huge hit with all travelers, even the veteran ones!

Sister Mary was typically the first to greet you upon arrival at Matthew 25. One year she was welcoming our group and explaining the ground rules for the guesthouse. She closed her instructions with, "If there is anything you forgot to bring that you need, just let us know." She paused for a moment to let that thought sink in. Then she continued, "And we will teach you how to live without it!" Not only was that unexpected from her, it was funny, and oh so Haitian!

A couple of years later Sister Mary had another classic bit of humor. She told us, "I still don't speak Creole, but I do drive Haitian!" You never knew when she was going to come up with one of these great one-liners!

———⟫●⟪———

On my second trip to Pendus, I was riding on top of the luggage in the back of our truck with several others including our interpreter Fritzner. As we were approaching Pendus, several young children came running out onto the roadway, chasing after our vehicle as it headed toward the church compound. I could not understand all that they were yelling, except I did understand "Blan" was used several times. *Blan* is the Creole word for "white."

Fritzner began laughing out loud. I asked him what was so funny. He said, "They are saying 'the whites are coming, the whites are coming!' It was being said with joy and excitement and not as a derogatory remark.

I have heard *blan* used many times in conversation. Most often someone would respond to my greeting with "Bonjou blan." No disrespect was ever intended. It was just an acknowledgement they were talking to me. It is like our use of *buddy* or *pal* in conversation.

———⟫●⟪———

On our first trip to Haiti post 9/11 we had to fly from PAP to Port-de-Paix. That meant we had to use the domestic airport adjacent to the main international airport. While our luggage was fed through a conveyor belt and scanner upon our arrival, there was absolutely no security provided. Almost every bag that went past the X-ray portion of the conveyor belt made the machine beep. No one did anything about it, except to put the next piece of luggage on and have it beep as it passed through!

It got so comical that when one package was too large to fit through the scanner, they simply picked it up and carried it around the machine and back onto the other end of the conveyor! The situation made us laugh when one Haitian lady placed her live chicken on the conveyor belt and it passed through. Again, the machine beeped! Alan Banning mused that they seemed to use the noise of the machine as a counter and not a security-detection device!

While there were several small planes being loaded at the same time, we were getting on a small commuter plane that seated only our group of twelve people and carried only our luggage, so we were not concerned about any safety issues. It was just funny to watch the charade of pretended security measures.

Two other humorous events happened on that same domestic flight to the northern coastal city of Port-de-Paix. Once we boarded our small plane, Sharon got concerned when she saw the pilot's window open as we began to taxi to the runway. Little did she know that we would not be flying at a very high altitude, so cabin pressure would not be a problem on this flight.

Also, the flight would not take very long as we seemed to skim just above the many mountains during the half-hour jaunt to Port-de-Paix. It was a cloudy, rainy day. Visibility was not great. As our little plane circled to land, Alan Banning looked out the window and quipped, "I think I see the landing strip, but I'm praying that it is not it!"

From our American point of view, airports and roads are all supposed to be paved surfaces. Once we left Port-au-Prince that ceased being the case in Haiti. The runway at the Port-de-Paix airport was a short gravel stretch of ground with water at one end and trees at the other. There were women doing their laundry along the end of the runway nearest the water. There did not appear to be sufficient length of runway to land even a puddle jumper such as ours. However, our pilot skillfully set our plane down, almost as smoothly as if landing on pavement. Our fleeting moment of anxiousness was for naught!

<hr />

Alan Banning and funny episodes seemed to go together on that trip. One night he was walking through the village of Pendus after dark with one of the interpreters. There was no electricity and therefore no lights anywhere outside the church compound. There also was no moon. It was so dark that Alan said he had difficulty seeing anything or anyone.

Serge was then a young teenage boy who spent as much time with our group as possible. Serge saw them walking together that night. He came up to Alan and said something that made the interpreter chuckle. Serge had said that Alan looked like a torch walking down the path! What he meant was Alan's white skin stood out, even in the dark Pendus night.

<hr />

On our first trip to Haiti, Father Cha Cha taught us a solidarity song called "Na Mache Men Na Men." It means "We Will Walk Hand in Hand." It is sung to the tune of "We Shall Overcome." It is an easy one for us to learn as four of the five lines are basically the same, repeating the main line, "Na mache men na men." The fourth line of the song is the only different one and, therefore, the most difficult line of the song. Father taught us this tune in Creole so we could sing it with the people wherever we might be.

We would then teach this song to each of our subsequent groups. Often the first few years, Father Cha Cha would ask the people at the chapel we were visiting to sing this song with us. We would all stand and hold hands as we sang. It was a very good song of unity.

One year we had just finished Mass at Massacre. Father had us stand to sing, which we did. It is a great feeling to be able to join in singing in their native tongue. After singing it through twice quite well, he said, "Now sing it in English." Of course, only the handful of our group would be able to do that so the volume level in the chapel dropped dramatically as the Haitians politely listened to us. We started with the first lines that we knew. We did fine with those.

Unfortunately, none of us could remember what the fourth line of the song was in English. Then the room got very silent as only our two Haitian interpreters were singing for that fourth line before the rest of us rejoined for the closing common line of the song. Everyone, including Father Cha Cha, got a big laugh out of us knowing the words of the song in Creole but not in our native English!

Benedict loved to play both the tambou and his saxophone for us. He would usually do it in the evening as everyone sat around the courtyard area and listened. I tried many times to video him playing the sax. I could always get the audio recorded. However, the video never turned out well as the lighting, even with the generator running, was not very good.

One day about thirty-forty minutes before sunset, we were sitting in the compound. I told Benedict to go get his saxophone and play for me so I could finally video him in the daylight. He ran back to his grandmother's house to get his instrument. However, he did not come right back. Soon thirty minutes had lapsed. I asked one young Haitian boy if he had seen Benedict. He said he had, that Benedict was heading toward the river. The river was not on the way back to the compound from his grandmother's house.

Finally, Benedict showed up, but the sun had already gone down. However, Benedict was dressed in his very best clothes, wearing a new shirt. It looked like one he would wear if performing a concert. He wanted to look his best for the video, so he went to the river to bathe before getting dressed and coming back! He did look very nice and played very well. I filmed him playing but got another great soundtrack and yet another dark, unimpressive video!

———✦———

These next two stories aren't as humorous as they are telling about life in Haiti. Our generator is only run in the evening to provide light for the church and courtyard area. It is not designed to run all day long. Whenever Madam Marcel needed ice, she would purchase it in Gros Morne, an hour drive away. Most of the time she needed ice, it was to chill our drinks.

In Haiti, ice is made in huge 450-pound hunks. It is stored wrapped in a burlap bag surrounded by what looks like sawdust. I have seen the beds of pickup trucks loaded with these big slabs of ice, being driven to their destinations. Ice made this way is most common in bigger cities as the rural areas do not have the infrastructure to make it. Obviously, it can melt before it is ultimately used for whatever the intended purpose is.

Once delivered to the "retailer" of ice, it may sit outside all day until all of it is finally sold, or it eventually melts. When you buy the ice, you simply chip off the amount you need from the bigger hunk. The nearest ice manufacturer is in Gonaives, nearly a two-hour drive away. Fortunately, the nearest "retailer" is in Gros Morne.

This day, Madam Marcel must have really needed ice as she sent one of the teenage boys on foot to Gros Morne to get it. While it is about ten miles to Gros Morne by car, I understand there is a more direct walkway through the mountain from Pendus that is only about seven miles. Either way, it is a long way to walk to get ice. What surprised me was the young man *walked* back with the ice. It was wrapped in burlap and carried on his head, as most things in Haiti are carried. I saw him carrying it into the compound. I was shocked that he did not ride a tap-tap or a moto back. There must not have been enough money to cover the added expense for a ride, so he simply carried it back to Pendus.

In Haiti, you always make do with what you have and do so without complaint!

⸻⟫●⟪⸻

The second such revealing tale occurred on my second visit to Haiti. We were staying at Hospice St. Joseph in PAP and had a free day to tour Haiti's capital city. As the driver arrived to pick us up, he pulled into our courtyard area. Our eyes were immediately opened to another reality of life in Haiti. I noticed there appeared to be lots of damage on the driver's side of the van.

Upon closer inspection, the damage wasn't from a collision. The entire left side had been riddled with bullet holes. There were at least fifteen such holes. Fortunately, the damage occurred a long time before when the vehicle was under prior ownership. Still, it was a little unsettling getting into the vehicle that morning. I commented that I hoped lightning would not strike twice! It didn't, but we were acutely aware that safety was always a concern in PAP.

⸻⟫●⟪⸻

St. Joseph Church has a cistern to catch water from the roof of the church. This water is then used for drinking, cooking, bathing, or cleaning. When our group is in Pendus, there is a much greater need for water just for the bathrooms, for showers, and for the toilets. If rain has not been plentiful, the cistern won't have enough water for the increased needs. When that happens, water is carried up from the river in five-gallon buckets on top of someone's head. The river is about two hundred yards from the compound. No matter the source of the water, it is a very precious product.

There were three fifty-five-gallon barrels on the roof over the bathroom. They were each hand filled, five gallons at a time. This chore is usually done first thing in the morning. Jean Claude stands on the roof and uses a rope to lower an empty five-gallon bucket to the ground. An assistant on the ground then fills that bucket, which when filled weighs thirty-five pounds. To help Jean Claude lift the bucket to the roof, the assistant holds the bucket as high as he can. Jean Claude sways the bucket dangling on the end of the rope back and forth. At the precise moment, he will swing the bucket out and up onto the roof in one quick motion without spilling any. He makes that almost look effortless from years of practice.

When we are in Pendus, someone from our group acts as his assistant on the ground. One day Roy Dejoie was that assistant. Jean Claude miscalculated the lip of the roof, catching the bucket and spilling the water all over Roy standing below. I told Roy that because water is so valuable, you only get one shower per day. Therefore, he already had his for the day. He quickly replied that this one didn't count since he wasn't actually "inside" the bathroom! I didn't think of it, but I should have countered with the fact that most rural Haitians don't even have a bathroom so they always bathe outside, so it would count!

———◆———

It is said that necessity is the mother of all invention. All the Haitians I know are great at making do with what they have. The year after we assembled 120 desks and 120 pews in Pendus, we found them using one of the extension cords we had left as the rope to lift the filled water buckets to the top of the guesthouse.

That did not surprise us at all. What caught our attention was the fact that they had cut off the plug end of the cord so they could tie it to the bucket handle easier. Since electricity was not something anyone had access to, the cord was simply more useful to them as a rope and would most likely never again be needed for its original purpose in Pendus!

———⟫●⟪———

Early in our twinning relationship we often used trucks to travel back and forth from Port-au-Prince. Since space was limited inside the trucks, several of us would ride on top the luggage in the bed of the truck. It is a great vantage point for a ride through the mountains. One year it was raining on the morning we were to leave Pendus. Because of the muddy road from Gros Morne, the two trucks coming to get us were late picking us up, causing some angst in our ability to get back to PAP before dark. Once the first truck arrived, we loaded up our luggage and waited anxiously for the other to come.

The intensity of the rain picked up. In anticipation of a wet and muddy ride home, I decided to change into my sandals, swimsuit, and quick-drying T-shirt. It would have been a futile effort to stay dry riding outside in the rain. With those clothes on, even if I got wet, those clothes would quickly dry out. I dug out my bag and changed in my room.

Shortly thereafter the second truck arrived. I asked Kyle to double check all the rooms one last time before we left. He came right back. He told me that Madam Marcel already had them locked. So we took off. About an hour later we had a flat tire. Of course, the spare tire was underneath the luggage. As we took each piece off the truck, I realized my bag was not there. I had left it in my room when I changed.

We did not have time to go back and get it and still get safely to PAP. Father Cha Cha asked me if I had my passport as that was the only thing I absolutely had to have. I did as I had left my passport and my plane ticket in the safe at the guesthouse in PAP. However, I did not have anything else. Things such as my wallet, money, camera, film and all my clothes were in my bag. Father said he would secure my bag and send it home when our March group came two months later.

As I rode to PAP, I had a very uneasy feeling that I would be wearing my sandals and swimsuit through the airports all the way home! It would be ten degrees when I got home to Indiana! Kyle looked at me and said, "Don't worry, Dad. You fit right in now. You have as much as the Haitians do!" That was funny, but also sad, as there was more truth to his words than we cared to admit.

The story ended up well for me as I borrowed a pair of pants, some socks, and a shirt from the others on that trip to go with my sandals for the journey home. It was weird traveling with absolutely nothing, not even a camera! I did call ahead to have someone bring a coat when we were picked up at the Indianapolis airport. Two months later the next St. Mary group brought my bag back to me.

I had a déjà vu moment the very next year. Once again I left Pendus dressed only in my swimsuit, sandals, and T-shirt. Only this year I was intentionally leaving my suitcase behind in Pendus.

On my first couple trips to Haiti, we would drive along the beautiful Caribbean coast between Port-au-Prince and St. Marc and wish we could get in the enticing blue water. Finally, on our third trip, we made plans to stop on the drive from Pendus back to PAP. We had noticed a couple spots where the water came right up to the edge of the highway. We could simply stop there and have thirty minutes of fun.

Coming from Gros Morne, the two vehicles were late getting to Pendus to take us to PAP. Sister Jackie knew we wanted to stop along the way but was worried about us getting back to PAP before dark. Therefore, we all piled into the first truck. Space was at a premium, so we even had people sitting in the bed of the truck. We left immediately after the first one arrived. Due to the tight space limitations, we could only take our backpacks with us. Sister Jackie and Barak, her driver, would come a bit later with our luggage. Hopefully, they would catch up to us before we reached PAP.

Because there would be no place for us to change along the highway, most of us took off from Pendus wearing our swimming suits. It would not take long to dry off when we were done. We would then finish riding to Hospice St. Joseph in our suits before changing back into our regular clothes after they arrived.

We made a couple stops along the way before finally reaching our water destination about 2:00 p.m. It was a very short stop, but our first dip into the crystal-clear water was so refreshing. We were quick enough that we made it back to PAP before dark. We also beat Sister Jackie there. Because she had not arrived, we could not take showers or change clothes. Suppertime came and she still was not there, so we ate while still wearing our swimsuits.

It was nearly 8:00 p.m. when we finally got word that Sister Jackie and Barak had car trouble and that they were stuck in St. Marc. Apparently, the differential in their vehicle went out. They did not have enough money or time to get it fixed. We were worried for their safety but also about getting our suitcases as we had an early flight in the morning. I could see myself going home this year to a cold Indiana in my swimsuit and sandals!

Sister Jackie called again and said she would try to get a tap-tap rented to get our stuff to us yet that night but she would be at least two more hours getting there. Therefore, Father Bob decided to have a "come-as-you-are" Mass while we waited. Good thing as we did not have anything else to wear anyway! It was my first Mass in my swimsuit! It was a very nice celebration as we spent a long time during the homily sharing our reflections of how blessed we really were.

Finally, the rented tap-tap with Sister Jackie arrived about 11:00 p.m. It was so loaded down that it could not make it up the hill to Hospice St. Joseph. We had to carry everything the last one hundred feet up the hill. Finally, we had everything. We could now get our showers and finish getting ready for our trip home the next morning.

On my first trip to Haiti, Sharon and Kyle were not with me. There was a quadruple wedding during our stay in Pendus. Lots of people attended the huge event. There were four young ladies who flirted with all the men in our group for the couple days they were in Pendus.

The next year, we were outside the church in Gros Morne. This time Sharon and Kyle were with me. Those four girls were also there. They saw me first and called out, "Jeff, Jeff." Surprised when she heard my name being called, Sharon said to me, "I think they are calling you." We walked over to greet them. In her broken English, one of them said she remembered that I was a lawyer. Kyle, however, said her pronunciation of lawyer sounded more like liar than lawyer! I then asked them if they remembered the others in our first group. They said yes to each of the men's names I mentioned but said no to every female's name! I then introduced them to Sharon as *madam mwen*, which means "my wife." One of the girls snapped her finger in disgust as she walked away from that apparently unhappy revelation.

Helen Hession was part of another funny story. On her first trip to Haiti she tried to introduce herself in English to a group of children in Pendus. They could never correctly understand her last name. They kept calling her Helen Haitian. They could not distinguish the difference in her name and Haitian. The back and forth between Helen and the children reminded me of the Abbot and Costello routine of "Who's on first?"

George White went with us in December 2010. It was his first time in Haiti. I was tickled by his many comments on the ride from Port-au-Prince to Pendus. Most of them started with the phrase, "This reminds me of when I was a kid!" George said that to seeing the rice fields, people carrying machetes, the sugarcane, homes with dirt floors, and many other sights. George grew up in central Alabama in the 1940s, so his week in Haiti turned out to be a very memorable one for him!

<hr/>

Many evenings, while in Haiti, our group will end the day with a reflective session that we reference as the Good, the Bad and the Ugly. No topic is off limits. The only limitation is one's willingness to share feelings on what happened. Many are very serious conversations. Often they are a bit humorous. Sometimes they are both. Tony Behr was on his third trip to Pendus with his third different child when he spoke up one evening, saying, "My 'good' is a selfish one. It is way cool watching my son Charlie here!" He added that it was very special seeing his son do all the things he had been doing that week, especially his interactions with the children in so many ways.

Charlie quickly followed by saying, "Yes, and he showed me how much he appreciated me by locking me in my room for two hours today!"

What had happened was Tony had locked his room before going to a meeting with the Pendus Central Committee. Tony did not notice that Charlie was still inside the room taking a nap. When Charlie awoke sometime later, he could not get out as the door only unlocked with a key from the outside. All the adults in our group were attending that same meeting. It took Charlie a long time to get the attention of one of the young Haitian boys to help get him out!

<hr/>

Father Wilner's birthday is December 28. Every year the nuns in Gros Morne threw him a birthday party. Even if he happened to be in Pendus with us, he would go back for the evening to be heralded at his own party! One year, Madam Marcel and the nuns decided to hold the party in Pendus and surprise him. That allowed our group to also be part of the celebration.

Unfortunately, Father disappeared late in the afternoon on his birthday that year without telling anyone that he was leaving. Nonetheless, after dinner that night Madam Marcel brought out the cake and popcorn she had made for his party. We sang "Happy Birthday" in his absence and then proceeded to enjoy his special treats!

Father was funny the next day when he returned to Pendus. Talking about his surprise party that was in Pendus and not Gros Morne, he said, "I was surprised twice!" We later learned that the nuns were on their way to Pendus the evening before when they passed him driving back to Gros Morne, so they simply turned around and went back. I had wondered why they did not show up for his party!

———⊰●⊱———

Shortly before his sixtieth birthday, Father Wilner Donecia's focus was changed from Pendus to Gros Morne. He still lived at the rectory in Gros Morne but not was actively involved with Pendus any longer. The bishop then appointed Father Joseph Telcin to take over as priest in charge of Pendus and its six chapel areas. He was only thirty-six years old. Always quick with a sense of humor, Father Wilner acknowledged, "I have one knee that can't go up the mountain and one knee that can't go down the mountain. This job is for a young man!"

———⊰●⊱———

One trip we had two doctors in our group, cardiologist Dr. Adel Yaacoub and pediatrician Dr. Jerry Wehr. We thought it funny that the only situation they both were apprehensive of encountering was the birth of a baby. Adel said that should be Jerry's job as he was the children's doctor and that a baby was a child! Jerry said it should be Adel's task as his role as pediatrician did not begin until after the child was born!

At the end of a long day of seeing patients, Sharon enlisted Dr. Wehr and Madam Marcel's help in playing a trick on Dr. Yaacoub. Sharon put on a backpack backwards, having it hang on her front instead of her back. She then put on a lightweight jacket and zipped it up to hide the backpack, giving her the appearance of being pregnant. Madam Marcel found a scarf and wrapped it around Sharon's head to make her look "Haitian." It didn't hide her white skin but that detail did not seem to matter.

Adel was still in the examination room when Jerry told him one last patient just arrived, a woman about to give birth! Adel immediately thought it was a trick until Jerry asked one of the interpreters how far apart the contractions were. The fake response was "Two minutes," which coincided with Sharon letting out a loud groan of pain. Adel's expression changed immediately. I had positioned myself to get a great photo at that precise moment. The look of concern was hysterical. It only lasted until he turned the corner to see it was Sharon made up to look pregnant. We all got a great laugh from it. Even Adel enjoyed it, saying, "It was a good way to end a stressful day!"

Dr. Adel Yaacoub and Sharon share a laugh at
the end of a day of clinic in Pendus.

25

Kyle Newell

Let your father and mother have joy; let her who bore you exult.
—Proverbs 23:25

OUR SON KYLE HAS BEEN a great inspiration to me from our many trips to Haiti. I have learned much from him. His ability to adapt and blend into a new culture is a marvelous attribute, one that I can only hope to emulate.

He was a seventeen-year-old high school junior when he first went with us to Haiti. Looking out the window of the plane as it descended, he described his initial feeling of PAP by saying, "It looks like a bomb exploded or a hurricane went through but no one did anything about it. They just continue to live there."

Despite that initial impression, Kyle fell in love with Haiti, its people, the culture, its history, its language, and its beauty. Haiti was not his first foray into another country as he had been to Spain the year before with his Spanish Club from high school. However, for such a young age, Kyle displayed an extraordinary sensitivity to and ability to adjust to another country and its way of life.

———◦———

From the beginning, Kyle had an acute awareness for many cultural aspects of the trip. At that point in his life, Kyle was a picky eater. He was not very adventurous when it came to trying new foods; so he brought peanut butter, crackers, and some cereal from home with him to eat. When it came time for our meals, he would always join us. However, he would not put anything on his plate that he would not eat. He knew how precious little there was for people to eat; he was not going to waste any of it. He never complained about being hungry or not having anything he liked to eat.

Luckily, most of our meals included bananas, bread, and peanut butter; so he could always eat something that was offered. Still he was sensitive to where he was. He refused to bring his food out to our table to eat it with us. He did not want to offend Madam Marcel and the cooks by such an openly defiant rejection of their meal. He would discretely eat later in the privacy of his room. Gradually over time, Kyle came to eat a variety of Haitian food.

What a great lesson he taught us about being culturally aware of your surroundings!

———◦———

Kyle further exemplified his ability to culturally blend in during that initial trip when he learned to play a popular Haitian card game called Casino. I saw him sitting with three young Haitian boys, patiently playing cards in the courtyard area. The boys were having a great time playing with Kyle, giggling and laughing frequently. He did not have an interpreter with him, but that did not hinder him from participating. I asked him what he was doing. He said, "Playing a game." I asked what it was called. He replied, "I don't know." I asked, "How do you play it?" He answered, "I don't know!"

Kyle explained that he had been playing one hand of the game after another for quite a while. Each time he pieced together another bit of information as he tried to figure out how to play the game based on what the boys were doing. Some of the rules would become obvious through that simple trial-and-error method. However, many of the intricate rules he would not learn until much later with the help of an interpreter. Still by the end of the first day, Kyle garnered enough information about the game that he could play well enough for the kids to stop snickering at his missing obviously easy plays. While they often laughed at him, they loved the attention he gave them by playing anyway. In the end, he gained their respect.

He later taught me and many others how to play Casino. Through the years, playing this card game has provided many from our groups an opportunity to interact and have fun with Haitians of all ages, without needing to speak Creole!

———⚬———

During his first trip, we were at Our Lady of Light Church in Gros Morne. There was a small basketball court on the property with a five-on-five pickup game being played. Kyle watched for a while before he was invited to play. He jumped at the opportunity to play a game he loved! He knew absolutely no Creole then but had no trouble communicating with his teammates. He could run give-and-go plays on offense or switch guarding an opponent while on defense without having to speak a single Creole word. Basketball has its own innate language that they were able to utilize during their play. It was fun to watch!

———⚬———

Initially, there was nowhere to play basketball in Pendus. There was a small grassy area in front of the St. Joseph School, but the game of choice was soccer.

There also was no equipment for the game in Pendus. Between Kyle's first and second trips to Pendus, St. Mary Cathedral sent two bank boards, rims, and basketballs on a sea container. There now was a place to play basketball in Pendus! It was not quite a court like we are used to in the United States, but it worked. They used two two-by-four pieces of lumber to make a pole to hang the bank board with a rim. It was a little wobbly but would suffice. The grassy courtyard area was not ideal either as it was not very level and had some rocky spots. It was not a very safe place to play basketball as it would be easy to turn an ankle. It would have to do as it was all that was available in Pendus.

Kyle knew that building even a small concrete basketball court would not be "next" on St. Mary's list of projects for a long time, if ever. Kyle asked Father Cha Cha how much it would cost to install an appropriately sized slab of cement at the school so a basketball court could be built. Father replied, "One thousand dollars." Kyle did not say anything about this to our group. In fact, I never knew he even had that conversation with Father Cha Cha until much later.

Kyle was then a senior in high school. He quietly returned to school and repeatedly told of his desire to build a basketball court in Pendus. He made his plea to anyone willing to listen to him, including all his friends and his teachers. He collected many small one and two dollar donations as well as a few larger five, ten, and twenty dollar ones. He repeated his story enough that he quickly raised the estimated $1,000. He collected the money so fast that he was able to send it with Father Bob on the next St. Mary trip, a mere two months later in March of 2002.

What was most inspiring to me from this scenario was Kyle's initiative not only to see a need but find a solution to meet that need without asking for any help. It never became someone else's project to handle. He took complete ownership of the entire endeavor. If a teenager can make such an impact, how much more could be accomplished if we all did the same?

⸺⬥⸺

Kyle so loved his early Haiti experiences that he elected to do his senior project in his Honors English class on Haiti. He developed a "How to Speak English" curriculum to teach to young Haitian children. However, this was not simply an academic exercise for him to turn in for a grade. He made plans to implement the class during the summer following his high school graduation! Kyle volunteered to spend the summer in Gros Morne through the Quest program.

His dedication to this endeavor was incredible as he first had to teach himself how to speak Creole. He found a few books he needed, including a comprehensive dictionary from the Indiana University Creole Institute. Slowly he began to learn how to speak Creole. It was difficult to master since he did not know anyone to practice speaking it with in Indiana.

He was meticulous in his preparation for spending the summer in Haiti. Kyle slept in a hammock on our front porch for several weeks before he left. He knew there would not be any air conditioning in Haiti, so he was preparing his body for the heat he would be enduring while away!

The Quest program had Kyle living with Sister Jackie and Sister Pat at the Kay Se house in Gros Morne so he would have some familiar faces around. His primary focus was to help run a summer camp that the nuns held for the poorest children in the town. While it was a day camp, it provided arts and crafts, swimming, games, and, most importantly, two meals each day for each of the campers.

His fluency flourished once he arrived in Haiti and was forced to predominately speak Creole. There were no interpreters available for him that summer! He continued his learning regimen by memorizing ten new words every night and then using them multiple times the following day. His process worked as he became fluent by the time he came home in August.

After working all day in the children's camp, Kyle then set up classes in the evening to teach English. He had several classes scheduled throughout each week while he was in Haiti. What surprised him the most was more adults signed up for his class than children! He said even one of the Gros Morne's three mayors took his class. After he got home, I asked Kyle how well his students performed. Smiling, he said, "I think my Creole was better than their English!"

The following December we were back in Gros Morne one afternoon. Everywhere we walked throughout the town there were children excitedly calling his name and running up to greet him.

He had so many of the campers following him around, I told him I would have to start calling him Haiti's Pied Piper!

———⟫●⟪———

God used Kyle to teach me another valuable lesson that "all things work for good for those who love God" as found in Romans 8:28.

Kyle was working on a master's degree in international development at Tufts University when he was on our December 2009 trip to Haiti. One of the requirements for that degree is to pass a proficiency test in a foreign language. Haitian Creole was an obvious choice for Kyle! There happened to be a professor in Boston who could give him that examination.

Kyle wanted to spend as much time in Haiti as he could on this trip so his fluency would be at its best when he took the exam after he got back to school. He, therefore, scheduled a four-week stay on this trip. This was the year our family met Andre Angrand six days early to experience travel to other areas of Haiti beyond our normal. It also was the year that he had his flight from JFK in New York cancelled due a ten-inch snowfall and had to drive to Atlanta to catch the next available flight. In all he was up over fifty hours as he struggled to get from New York City to PAP. Little did we know he would narrowly miss a harrowing tragedy on his way home as well.

The end of the mission trip for Sharon and me (and the rest of our team) was January 3, 2010. Kyle's return flight was not until January 18. Therefore, he stayed in Gros Morne when our group drove back to PAP. He has many friends in Gros Morne who he wanted to spend some time with after we left. He would later travel to PAP before flying home. All the while he could continue practicing his Creole.

The day after I got home, Kyle e-mailed me and asked if I could move his return flight home up a week earlier to January 11. Our travel agent easily got that done. Kyle did not tell us until after he landed at JFK late on January 11 that he came home early because he was not feeling well. He had contracted level-one malaria after we left Haiti but was feeling better now.

I never thought I would thank God for Kyle getting malaria, but I did the next day.

Kyle spent his last night in PAP at a home of a Tufts University graduate who lived in PAP. That house was destroyed the next day, January 12, when the 7.0 earthquake devastated the PAP area of Haiti. Had Kyle not been sick and come home early, this story may not have ended so well. Was it purely fortuitous or God's hand at work when Kyle asked to come a week early, as he could have asked for five or six days instead? That would have put him in the middle of that tragedy.

All I could think was *Gras a bondye*. "By the grace of God" we dodged a bullet!

By the way, Kyle passed his Creole proficiency test later that month.

———————⋙●⋘———————

Through the years, Kyle has been to Pendus as many times as I have. There is a special connection between Madam Marcel and him. If he isn't readily present when we show up in Pendus, her first question to me is "Where is Kyle?" Whenever there is dancing in our courtyard area, Kyle makes sure to get Madam Marcel involved, including dancing the first dance with her. They love to tease each other as well. A true affinity exists between the two of them.

Often Madam Marcel makes french fries or boiled potatoes as part of our meals as she knows he likes them. During one of the more recent trips to Pendus, Kyle was served a special plate for breakfast, with different food than the rest of us.

I made a comment that he was being spoiled again by Madam Marcel. Sheepishly, he grinned and said, "It does help to know the cook...and Creole!"

———————⋙●⋘———————

On the other hand, Kyle has also told Sharon and me that sometimes we are lucky not to speak Creole. Kyle has a close connection with the younger Haitians, particularly in Pendus. He spends a lot of time with them and can build a relationship easier with them because of his ability to speak Creole. Whether he was told directly or overheard it as part of a larger group conversation, Kyle said he is aware of some very sad or unfortunate situations the children find themselves in, simply as part of their daily lives.

Kyle has never failed to impress me how easily he adapts to different cultures. It seems so effortless for him to live, work, and play in environments totally different from those in which he grew up in.

After graduation from Tufts, Kyle accepted a job offer and moved to Port-au-Prince. He had no hesitation about living in Haiti. He actually embraced the opportunity. He would be the top employee for a startup plastic recycling business. Six months later, he uprooted and moved to Johannesburg, South Africa, to start his own business consulting company. As part of his work there, he has traveled to over twenty countries on that continent.

He makes such moves appear so easy. He welcomes the challenge of learning new languages, which in turn allow him to seamlessly "fit in" new cultures. His ability to assimilate into new and different ways of life is a trait we all should have. Our world would be a much better place if we all had similar skills.

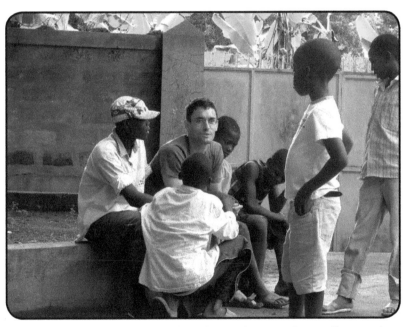

Kyle has a unique ability to blend in with new cultures all around the world. His ability to speak Creole helped him do so in Haiti.

26

Basketball Game in Gros Morne

I have competed well; I have finished the race; I have kept the faith.
—2 Timothy 4:7

PARTICIPATING IN A BASKETBALL GAME against the team from Jean XXIII High School in Gros Morne was one of the best cultural experiences I have had in Haiti. Not only did I get to play a game that I truly enjoy, I was at the same time literally in the middle of a Haitian party. In every way, Kyle was responsible for this event.

Despite Kyle previously collecting money for a basketball court in Pendus, there were many reasons the project did not get started right away. About a year later, Father Cha Cha called Kyle and asked if the basketball court could instead be built in Gros Morne at Jean XXIII High School, named after Pope John XXIII. Father thought it would get more widespread and frequent use at the high school where over three hundred students attended. The older students were more apt to utilize the facility than the elementary children in Pendus. Kyle quickly agreed.

It took several years to get the basketball court built as it cost considerably more than the initial $1,000 donation that Kyle had amassed. There were several factors forcing the cost to escalate. First, this court would now be regulation sized, so more concrete would be needed. Second, the terrain of the school complex was not conducive to such an endeavor. Jean XXIII is built on the side of a mountain.

The flattest, most level part of the property is immediately in front of the school. Because soccer is the country's favorite sport, that space was reserved for soccer games. A third factor added to the extra time required to get it built. Rarely in Haiti is money borrowed to build something and then paid back later. Instead, the money is saved up before it is spent. It took time to raise the additional money needed for this project.

The area to the south of the school was selected for the basketball court, where there was a much steeper slope to the mountain. The drop-off from one end of the court to the other was over nine feet, requiring a lot of prep work before the court could be finished. There was so much foundation required at the downhill end of the court that they built two locker rooms and a concession stand under that end of the basketball court with very little extra excavation needed!

To keep players safe on the court, they built three rows of tiered seats around three sides. The seats were all concrete with a short wall behind the top row. There would be no way for any players to accidentally "fall off" the edge of this court! The one side without seating had an eight-foot concrete wall with enough space for a scorer's table and two team benches. To top off the project, there were six light poles placed surrounding the court, allowing for games to be played at night when it was cooler. It was an impressive facility, especially for the northern mountains of Haiti.

The dedication game for this court was between Jean XXIII High School and the high school from Port-de-Paix. Father Cha Cha was then the priest in Port-de-Paix following his tenure in Gros Morne. He, therefore, was the coach for the visiting team and Father Wilner the coach of the home team in that first event at the new facility. Several concerts and other gatherings have also been held on this court, so the facility is used often.

Once the court was completed, Kyle dreamed of having a game between our mission group and the Jean XXIII high school team. It would be a fundraiser for the school as admission could be charged and concessions sold. Even before our group left for Haiti that next year, Kyle began to arrange with the principal for such a game to be played.

To accommodate the game logistically, we left Pendus one afternoon earlier than usual at the end of our trip. We stayed at Gre Pin, a Montfort retreat area and an agriculture center just outside Gros Morne. This would save unnecessary travel back and forth from Pendus as we would play the game that evening at the nearby school and then drive on to PAP the next day as originally planned. Kyle went to Gros Morne a day before the rest of us to make sure everything came together for the event, spending the night at Kay Se, where he lived in the summer of 2002. He also spent time playing basketball with the Jean XXIII team while he was there.

Our group that year had three who played basketball—Kyle, Frank Donaldson, and me. We also had two of our doctors, Don Clayton and Mike Holmes, who were willing to play in the game. To fill out our team we also had two of the interpreters play—James Metallus and Serge Fortune. With seven players available, we felt comfortable that we could compete and not wear ourselves out! Besides our age, we did have one other obstacle to overcome. Most of us would be playing the game in our hiking shoes as we all did not bring tennis shoes on the trip.

We arrived at Gre Pin at 5:00 p.m. We got unpacked and immediately sat down to eat because our game was scheduled to start at 7:00 p.m. Kyle had been there waiting for us since noon as he did not know for sure when we would get there. He said he was starving. Unfortunately, we only had pasta to eat, which was not a favorite of Kyle's. I saw him only eat bread and peanut butter.

Before I finished up eating, Kyle came to me and said, "I am not going to be able to play tonight!" I thought he was teasing me. He wasn't. He said he suddenly did not feel well. He had a fever and felt like he was going to throw up. Don said he was starting to feel the same way. We were not sure what either was suffering from—malaria, dengue fever, or simply some sort of food poisoning. We found a bed for Kyle (since he was staying at Kay Se). Sharon immediately said she was staying with Kyle and not going to the game.

Our basketball team was now down to just five players. Three of us were over fifty years old, and Serge had never played the game before. Thankfully, James, who was twenty-five years old, was a really good player and Frank had been a very good player in his youth! What had started out as a fun prospect—with Kyle, we would have been very competitive—was now looking pretty grim. We did not want to get embarrassed!

We loaded into our vehicle and headed into Gros Morne to the high school. On the way, we passed Sister Jackie coming toward us. She thought we would need two vehicles to transport everyone, but with two sick players and two staying behind to be with them, we didn't need the second vehicle. She still went to Gre Pin to check on both Kyle and Don.

It was nearly 7:00 p.m. and well past dark when we arrived at the school. Only two of the six lights were on over the court. However, the music system was already blaring! It was the scheduled game time, but only a few guys playing the music were there! We were there over thirty minutes before someone showed up with a basketball so we could begin to warm up! Finally, the other team showed up about 7:45, decked out in nice red uniforms. There were seven on their team. I knew we were in trouble, especially if they played up tempo and substituted a lot.

Before long, Father Wilner arrived, along with over five hundred paying customers. It seemed like a party immediately broke out! It did not take me long to realize that the basketball game would not be the focal point of the evening. Mingling with friends and listening to the music would be! The atmosphere was electric. The music was loud but very good. It was impossible not to want to start dancing! The Haitian beat is contagious.

First thing Father said to me was, "Where is Kyle?" I told him Kyle was sick and did not come. He responded, "Oh. Oh. You lose!" I guess the local odds-makers could see the writing on the wall!

For the only time the entire evening, the music stopped as both sides were individually introduced. I fully expected the lights to go dim and have the home team introduced by spotlight, like a pro basketball game. It didn't happen!

The ref spoke a little English but used mostly Creole. He said we would play four fifteen-minute quarters with a running clock. I did not see a clock anywhere. It must have been kept by someone's wristwatch. That would make a difference throughout the game as we never knew how much time was left or when to hold the ball for a last shot.

Like any outdoor court in America, the concrete could be slick in spots. There also were a few places with rough cement. Knowing those locations are simply part of home-court advantage. There were also good and bad spots in terms of lighting. The lights were low enough that many times a passed ball could be lost briefly in the glare of the lights. Those factors, coupled with fact that Frank did not play with his glasses on for fear of them getting broken, caused many of our normal basketball moves not to look very fluid.

To keep score they simply had a chalkboard leaned up against the wall between the two team benches. There were two columns, one labeled "Jean XXIII" and the other "Indiana." Someone had to erase any prior score and write a new number after each basket. Without any subs, we had to keep an eye on the scoreboard. I wasn't afraid of cheating, but most of the folks there seemed much more interested in the music and socializing than in paying attention to the game!

At last the game started. The music was very loud. It was impossible to talk to each other on the court. You simply could not hear even if you screamed at each other. Being old teammates, Frank and I suggested an opening play. James would jump center and tip it to Frank. I would break for the basket. Hopefully we would catch them off guard. It worked too, except that as I went up for the uncontested layup, I hit one of the slick spots and fell on my butt. The ball still went in, and I was not called for traveling, so we led 2–0 moments into the game.

We actually led 8–3 at one point, and hope sprang within us that we just might stay competitive. The home team stayed in a 2–3 zone defense and did not press us, allowing us to walk the ball up the court on each possession. That helped conserve some energy!

The first two quarters seemed about right for a fifteen-minute running clock. They led us by eight at halftime. Of course, the party atmosphere increased at halftime. Many in the stands came onto the floor to either dance or shoot baskets, meaning we were not getting a chance to warm up for the second half! Concessions were being sold. I wished I could have seen all that was available. I did notice soft drinks, beer, and rum in the stands along with some food.

We kept the score close in the third quarter, trailing by only four points. James turned out to be a very good basketball player. He was the biggest player on the court, and the home team nearly always had to double team him to limit his effectiveness. At the end of the third quarter, we had a bigger break than we did at halftime. First, the ref tried to tell me it was halftime, which I knew was incorrect. Then he said, "You looked tired so we thought you needed a rest!" That I could believe! I think the truth was there were still concessions to sell and no one wanted anything to go to waste! After all, this was a fundraiser and everyone was having a wonderful time! No one wanted it to end.

Finally, the last quarter started. At one point, we were behind 55–51. I hit one of two free throws, and Frank a three-pointer from the corner to tie the game. Of course, there was no way to know how much time was left. One member of our group later told me the last quarter lasted over forty minutes! They came down and hit a three pointer on their next possession to regain the lead they would not relinquish. The final score wound up 64–55. It was a good showing and a competitive game. We were all absolutely drained.

I know I will never forget this experience. I only wished Kyle could have played since it was all his idea. I think the final box score wound up with James scoring 32; Frank, 20; and me, 3. Mike and Serge did not score. I don't think either of them even took a shot!

After the game, I learned that Sister Jackie had brought Kyle and Sharon back to Kay Se with her. Her house overlooks the basketball court where we were playing. Sharon said she came out a couple times to watch from the balcony of Kay Se but spent most of the evening sitting by Kyle in his room.

Kyle later told me he could hear the music all night. By the start of the last quarter he began to feel a little better. He told Sharon that he wanted to pull a Willis Reed and come out and lead our team to victory! Sharon surprised me when she said she understood that analogy to the 1970's New York Knick's legend coming back from injury to inspire his team to victory. Kyle then thought it prudent to not take any chances and stayed in bed.

The next day I was walking the streets in Gros Morne before we departed for PAP. One young boy recognized me and said, "You were in the game last night. You played well!" I guess people were paying attention after all.

Site of the charity basketball game between the St. Mary mission group and the Jean XIII High School team, this full length court sits on the mountainside next to the high school in Gros Morne, Haiti.

27

Haitian Crosses

Own only what you can always carry with you: know
languages, know countries, know people.
Let your memory be your travel bag.
—*Aleksandr Solzhenitsyn*

MY MEMORIES OF HAITI ARE both many and wonderful. But upon returning from a trip, it is easy to get right back into a normal routine and forget many of the things that have touched my heart. I try hard not to let that happen.

Writing a journal as soon as I return is a big help remembering details, especially since I have been so many times. However, wearing a Haitian cross every day is the best way for me to generally remember Haiti and my commitment to many relationships built through the years. It helps me recall those memories every time I put it on and take it off. There also is a special symbolism in the fact that it is near to my heart when I wear it.

On my first visit, I bought a cross made from a steer's horn. I wore that for a couple years before it broke. Thereafter, St. Mary parishioner Doug Granlund began making ceramic crosses for each person going to Pendus every year. About a week before each trip to Haiti, we would have a "send-off" blessing at a Mass at St. Mary. In addition to the blessing the travelers received, the priest would also bless those crosses before we passed them out.

One year Doug was unable to make his crosses for us, so I contacted Duane Sellers, a good friend who is actively involved in his church's Haiti ministry. I knew Duane also made crosses for people going to Haiti with his church. I told him of my predicament and asked if I could buy some crosses from him. He responded, "I will not sell any to you, but I will make them for you for this trip only!"

His crosses are unique because they are made from a blend of two types of wood, one from Haiti and the other from the United States. He sent me the following e-mail:

> The crosses were born from the desire to have a physical piece of Haiti with me all year round. Around 1999, I brought back some wood from Baudin with no specific plans for it. After some thought, I decided that I would make some crosses for the people that went on the trip with me that year. The crosses were made from 2 different woods. The predominant wood (outside cross) was Haitian; the small inner cross was American, representing a blending of our cultures and the lives of the people who traveled there. After sharing these crosses with those on that trip, it became my desire to give a cross to all future missionaries traveling to our sister parish in Baudin from St. Toms.

I loved the phrasing of his "desire to have a physical piece of Haiti with him all year round." That was exactly what I was trying to do too. I just never expressed it so eloquently! When I am awake, I always have a Haiti cross on.

There are two other ways I also try to keep Haiti at the forefront of my thoughts. I have some artwork from Haiti in nearly every room of my home and my office. Most of the items are either paintings or wood carvings. Some are photos I have taken and had framed. Every time I notice one, I am reminded of my experiences in Haiti. Hopefully those reminders help keep my priorities in a proper order.

Another way to remember Haiti is through prayer. I have memorized the Lord's Prayer in Creole. I say it in Creole every morning. I also recite it to myself right after saying the Our Father in English at every Mass.

These are small ways for me to keep Haiti forever on my mind and in my heart. Remember what we are told in Deuteronomy 4:9. "Do not forget the things which your own eyes have seen, nor let them slip from your memory as long as you live."

Crosses are blessed and worn by each member of
St. Mary Cathedral's mission groups. For me, the
cross is a great reminder of the many relationships
made and lessons learned while in Haiti.

28

First World Problems

For where your treasure is, there also will your heart be.
—Matthew 6:21

MANY STUDENTS HAVE TRAVELED WITH us to Pendus through the years. After their return, I often heard from their parents that they don't complain about as many things as in the past. That is a good thing! I would like to think it is true for me as well. Most likely, this phenomenon is a product of having personally witnessed an example of how over half of the world actually lives. When we immerse ourselves in a new culture, we gain a new perspective on our situation in life.

The term *first world problem* has been defined as a relatively trivial or minor problem or frustration when contrasted with more serious problems that those may be experiencing in the developing world. The two words that jump out at me are *trivial* and *frustration*. I am as guilty as anyone when it comes to complaining about not finding a parking spot, not getting a better seat at an event, not getting good service at a restaurant, having too many commercials on television, and on and on. Most of my daily problems are really trivial. They are truly frustrations and not problems, a confusion frequently made in America.

Sharon had an experience that drove home the first world problem issue extremely well. It occurred on our December 2010 trip.

Before we left for Haiti, we knew that we would be attending Fritzner's wedding on our last day in Haiti after first spending our week in Pendus. It made it very difficult to pack for a trip to Pendus *and* for a wedding as the clothes needed for both endeavors are not the same! We only have one carry-on for our personal needs. Our check-in luggage is for taking items needed in Pendus. There isn't enough room to also take extra clothes and shoes suitable for attending a wedding. However, somehow we made it work.

At the last moment, as Sharon and I boarded our flight in Indianapolis early on the departure date for the trip, we were forced to check our carry-ons just as we were about to enter the plane. We were told that our bags were too big, that the plane was extremely full and there would be no more room available for them on board. It did not matter that we simply wanted to put the carry-ons under the seat in front of us and rest our feet on them. That space would always be available! The airlines took them from us anyway and gave us a pair of luggage receipts so we could claim them later in the day in Miami. I told the lady that was not a good solution as we were ultimately going to Haiti and our layover in Miami was a short one. There would not be enough time to retrieve them in Miami. I did not prevail.

We were both upset. There obviously was discretion allowed at the gate in deciding what could be taken on board and what could not, as we saw many carry-ons on the plane much bigger than ours. Haiti can be a daunting experience even when you have all the necessities you planned to take with you. Now the prospect of losing ours was frightening to both of us.

As we sat in our seats before taxiing, one of the stewards came and gave me a new baggage claim for our two carry-ons. It now said to get them in PAP and not Miami. I now held receipts to pick them up in both cities so there was one more opportunity for them to be mishandled en route!

This was our first trip to Haiti after the earthquake. The PAP airport had suffered massive damage. The building's temporary configuration was all-new while permanent construction was still ongoing. We made it through immigration and were waiting on our luggage to be carted from the airplane. Slowly a few of our suitcases appeared.

That was encouraging. Eventually more were spotted either on the conveyor belt or sitting off to the side. Finally, I found my carry-on. I was surprised and elated. However, we could not find Sharon's bag.

After thirty minutes, we had all our bags except Sharon's so I went to the lost baggage counter. Luckily there was a Haitian lady there who also was missing her suitcase. She spoke English well and offered to help me. It complicated things that Sharon's claim ticket was a handwritten one and not a normal bar-coded one. The airlines lady could not locate Sharon's bag in her computer. She wound up giving me a claim number and paperwork to come back in the morning to see if Sharon's bag would arrive on the early morning flight from Miami. My hopes weren't very high. It was worrisome that her bag was not showing up in the airline's computer.

Needless to say, Sharon was not very happy with the prospect of spending a week in Haiti with no clothes other than those she was wearing. In addition, she did not want to go to Fritzner's wedding without proper attire. It was an event she was greatly looking forward to attending. Luckily, she had all her medicines in her backpack she had been able to keep the whole time.

Our sleeping arrangement at Matthew 25 had the women in one room and the men in another, so Sharon and I did not share a room. Sharon said several of the other women had offered to loan her some of their clothes to help get her through the week. Despite the generous offer to help, she could still only foresee a bleak week ahead.

Then Fritzner came up to her and gave her a big hug. He comforted her and told her that everything would be okay. Suddenly it dawned on Sharon that Fritzner spent over four months after the earthquake with only the clothes he was wearing on that fateful day and that he was still living in a small tent with his children. In an instant, all her worries and concerns seemed so minor in comparison to his daily reality. She now had a proper perspective on her situation. It was a valid frustration but was not insurmountable.

For the first time, Sharon was at ease with whatever was going to happen that week, even if it meant not getting her clothes back. She is very creative. I am certain she would have found some way to get more things to wear. While there are no stores in the mountains to go shopping, there are women who make dresses and other clothing. I am sure she would have found a suitable solution by the wedding day.

However, I will never know what resolution she would have come up with as her story ended well. We went back to the airport the next morning, and her bag had come on the early morning flight from Miami. As I came out of the airport carrying her bag, I got a photo of her million-dollar smile, acknowledging that her "first world" ordeal truly had a happy ending.

It also taught us both a valuable lesson on perspective.

Being in Haiti helps Sharon shed the normal concerns of daily routines, allowing her to treasure what is truly important in life.

29

A Little Goes a Long Way

Give something, however small, to the one in need.
For it is not small to the one who has
nothing. Neither is it small to God, if we have given what we could.
—St. Gregory Nazianzen

DURING MY FIRST VISIT TO Pendus, I met many of the local residents. We were even invited inside to see several of their homes. One such home we visited was that of Jean Claude Alexis. Actually, it was his mother's small four-room home. He lived there along with several other relatives. Jean Claude helped take care of his mother.

The house was close to the church compound, located just down the hill from the church as you walked toward the Pendus River. It was in a beautiful setting, nestled within a bend of the river. With a great source of water nearby, there was plenty of vegetation, such as mango trees, avocado trees, and several varieties of crops. Some cows and pigs were also nearby. It turned out that many of Jean Claude's siblings and cousins also lived in that same immediate area.

The dimension of the exterior of his mother's house was no more than twenty feet by twenty feet. It was made of concrete block walls with a dirt floor and tin roof. The roof looked old and weathered and had many holes where sunlight came through in good weather and rain came through in the bad. Inside there was only one twin bed and several mats for sleeping on the dirt floor. The wooden rafters had a few boards resting across them. Jean Claude said the boards were to put on the ground to sleep on when it rained and the floors got muddy! Remember, the Haitian proverb "Kay koule tronpe soley, men li pa tronpe lapli," which translates as "The house that leaks can fool the sun but it cannot fool the rain."

On the last night in Pendus on that first trip to Haiti, we were sitting in the courtyard area. We invited Jean Claude to sit and talk with us. He had been around all week, helping wherever he could but never at the forefront of things. He would set up chairs when needed, sweep and clean, haul water to the compound, play the tambou, and many other tasks. He could not speak any English so that added a degree of difficulty to his ability to comfortably blend in with our group.

Using our interpreters, I asked Jean Claude to tell me about himself. His response was not what I was expecting. He said, "I am twenty-nine years old. I have no job. I am not married, and I will probably never be married." I was at a loss for what to say next. I had plenty of questions that I wanted to follow up with, but I did not want to offend any cultural norms by prying into what he meant by what he said, so I let it go.

The next morning, just before we were ready to leave Pendus, I asked Father Cha Cha what Jean Claude's words meant. Father told me that Jean Claude had minimal education, which is common in the mountains of Haiti. There were no paying jobs for him locally, especially without any education. Father continued by saying without a job and income, he was choosing not to get married as he would have no way to support a family, particularly with the eventuality that there would be children. Since his situation in life would never change, he probably would not ever get married. It broke my heart to hear it put that way, but it was a stark reality.

I immediately asked Father if St. Joseph Church could use a janitor or caretaker. It seemed to me that he would be perfect for that job and probably was already doing many of the tasks a caretaker would do in Pendus. Father replied that they could use someone in that role and that Jean Claude would make a good caretaker. But he quickly added, "We do not have any money to hire one." I then asked him how much it would cost for the church to hire someone. Father's answer floored me. "About $30 a month in American dollars," he said. I could not believe it would cost so little.

The first thought I had was that I wasted more money than that on frivolous things each and every month! Just drinking water for lunch every day, instead of paying for a beverage, would save enough money to pay for his salary. We could easily afford that. So I reached for my wallet and handed Father $30 and said, "Please hire him. I will send the money needed for the rest of the year's salary after I get home."

When I got home, I explained to Sharon what I had done. She instantly was in complete agreement for us to do this. We promptly sent the rest of the year's salary to Father Cha Cha to continue to employ him.

Eight months later, Sharon went with me to Pendus for her first trip. Jean Claude took us to see his mother and her house. Jean Claude already had a new tin roof on the house so it was now water-tight. They now had a truly safe haven to weather out a storm and stay dry, not to mention not having to sleep on a muddy floor when it rained.

Since very little is wasted in Haiti, Jean Claude used the old tin roof to cover the "kitchen," which was nothing more than a detached stick shelter that originally had a thatch roof. It was a separate structure for several reasons. First, it would prevent the smoke from the cooking fires from filling the living quarters of the home, and second, it served as a safety measure to keep a potential fire from destroying everything! Now it too was an improved structure.

To this day, Jean Claude still serves as St. Joseph's caretaker. His life story continues to get better. Several years after he started working, Jean Claude got married. His lovely bride is named Marimat. They have built their own home immediately adjacent to his mother's house. It also is built of concrete block with a tin roof and has a big garden area to grow a supply of food for the family. More importantly, his house has a concrete floor!

Jean Claude and Marimat are now the proud parents of three young sons. The oldest was born in 2011 and is named Jean Claude. The second was born in 2013. His name is Jean Wilson. Even though I could not be there for the baptism, they named me Jean Wilson's godparent, an honor I will always cherish. The youngest was born in August 2017 and is named Adensley.

While Sharon and I may have been giving from our superfluous goods when we started donating to St. Joseph Church so a caretaker could be hired, we have learned that it does not take much to make a tremendous difference. The modest sum through the years has made a huge impact on the life of Jean Claude and his ever-growing family. All he needed was a chance to get started!

St. Gregory the Great once said, "When we attend to the needs of those in want, we give them what is theirs, not ours. More than performing works of mercy, we are paying a debt of justice."

Jean Claude Alexis family; from left, Adensley, Marimat,
little Jean Claude, Jean Claude, and Jean Wilson.

30

Never Too Small

Kindness is the language that the deaf can hear and the blind can see.
—Mark Twain

WE ALL DREAM OF HITTING the home run that wins the game in the last inning. However, most games are truly won when every player does the little things throughout the game that often go unnoticed, seemingly minute things such as hitting the cutoff man, throwing to the correct base, knowing when to advance an extra base or when to stay put, or properly executing a sacrifice bunt. These small acts rarely show up in the stat line, but they are ultimately critical to the game's outcome.

Life is much the same as my baseball analogy. Most people like the feeling of making a big impact. However, those huge moments are frequently beyond our means to achieve. Most difference-making moments are more often found in less dramatic situations. Frequently, those moments are random acts of kindness that can occur at any time. Scott Adams, creator of the Dilbert comic strip, once said, "Remember there's no such thing as a small act of kindness. Every act creates a ripple with no logical end." I love the imagery of the ripple effect, that one act can lead indefinitely to another. This notion is embodied in the *Pay It Forward* movie that became popular shortly after the turn of the twenty-first century.

Mother Theresa gave us an alternate, yet insightful, way to look at this when she said, "Not all of us can do great things. But we can do small things with great love."

Simple acts of kindness can have a bigger significance than most of us would ever expect. Little things such as saying hello, opening a door, or sharing a smile with a passerby can have a lasting effect on the recipient. None of those require much more from us than to pay attention to the moment. Remember the lesson I learned from Fesson that I related earlier in the book. Simply remembering his name was all he desired from me. Being worthy of being noticed, remembered, and called by name is important to all of us! How comforting is it that God calls us each by name? See Isaiah 43:1.

I understood this lesson about small acts in a more profound way on a recent trip to Haiti. I take lots of photographs on every trip I take to Pendus. I like to print many of the pictures and give them to the person on my next trip. Printed photos are not very common in Haiti, especially in rural Haiti. People appreciate receiving them. Giving a photo is a relatively small gesture of kindness, without any deep implications. At least that was what I thought.

Martial Dareus was an active member of the parish at the Kayimit chapel. He was also a friend. He died in 2015 before my December trip to Haiti that year, leaving behind a widow and nine children. During our visit later that year, Sharon, Kyle, and I decided to stop at their house to give our condolences to the family.

Madam Martial was home along with six of her nine children and one grandchild. I greeted her with my best Creole. I began by telling her that Father Cha Cha sent his sympathies and had given me some money to give to her. Upon my mentioning of Martial's name, she broke down and began to weep uncontrollably. She was nearly inconsolable for several minutes. Both Sharon and I hugged her to try to ease her obvious pain. It did not seem to help.

After a short time, her daughter brought out a family album and shared those photos with us. The entire album did not have more than twenty-five pictures in it. I was surprised when two of the pictures were photos of me with Marital that I had given him in the past. There was not a complete family photo in the entire book. In fact, I don't think each of the children even had a picture in the album. A few did but not all. Until that moment I did not fully realize how even something so small or insignificant as a photo could have such importance to the recipient.

When Madam Martial finally composed herself, I gathered the family to take some photos of her with her children and grandchild. Without question, I took copies of those photos for each member of the family on my subsequent trip to Pendus. I had to leave them with Father Sylvio to deliver to her since we did not get to Kayimit on that visit.

British philosopher Edmund Burke summarized my underlying sentiment for this chapter well when he said, "Nobody made a greater mistake than he who did nothing because he could only do a little."

As an outgrowth of my experience with Martial's family, we decided to take family portraits on our 2016 trip. Pam White made her first visit to Pendus that year. She brought a color printer with her along with enough ink and paper to print over four hundred four-by-six photos.

We scheduled the photo session for Sunday, January 1, 2017, following the Mass at St. Joseph Church that morning. That time would provide three benefits for this first-time endeavor. First, it would allow for the most people to be in the church courtyard area at a common time as they would already be there for the church service. Second, since most Haitians wear their best clothes to church, it would allow them to look their best for the keepsake photos! Last, but not least, many people travel home for the New Year's holiday so potentially more members of the family could be available for the photo shoot.

Pam scouted the courtyard area for the best location to take the photos and found the perfect spot. It was in the shade but still had plenty of natural lighting. It also had a ledge where we could have folks stand if needed to fit everyone into the picture or simply adjust for various heights of the family members. The best feature of this spot was the exterior wall of the church was painted a solid blue color. This made for an ideal backdrop on all the photos taken that day, giving them a look of having been taken in a professional studio.

Pam arranged each grouping of family members while I took the photographs. I took several of each grouping just to make sure we had a good one to print. We had to run the generator in the compound to provide power for the printer. Cyle Newton worked the printer. In less than an hour after all the photos were shot, everyone had them to take home with them.

Pam said the smiles from some of the women receiving the printed photos made the entire day's effort worthwhile. Sometime later that afternoon, Steve Fields, another member of that year's group, was walking down near the river. One of the local residents walked by, waving his photo at him with great joy.

This is one of the photos I had given to Martial
that became part of his family's photo album.

31

Give Me Eyes to See

Open my eyes to see clearly the wonders of your teachings.
—Psalm 119:18

ANOTHER FAVORITE HAITIAN PROVERB OF mine is "Sa je pa we, ke pa tounen." It means "What the eyes cannot see, the heart cannot feel."

I am thankful that God has prompted me to go beyond my comfort zone and travel to Haiti. Without being physically present, I could never have experienced the many stories I have related in this book. But God has done more than physically transport me to a new location. He has moved me spiritually. He has granted me eyes to see and a heart to feel in ways that never existed before. I am equally thankful for that too! How many times in our daily lives have we experienced a situation in which we simply fail to notice what is going on? Or even if we do notice, we don't appreciate the significance of what is happening? How easy is it to miss the hand of God in most situations?

As I mentioned early in this book, I find it much easier to notice Jesus in others when I am in Haiti. That also applies to seeing God's hand at work in what is transpiring at any particular moment. The following are some more examples of such occasions.

⟶⊷⊷⟵

We held a medical clinic at Massacre on January 1, 2007. It had been three years since we hiked to Massacre due to weather-related issues. One year it was too wet and muddy to hike, and the next year it took us three days just to get from PAP to Pendus due to heavy rains and high-flowing rivers, thereby cutting our stay in Pendus. As such, we had a larger-than-normal turnout for that year's clinic near the top of this mountain.

A young man, probably no older than thirty, carried his mother in his arms to our clinic. She had previously suffered a stroke and was unable to walk. I had no idea how far he carried her, but any distance at all on that mountain would have made it a very difficult hike. There was no immediate medical issue with his mother; he just wanted her to get a medical examination since we were there.

I watched as he carefully carried her into the classroom that was turned into a temporary clinic room. He gently sat her down on one of the school benches and held her hand as he sat beside her. Emily Hilycord, a masters student in Purdue University's School of Nursing, thoroughly examined her. There was nothing that could be done for her in this rural mountain setting. After finishing with her, Emily leaned over and cradled the woman's head in her hands as she softly kissed her on the cheek. She smiled back at Emily.

Satisfied, the young man carefully picked his mother up and carried her home. Both the son's devotion for his mother and Emily's gentle, loving attention to a stranger were great evidence of Jesus's presence in that moment to me. Both of their actions spoke loudly to me about the human dignity of each and every person and how we are to love one another.

Human dignity was also at the forefront when we visited Mother Theresa's Sisters of Charity Home for the Dying, located just outside Gonaives. The facility had fifty beds. We were told it sees over five hundred patients per year. There is no cost to anyone to stay, to receive care, or for medicine. We also learned that most of the patients there were suffering from AIDS, tuberculosis, or cancer.

We met one patient named Etelius Pierre. He was confined to a wheelchair. The nun that was showing us through the facility instantly knew his name, his family history, and all about his illness. She told us that he has no one to visit him as his wife had already died and his son never comes to visit. He cried when we simply came up to talk with him and pat him on the shoulder. He told us he was "waiting to die." It was very difficult for me to witness.

Dr. Adel Yaacoub, a Lafayette cardiologist, was on that trip. He said that he was very impressed with the facility. Not only was it very clean, he said, "There was great dignity in the care" being given. The nuns gave a great testament to the value of every life and that no one there would ever die alone.

Sharon's education and background is in early childhood development. Her only medical experience comes from being a loving mother, which by itself qualifies her to assist on our many medical missions. She helps with intake information, takes blood pressures, works in the pharmacy, and performs any other task that is needed to support the doctors and Madam Marcel.

She was helping on one of the early medical missions at the dispensary in Pendus when a young Haitian boy showed up. She estimated him to be no older than twenty. Age is often difficult to guess as most Haitians are smaller than their American counterparts of similar age! He was shivering severely. As they began to attend to him, Madam Marcel pulled Sharon aside and told her that he had AIDS and that she should not touch him. Another Haitian woman came over and gave him a blanket to help comfort him. After checking him, Dr. Adel Yaacoub said that the boy needed to go the hospital in Gros Morne right away.

The boy sat outside the dispensary shivering as he waited for a truck to come drive him to the hospital. Sharon said that he looked so scared and alone. Her maternal instinct told her to hold him to comfort him, but she couldn't. This was her first close encounter with someone suffering from AIDS, and it frightened her. She did not know how contagious it could be as accurate knowledge of the disease was still in its infancy.

After he left for the hospital, Sharon said she felt so sorry that she could not do anything for him. She had sensed the presence of Jesus in the situation and still froze.

Sharon had another opportunity to witness God's hand at work when she was again helping Madam Marcel. One evening after dinner, we received word about a patient at the dispensary who was about to have a baby. Sharon quickly joined Madam Marcel in walking down there. Both of our sons were born by cesarean section, so Sharon had never experienced a natural birth before.

The young lady was already lying down when they walked into the delivery room. Her grandmother was with her. Madam Marcel was calm, exuding the confidence from having delivered hundreds of babies. Still, Sharon's heart was racing in anticipation of what was about to happen.

Sharon comforted the soon-to-be mother by rubbing her head and swatting bugs away. It was very warm in the room. Madam Marcel gave Sharon a flashlight to hold as it was getting dark and instructed Sharon to watch for the head to crown. Sharon realized that the bed was not very long and a bucket sat on the floor at the end of the bed. Sister Jackie finally arrived to help assist.

Then the young lady said something that made both Sister Jackie and Madam Marcel laugh. Sharon asked what she said. Sister Jackie replied, "Why did I tell him yes?" Sharon chuckled as well. The patient made no more sounds until she began to hum softly. She did not seem to be contracting and was not pushing the infant out. Madam Marcel started to knead the young girl's stomach and thighs, then began to hit her harder to try to her get to push. She was not pushing.

Sharon was certain by this point in the procedure that if they had been back in the United States that a C-section would have been performed. That was not an option in rural Haiti. Madam Marcel had to cut her several times and reached in to pull first the head and then the baby's shoulders out. Sharon had finally witnessed her first natural birth. It was a girl! Madam Marcel immediately focused all her attention on the young infant. The umbilical cord was wrapped around her neck. No one could possibly know how long the baby had been without oxygen. It seemed to take minutes before Sharon heard a cry. The beautiful sound completed the miracle of new life.

The young mother began to shiver. It was evident that she was in shock. Sharon was asked to rub her down with alcohol while Madam Marcel dressed the baby in a pretty little dress and handed the little girl to her grandmother. Sharon continued rubbing down the mother. The new mother was moved into the overnight room of the dispensary. Sharon commented to Sister Jackie that the young lady had not yet been sewn up. To Sharon's surprise, Sister Jackie responded that probably was not going to happen.

Sharon later reflected on this experience, "It showed me the miracle of life and that Madam Marcel was truly an angel living in Pendus. I realized all the hardships these women must endure all the time. They do not complain at all. They simply go on with life and accept what happens to them. Jesus is in them, and they trust in Him."

It is very fitting that the wall overlooking the birthing table was painted with a scene of the Holy Spirit in the form of a dove hovering over a newborn baby. Above are the words, "Sila a se petit mwen renmen an, nan li mwen Jwenn plezi mwen." This translates to "This is my little one whom I love, in him I find my pleasure." What a wonderful setting for a birthing room!

———⟫●⟪———

God's presence was felt again during another birth experience on our December 2010 trip. This was our first visit to Haiti after the earthquake the prior January. Despite the dispensary in Pendus suffering only some cracking in the ceiling and walls, Madam Marcel was still operating out of temporary tents in the compound court-yard area. She had moved all the important equipment and records into a small adjacent concrete building that had not been damaged. Since the dispensary was built entirely of concrete, she remained hes-itant to return inside.

One of the biggest problems post-earthquake was the outbreak of cholera in Haiti. The epidemic was felt throughout the country and not just near PAP where the earthquake was centered. The big-gest tent in the courtyard was used to quarantine the cholera patients. At one point, there were over thirty cholera patients in the dispensary at the same time.

I asked Madam Marcel how she was able to find enough beds for all the patients. She replied that she simply told each patient to go get a bed from home and bring it back to the dispensary (and then take it back once recovered!) She added that there had been more than two hundred patients there over the past three months and that five people had died from cholera. She said that cholera attacks the body so quickly with violent vomiting and diarrhea that a person without medical attention can die from severe dehydration in less than twenty-four hours. The first medical response is rehydration salts and IV fluids followed by Cipro or a comparable medicine. It was a scary situation throughout Haiti, especially in remote areas that did not have any medical care nearby.

Luckily, there were no cholera patients there when we arrived right after Christmas that year.

Sister Jackie and Sister Pat wanted us to help convince Madam Marcel that it was safe to utilize the dispensary building again. One of the ways we were able to accomplish that was to help in the transi-tion back into the dispensary. Sharon and the seven nursing students spent half a day scouring the entire building with a bleach solution to sanitize it, making it safe to use once again. Talk about many hands making light work! This endeavor would have been overwhelming for Madam Marcel without this assistance.

Our entire group then helped carry shelves, desks, chairs, medical supplies, and all the medical records from the outbuilding back into the dispensary. The dispensary was now back in business, and Madam Marcel was quite happy!

After a short break for a meal, Sharon and the seven nursing students were back finishing up at the dispensary when a lady arrived about ready to deliver a baby. Madam Marcel and the two nursing school instructors were not there. Initially, the students looked to Sharon for guidance since she was the only one with a birth experience in Haiti. The eight of them went to work getting the woman ready for delivery. Thankfully, Madam Marcel arrived just before the baby was born.

The seven-and-a-half-pound boy was not breathing at first and was turning blue. Madam Marcel calmly prodded and kneaded the baby for several minutes before he finally began to breathe on his own. Sharon described the newborn's attempt to breathe like a sound of a car that sputters, then stops several times before finally taking off.

One of the nursing students assisting was Kelly Kruekeberg. Afterward she wrote, "If this baby were in America he would have been sent to NICU immediately and oxygen been given, but here in this tiny clinic in the middle of nowhere there was no oxygen in sight. We prayed the whole time Madam Marcel was recovering the baby, asking God to have grace on him and allow him to take his first breath. Finally, after what seemed like fifteen minutes, the baby took his first breath and started to cry."

Before the evening was over, one of the nursing students saw the woman put her clothes back on, pick up the baby, and walk home. Such is life in Haiti.

———⇒►●◄⇐———

Cholera was still a problem a year later. Claire Allen was one of four nursing students that year. All four were at the dispensary when a thirty-one-year-old cholera patient arrived. The woman was so lethargic that she could barely move. Madam Marcel quickly got an IV started and told the man who brought the patient to the dispensary that he needed to take her to the hospital in Gros Morne immediately. If he didn't, she would die. Within an hour they were gone.

Two days later our group was in Gros Morne. Following her graduation from St. Elizabeth School of Nursing, Kelly Krueckeberg was volunteering at Alma Mater Hospital in Gros Morne. She gave us a tour. Since it was New Year's Day, Kelly explained that many of the patients were sent home to be with family for the holiday.

The one area that still had lots of people was the infant care unit. There were several mothers helping take care of their children. In Haiti, hospital care does not include food. The family must provide food for the patient.

Claire asked Kelly about the cholera patient who was recently sent from Pendus, so Kelly took us to where the cholera patients were located. Because of the quarantine, the woman could only come to the entrance of the ward and not all the way to where we were standing. Claire was ecstatic, saying, "She looks so good! She was at death's door when I saw her last. It is amazing how different she now felt." The woman also said that she was hungry as she did not have any family there to provide for her.

Claire immediately left the energy bars she had in her backpack with Kelly to give to the woman. When Claire got back to Pendus later, she gave Kelly another Ziploc bag with other snacks to take back to her for the duration of her stay at the hospital.

<hr />

One afternoon during one of our early trips to Pendus, our son Kyle got sick. His stomach was upset, and he did not want to eat anything. He also had a slight fever. At that point in his life, Kyle was a very finicky eater and did not like to try new things. He had been to Haiti several times by then, including his summer in Gros Morne. During that time, he had built up a special bond with Madam Marcel.

When she realized that Kyle was not feeling well, she mixed up a concoction for him to drink, the ingredients of which are still a mystery to me. Only Madam Marcel could have offered this strange remedy and have Kyle drink it. I am sure both Sharon and I would have difficulty getting him to drink it. But for her, he did drink it. Almost immediately he vomited but said thereafter he did feel better. By the next morning, he was back to normal.

Taking medicines at home was not an easy thing for Kyle, but the trust he had built with Madam Marcel overcame any hesitation he may have had while in Pendus. While Kyle may not have thought this story involved divine intervention, as a parent I sure did! God's fingerprints were all over his quick recovery.

Sometimes too many pieces are in precisely the right place at precisely the right time for God not to be involved.

We had one of our larger medical teams on the December 2006 trip. Dr. Dave Schmidt, a cardiologist, was joined by Mollie Hanlon, a PhD nursing student at Purdue; Emily Hilycord, a master's level nursing student at Purdue; Josee Angrand, a nurse with many years of experience in both Haiti and the USA; and Paula Max, a pharmacy tech from St. Elizabeth Hospital in Lafayette. That group had several significant encounters that week. I will focus on two of them.

For the first time, we decided to take a medical clinic on the road instead of holding it in the dispensary in Pendus. We thought this would help get medical care to people in areas not conveniently located to Pendus. We planned three road clinics for the week, one each at the chapels Kayimit, Montbayard, and Massacre.

The first was at Kayimit's chapel, the only chapel of those three that was accessible by vehicle. Despite being located only six miles from Pendus, it was a thirty-minute drive! Our main problem was we only had one vehicle available that morning and we needed two vehicles to get our entire group and supplies needed to Kayimit and back. So Father Wilner drove us there in two shifts.

While waiting for the second half of our group to arrive, we set up three examination stations at the chapel, one each for Dr. Schmidt, Mollie, and Emily. Each would have their own interpreter. Josee would then act as the floater, helping wherever needed. She was especially helpful in noticing which patients needed the most immediate attention to make sure they were seen during our stay. Her ability to speak Creole was invaluable!

One of the first patients seen that morning had meningitis and needed to be taken to the hospital in Gros Morne, which was another thirty-minute drive from Kayimit. Using the only vehicle in the area, Father Wilner drove the patient and his mother to the hospital.

We were going to have a Mass at the end of our clinic, but because Father was so late getting back from the hospital, we did not do so. Father was still going to have to make two trips to get us all back to Pendus, and it was getting late. To help in the logistics of getting everyone back to Pendus, about half our group elected to join me in hiking back. That allowed Father to only drive that distance once. Of course, I made sure there was a resident of Pendus familiar with that area walking with us so we would not get lost! It was a trail that I had never been on before. It was a spectacular walk back with the vista of the mountains and the setting sun!

We continued our walk until the last river crossing in route to Pendus. Father Wilner was there waiting to drive us the final two miles. It was a good thing he came back for us as it is much more difficult to hike in the mountains in the dark.

When we finally arrived back, the medical team was summoned to the clinic. There had been an automobile accident earlier that evening. A tap-tap had lost its brakes as it descended the steep incline that made a sharp ninety-degree turn down toward the Pendus River near where Father Wilner had picked us up. It crashed into the earthen wall and several of the passengers were hurt, including one young woman quite severely.

Dave, Josee, Mollie, Emily, and Madam Marcel did a wonderful job attending to the patient. At one point her blood pressure was only sixty over thirty. They knew she needed to get to the hospital in

Gros Morne as quickly as possible. An old World War II army surplus stretcher has been previously sent to Pendus on a sea container. Six people carried the woman on it from the dispensary up the hill to the closest place a vehicle could pick her up.

Madam Marcel's assistant traveled in the bed of the truck with the patient. She held the IV elevated and continued to monitor the patient during the hour drive over the rough mountain terrain back to Gros Morne. As they left, we were not sure if she would survive. The jostling of the drive itself can be unsettling, let alone when in her condition. We heard later that thankfully she did survive!

———◆———

The second significant medical story from that December 2006 trip came during our road clinic to Massacre. As mentioned, it is a grueling two-hour hike up the mountain to reach Massacre from Pendus.

One of the last patients to be seen at this clinic was a little girl who was carried there by her father. She was listless and did not respond to Mollie's attempt to wake her. Her father said that her fever had lasted for several days. This father was raising four young children by himself as the mother had left. Mollie convinced him to take his daughter to the dispensary. If Madam Marcel could not help her, she could at least get her a ride to the hospital.

I know how difficult a hike it is between Massacre and Pendus. I cannot imagine how hard it would be to carry a child over that terrain, especially one who is limp and unable to hold on to her father.

It was nearly 5:00 p.m. and dusk when we got back to Pendus. The father had made it to the dispensary. The medical team and Madam Marcel rehydrated her orally. By the end of the evening, the little girl began to respond. I got a great photo of Dave gently cradling her in his hands as he continued to examine her. She and her father would both spend the night in the dispensary and go home the next morning.

Dave gave the father some food and water. He only ate a small portion of what was given to him, saving the rest to take back to his other children the next day.

<hr />

It is no coincidence that all my examples of seeing Jesus involved the sick and the infirm. After all, Jesus told us in Matthew 25 that not only was he present when someone visited and attended to the sick, but also that it was Him that you would be caring for!

A bit of a twist on the Haiti proverb that I like so much would make it read: "Once your eyes do see, it is difficult for your heart not to care and respond."

This little girl was severely dehydrated upon her arrival at the dispensary. The hand of God was evident as Dr. Dave Schmidt gently examines her during her recovery.

32

Empty Plates

For their hunger, you gave them bread from heaven.
—Nehemiah 9:15

GOD USES A VARIETY OF ways to teach me a lesson in Haiti. The most unusual one came on my most recent trip to Pendus. He used a trash can filled with empty plates to grab my attention!

The plates weren't empty because they had not yet been used. They were empty because every bit of rice, beans, and chicken originally served on them had been eagerly eaten and then properly disposed of in the container. My favorite photo from this trip was of the inside of the fifty-five-gallon drum that we used as a trash container. There was not a grain of rice left on any of the dozens of plates discarded after the meal!

Father Sylvio had always wanted to be able to invite the children of the community into the church compound and provide a meal for them. The summer and fall seasons of 2016 were not kind to the Pendus area. Drought conditions diminished crop production during the summer. Then Hurricane Matthew's massive rains ruined much of the remaining crops in October. Having sufficient food was a critical issue throughout the area. Our December 2016 trip would be an ideal time to implement Father's dream.

There are often food issues in the Pendus area, especially after natural catastrophes such as hurricanes and the 2010 earthquake.

The priests' solution is not to distribute food directly to families. Instead they feed the schoolchildren. Meals are not otherwise provided at any of the schools in the Pendus area on a regular basis. When the children go home, they do not eat again, leaving more food for the rest of the family to share. This form of rationing meager resources allows more families to benefit. This method of handling hunger issues has worked throughout the years under the leadership of each of our four priests in Haiti.

Octa, one of our interpreters, owns a small store in the Port-au-Prince area. I ordered sufficient rice, beans, and cooking oil from him well before our trip. Octa had all of it delivered to the airport upon our arrival so we could take it with us on our bus to Pendus.

A close friend from back home heard me describe what we planned to do and donated the money to cover the cost of this endeavor. This reminds me of the words from one of his favorite books in the Bible, Sirach, found in 18:25, "In the time of plenty, think of the time of hunger; in the days of wealth, think of poverty and need."

Sharon planned to make the day extra special by bringing several games and activities for the children to participate in before the meal. It would truly be a festive picnic atmosphere. Father arranged for the woman who cooks for St. Joseph School (whenever meals are served there) to cook this special meal for the children. She had us buy some chicken when we were in Gros Morne earlier in the week to augment the menu. Father provided the Styrofoam plates and plastic spoons. Someone had a battery-powered CD player that provided ample music for the day.

Soccer is the favorite sport in Haiti. Dozens of boys played throughout the day. One of the other games Sharon brought was a Velcro toss and catch set. The Velcro balls would simply stick to the Velcro mitt when caught. I am sure the children had never seen anything like it before, yet they had great fun with it. Separately, I asked both Kyle and Benedict later how the children would describe this activity at the end of the day when their parents asked, "What did you do today?" I laughed when both replied exactly the same in Creole. They would simply say, "M'ap jwe avek blan yo," which means "I was playing with the whites!" Children are the same everywhere, skipping all the details!

Sharon, Pam White, Ellie Fields, Mary McKee, and Cyle Newton helped Madam Desira prepare the food for the day. They peeled onions, stirred the rice and beans, cooked the chicken as well as help serve the food.

Father gathered the children in a group in the middle of the school yard. He said a blessing, then had them say the Our Father and Hail Mary prayers. He also told them to throw the trash when they were finished (Styrofoam plates, plastic spoons, and plastic drink containers) into a fifty-five-gallon barrel that we set out in the middle of the school yard. I was concerned about cleanup when we were done. There are several reasons Haitians do not have much waste in the normal daily activities. First, very few items are store-bought. Most are homegrown. Natural wastes such as banana peels and coconut shells can be given to animals to eat. Often, when we pass out candy at a function, the wrappers simply are tossed on the ground. It is not like there is a wastebasket somewhere that will eventually be emptied into a garbage can and picked up for disposal by anyone. Community trash typically is raked into a pile if it becomes excessive and burned in place.

Father then had the children line up by age, beginning with the youngest. Benedict and Kyle helped lead a dozen children at a time, single file, to receive their plate filled with a mound of rice and beans and topped with some chicken (some still on the bone and some not). Each plate was filled to capacity. They would then go sit in the shade of the trees to enjoy their feast. We distributed drinks such as Tampico and Coca-Cola. The youngest ones were told to share an entire drink, which they did without hesitation. The older children got an entire drink for themselves.

Over one hundred children were fed. They all sat quietly and enjoyed their meal. Every child paced themselves, savoring each and every bite of precious food. There was no loud talking or jovial noises. The children did not pester or disturb each other. In addition, if an older sibling finished first, he or she provided any assistance the younger one needed to finish eating his or her plateful. I saw no spillage of any food or drink.

I watched the younger children eat. They carefully balanced their plate on their little laps, looking around with a sense of amazement that this was really happening for them.

I was pleasantly surprised when the first child who finished got up and walked to the fifty-five-gallon drum and tossed his plate into it. Soon another followed...and another. After several dozen children had done as previously instructed, I ambled over to look inside the drum. What I saw amazed, and impressed, and humbled me. There was absolutely no food in the container, only the Styrofoam plates, plastic spoons, and plastic drink bottles. Some of the plates looked like they had been cleaned before being discarded. Even the juice from the sauce mixed with the rice and chicken was not readily apparent on the plates. They ate every last bite. There was no food wasted this afternoon. Not even by one child, not even by the youngest one!

I could not help but think how much the children needed this meal. I could also not help but feel how blessed I am to never have been so hungry in my life that I would literally lick my plate clean. I also could not help but think of the hopeful words from Revelation that at the End Times: "They will hunger no more and thirst no more" (Rev. 7:16).

A peek inside the trash barrel shows that no food was wasted.

33

Education

*The heart of the discerning acquires knowledge, for the ears of
the wise seek it out.*

—*Proverbs 18:15*

HAITI'S CONSTITUTION PROVIDES THAT A public education be offered
free to all people. The Haitian government, however, has never been
able to fulfill this obligation. In fact, over 80 percent of all primary
and secondary schools in the country are currently provided by the
private sector, most of which are religious-based endeavors.

The percentage of Haitian children attending school is among
the lowest in the world. According to the UNICEF Humanitarian
Action Report 2008, only 67 percent of the children in Haiti are ever
enrolled in elementary school. Only 70 percent of those continue to
third grade and only slightly more than 21 percent reach the secondary level.

The people of the Pendus area recognize the importance of
educating their children. The Catholic Church runs primary schools
(through sixth grade) at St. Joseph in Pendus as well as in the chapels
at Massacre, Montbayard, Savanne Carre, and Mayombe.

The first five years of our twinning relationship, we were not
involved in education other than sponsoring a few children to go to
school. In 2005, however, Father Cha Cha told us that their funding
source for paying teacher salaries had dried up. It had been coming

from a French foundation suffering from the worldwide economic downturn over the past few years.

St. Mary Cathedral stepped up and began raising $18,000 per year to cover the salaries of the thirty-five teachers at all the local schools. Five hundred dollars per year in salary for each teacher does not seem to be much, but it is one of the highest incomes in these remote mountain villages of Haiti.

Most every December since, our group has met with the Pendus Central Committee. It is comprised of representatives from Pendus and all six chapels. Despite the dire need for capital improvements and other projects, their unanimous choice as the top priority for St. Mary to assist with each year has been to continue paying the teacher salaries. By sponsoring the teacher salaries, the schools can keep tuition costs much lower for the parents to send their children to school, meaning more students are able to attend. The parents' portion helps pay the teachers a continued stipend during the summer months when school is not in session.

The local community clearly embraces Benjamin Franklin's thought when he said, "An investment in education pays the best interest." St. Mary's parishioners agree!

The St. Joseph School children proudly wear their
school uniforms at morning assembly.

34

Earthquake 2010

The memory of the just will be blessed.
—Proverbs 10:7

Tragedy struck Haiti on January 12, 2010. Just before 5:00 p.m., a 7.0 earthquake centered about 10 miles west of Port-au-Prince devastated Haiti. By midnight there were seventeen aftershocks of at least 4.5 in magnitude, with seven of them over 5.0 on the Richter scale. There were over a hundred aftershocks in the next few weeks. Every major landmark in Port-au-Prince suffered damage. Over two hundred thousand people were killed and over one million were homeless, simply sleeping outside on the ground. Tent cites sprang up as people tried to regain some sense of normalcy. Many people whose homes were not destroyed still slept outside for fear of further tremors and possible collapse.

Pendus is located about 120 miles northwest of PAP. The earthquake could be felt there, but the major destruction did not occur there. There were a few buildings in the area that were greatly damaged, such as the Fonkoze office in Gros Morne. However, most of the visible damage suffered in Pendus was limited to cracks in the walls of the concrete buildings, such as the dispensary. The total extent of the damage may never be fully known due to the remoteness from Port-au-Prince and the few people with expertise available to make such determinations.

Fortunately, Pendus's distance from the epicenter of the disaster kept the injuries and fatalities to a minimum. Father Wilner Donecia was in PAP for an annual Montfortan priest retreat when the earthquake hit. He was unharmed, but ten of the Montfortan seminarians were killed, as was the archbishop of Port-au-Prince. Four of the interpreters used by St. Mary's over the years were also in PAP when the quake hit. It took one week before we finally heard from each of them: Fritzner Guerrier, Roody "Octa" Pierre, Serge Fortune, and Sergo Castin. All four had survived. The only injury was to Serge's shoulder as he escaped from a falling wall in his room during the quake. However, each of them lost their homes and most of their possessions.

I remember precisely when we heard from Fritzner that he had survived. With tears in my eyes, I typed the simple message, "Li la" ("He is there"), to everyone who knew him. Father Wilner added a bit of humor to his first message to us, simply saying, "Mwen pa mouri," or "I am not dead!"

"Like cold water to a thirsty soul, so is good news from a far country" (Prov. 25:25).

Immediately after the quake everyone wanted to help. The next day Andre Angrand, Josee Angrand, Sharon Newell, Helen Hession, and I—all from St. Mary—met with about a dozen others in Indianapolis to coordinate a relief effort. Our group called itself Indiana HERO with HERO standing for Haiti Earthquake Relief Organization. Our goal was threefold: first, to help get medical personnel to Haiti; second, to help get medical supplies to Haiti; and third, to raise money for many other relief needs. Transportation to PAP, even for critical medical personnel, was nearly impossible. Haiti had only one international airport in the country at that time, and its radar and communications systems were damaged. Furthermore, its lone runway was not sufficient to accommodate the instantaneous world-support effort. The main port area also suffered great damage, further hindering relief efforts.

Many from Lafayette, including Dr. Rita Mankus; Dr. Don Clayton; and nurses Mindy Clayton, Josee Angrand, and Chloe

Harshman traveled to PAP to help with the immense medical needs. Medical people from Kokomo, Noblesville, Indianapolis, and other central Indiana cities also made it to Haiti in the weeks after the earthquake. Each one had to fly to the Dominican Republic and then bus over eight hours to Port-au-Prince. To put this in perspective, it would be like flying to Atlanta and then busing to Indianapolis, clearly not an easy or convenient trip!

We began to raise money from many places to help with the relief effort. Both St. Mary Cathedral and St. Lawrence Church in Lafayette took up special collections. Together the two churches raised over $27,000. E-mails to friends, relatives, and acquaintances, which often then got forwarded onto others, brought in another $10,000. It was amazing as mail brought donations from as far away as California and Texas. The Pine Village Elementary School collected and donated over $600 to the cause! The outpouring of support was heartwarming.

Some of the first money raised was sent to Matthew 25 Guest House, Visitation Hospital, and Deep Springs International to help with immediate needs. Matthew 25, the guesthouse run by the Parish Twinning Program of the Americas and a place many of us stay as we come and go from Port-au-Prince, suffered structural damage. However, its adjoining soccer field immediately became a triage area for the medical folks staying there. Sister Mary Finnick, who is also a nurse, and many other medical folks there quickly had over one thousand patients staying in makeshift tents on the soccer field.

Visitation Hospital, also run by the PTPA but located about two hours west of PAP, saw a great number of patients from the earthquake. Deep Springs International provides a simple one-bucket, in-home water purification systems throughout Haiti. It had an immediate response effort in Leogane, an area close to PAP that was almost entirely leveled. Leogane was the epicenter of the earthquake. In all, Deep Springs raised over $200,000 to provide emergency water to many affected by the disaster. We were also able to send many medicines down with some of the medical folks who could make it to Haiti.

Money was also sent at the request of Father Wilner to help with humanitarian efforts in the Pendus area. After the earthquake, the costs of many essential staples such as rice, cooking oil, and other necessities tripled or worse. Many could not afford such items at normal prices, let alone at the newly inflated ones. To help many strapped families, he provided meals to all the students in Pendus and surrounding chapel areas for the final two months of the school year. When a family eats only one meal per day, it was a great help to have the children eat their meal at school, leaving more to eat at home for others in the family.

With many refugee families moving home and away from the destruction of PAP, there were fifty new students enrolled in Pendus schools who needed help with the transition, having lost all they had in the earthquake. Father Wilner also used some of the money for medical needs of the returning refugees.

Amputations were common after the earthquake. Many of the injuries incurred during the earthquake were crushings because of the collapsing of concrete buildings. Julie Lidester spearheaded an effort to collect wheelchairs, walkers, crutches, and canes. St. Anthony Health Care made a major contribution of such items. In late April, Frank Donaldson and I drove a van loaded with nearly one hundred such wheelchairs, walkers, and canes to Nashville, Tennessee, to be sent by the PTPA sea container to the Visitation Hospital.

The Lafayette Latino community also contributed, holding its first annual Carnival Latino in early May. Kimberly Huesca and Berna Turuno organized a fun-filled day that raised over $ 2,000.

Members of the Friendship Bible Study, sponsored by the Thorntown United Methodist Church, uniquely responded to the earthquake relief effort. This group's members are adults with special needs. Using both their own money and donations of others that they collected, they purchased and packaged toiletries, school supplies, and sewing items to be sent to Haiti. In all they assembled fifty such kits. "These are people who are mentally challenged," said Linda Prage, one of the leaders of the group. "We did a lesson about being a servant and kind of got the idea that helping Haiti would be a good project. It was precious to watch them take such care to pack everything." She added, "It was a big job for them!"

This great outpouring of support brought to mind the Haitian proverb, "Se nan nale ou konnen bon zanmi," which simply means "Good friends are recognized in adversity." Haiti sure has a lot of good friends in Indiana.

The Cathedral of Our Lady of the Assumption in Port-au-Prince was one of hundreds of building destroyed in the January 12, 2010 earthquake.

35

Piti Piti Swazo Fe Nich Li

A possibility is a hint from God. One must follow it.
—Soren Kierkegaard

"Piti piti swazo fe nich li" is a Haitian proverb that means "Little by little the bird builds its nest." It fits perfectly to what has been accomplished in the twinning relationship between St. Mary Cathedral and St. Joseph Church. It applies both to the many relationships that have been nurtured as well as the infrastructure that has been built.

Our parish twinning relationship all began with a possibility: imagine what could happen if the parishes of St. Mary and St. Joseph twinned together. I always said, "Look what happened the first time Mary and Joseph got together two millennia ago!" I know that in the case of our two churches, no one could have honestly foreseen all that has transpired over the years.

About three years into our twinning relationship, Haitian Bishop Emanual Constant came to visit Father Cha Cha in Pendus. His reaction to seeing all the improvements made in that short time was hilarious. He said, "My goodness, Cha Cha, what did you do, rob a bank?"

Whenever you step back and take a snap shot view of what has been accomplished, it does look like a lot. It would be overwhelming to try and duplicate what was done, especially in the early years. As that Franciscan Benediction goes, we "were able, with God's grace, to do what others claim cannot be done." We are reminded in Proverbs 16:3, "Entrust your works to the Lord and your plans will succeed."

Our focus was on community projects, ones that benefited the most people. Infrastructure was desperately needed in Pendus and the six chapel areas. Prioritizing the many competing needs required a delicate balance in the early years because there were so many of them.

Much like the Haiti proverb above, St. Mary set about to do one project at a time. With insightful leadership provided by our Haitian priests in conjunction with the Pendus Central Committee, we would tackle their top priority, however long it would take, before moving on the next endeavor on the list. We did not try to "bite off more than we could chew" at any one time. Little by little the accomplishments began to add up.

Former president of the University of Notre Dame, Father Theodore Hesburgh, talked about such leadership, saying, "The very essence of leadership is [that] you have a vision. It's got to be a vision you articulate clearly and forcefully on every occasion. You can't blow an uncertain trumpet." Each of the four Haitian priests has exhibited such vision throughout the years. Many of the projects we have accomplished over the years are featured in other chapters of this book. The following will focus on some of the other significant ones.

St. Mary sent a modest sum to Father Cha Cha before our first visit to Pendus. He used it to build a four-room guesthouse, which included a bathroom at the end of the structure. The floors and ceiling were concrete and the walls made of concrete block. By American standards, it was a spartan building. However, it was much better than I ever envisioned we would have in the mountains of Haiti. I thought we would be sleeping on mats on dirt floors, not a bed with a mattress in a weather-protected room!

As Father Cha Cha told Theresa Patterson before the twinning relationship began, he wanted as many as possible to come and spend time with the people of Pendus. He knew that a minimum level of comfort would greatly enhance our experience and therefore bolster our willingness to return. Sagely, he understood that regular visits are the backbone of a creating a strong twinning relationship. In addition to housing our visiting teams, the guesthouse also is used by St. Joseph teachers when we are not there. Several teachers live a few miles from Pendus and walk each way to school. Staying at the guesthouse allows them not to travel so much during the week when school is in session.

After the initial trip to Pendus, another similar sum was sent to Father Cha Cha, as well as a sea container, which included a diesel-powered five-thousand-watt generator. Before the return trip in December later that year, many improvements were completed to the St. Joseph school and church compound area, including erecting two small concrete buildings. One housed the generator and another created space for storage and a small kitchen for the school. Other finished projects include the completion of an eight-foot concrete block wall to enclose the combined church-school compound; painting the school; wiring from the generator room to the rectory, church, and guesthouse; painting the iron-window coverings; and installing screens in the guesthouse.

——➤●◀——

St. Mary's first major undertaking was to build a new chapel and school at Massacre. It was completed in early 2001. The original chapel was approximately twenty-five feet by forty-five feet in size with palm-woven sides. It was dirt floored but did have a tin roof. However, this small space also doubled as a school for over two hundred students. There were five classes held in the area, each facing a different direction with its own blackboard. It must have been very difficult to conduct so many classes simultaneously. The noise levels alone would complicate a routine day's activities.

As many as four students shared each four-foot desk in that school. Thinking of how that cramped scenario would have played out in the USA, Sharon asked the principal how they handled discipline problems in that tight space. His answer surprised us. He said, "We don't have any discipline problems."

The new construction would provide a seventy-five-foot-by-thirty-five-foot chapel with four twenty-foot-by-twenty-foot adjoining classrooms. There would be a covered overhang connecting each of the classes to the chapel. While Massacre is located high up the mountain, the site for this project was located slightly downhill off the path into the village. To accommodate this elevation change, concrete stairs were added from the path down into chapel. While the Haitians did not need the steps to traverse the slope, they did help prevent mud from being tracked into the new facility.

This was our first construction experience in the mountains of Haiti. Remember, Massacre is not accessible by vehicle. It is a two-hour hike up the mountain from Pendus. Therefore, all the material needed, such as bags of concrete, concrete blocks, and tin roof, had to be carried up to Massacre by the locals. The people of Massacre also contributed to the construction by gathering rocks, sand, and water.

The most amazing aspect of all the projects over the years has been how quickly they could be completed. We did not send the money for this endeavor until late fall of 2000. When we visited in December, we observed the newly laid foundation for the chapel and four-room school. The March 2001 group joined Father Cha Cha in celebrating the first Mass at the newly completed chapel and school.

———————

The second major community-centered project was building a dispensary in Pendus. The original space used by Madam Marcel to conduct her clinic was a small building comprised of two ten- foot-by-ten-foot rooms side by side each other. Needless to say, the space was cramped.

Several of the doctors, who already had been to Pendus, met with Father Cha Cha at a Lafayette restaurant during his visit to

St. Mary in August 2001. They drew up their plans for the new dispensary on a napkin. Those rough sketches became the springboard for what was ultimately built. Construction began in the fall of 2001. The formal dedication for the Dispensary of Saint Mary of the Immaculate Conception was held during the March 2002 trip to Pendus.

The dispensary has a large waiting room across the front as you step inside. In addition, there are two examination rooms, a birthing room, a pharmacy, office and records rooms, an overnight room for patients, and a small indoor bathroom. The wall in the birthing room is where local artist Jean Saul painted a newborn baby lying on a bed with the Holy Spirit in the form of a dove descending upon it. A beautiful setting for both mother and baby!

The dispensary is located on a two-acre plot just east and downhill from the St. Joseph Church complex. It sets between the church and the Pendus River and is surrounded by an eight-foot-high concrete block fence with barbed wire on top for additional security. The courtyard area in front of the dispensary is shaded by a huge one-hundred-year-old mango tree, whose branches form an umbrella over most of the courtyard. It makes a peaceful and comfortable waiting area for extra patients on a busy day.

There also is a small three-room outbuilding that can be used as either a guardhouse for the complex or a place for traveling doctors to stay while visiting the dispensary. A cistern was also built behind the dispensary to collect water from the roof. Banana trees were planted throughout the grounds, making it look like a tropical forest. The food provided is an added bonus.

———◦◦◦———

St. Mary sent a second sea container to Haiti in late 2002. We had its contents shipped to Port-de-Paix instead of Port-au-Prince for two key reasons. First, Port-de-Paix is much closer to Pendus. Second, Father Wilner was then the priest at the Catholic Church in Port-de-Paix. He would be able to gather the items from the ship and store them until Father Cha Cha could arrange transportation for them. There was no such helpful connection in PAP.

Among the many things sent were some used scaffolding and 120 gallons of blue-and-white interior paint, colors that matched our recently renovated St. Mary Cathedral in Lafayette. These colors were popular in Pendus and created another connection between the two churches. In 2003 Father Cha Cha had the interior of the church finished, adding a ceiling in place of the exposed wooden trusses and completely repainting the church both inside and out. Since then, the high-quality interior paint has survived the heat and humidity of Haiti quite well.

This sea container also contained all the prepackaged desks and pews we would assemble on our next visit to Pendus. (See further elaboration of this project in Chapter 17.) Once the pews were assembled and put in place, the interior of St. Joseph Church looked beautiful.

———⟫•◦•⟪———

St. Mary parishioners' first visit to Mayombe was in December 2001. This was when the woman said, "What God has brought us today, no flood can wash away." Its chapel was in very poor shape as it had an uneven dirt floor and part of its roof was missing. Not only was it very small (only twenty feet by twenty feet), but it also was not a safe worship space for the community.

By August 2002 enough money was collected and sent to Father Cha Cha to begin construction of a new, bigger chapel in Mayombe. Again, all the needed materials had to be carried by individuals up the rugged mountainside and the villagers helped with collecting sand, rocks, and water.

The finished chapel measured thirty feet by fifty feet with a complete roof. The village finally had a protected community gathering space suitable for worship and other events. Wind and rain would not be a problem any longer in Mayombe. A small room adjoined the chapel, providing a place to stay for a priest when he visited the area. It could also be used as a sacristy. The high-quality interior paint that was sent on sea container in late 2002 was also used to paint the exterior of this new chapel. Despite the extreme exposures on that mountaintop, it has withstood the test of time since then. As is customary in Haiti, a concrete block wall was also completed around the compound perimeter. Construction was again completed quickly as our December 2002 group joined Father Cha Cha in celebrating the first Mass at the new Mayombe chapel.

———=⟫●⟪———

Kayimit's chapel is located near the intersection of the Gonaives to Port-de-Paix highway and the cutoff road that heads north to Pendus. It is a bit misleading to call either a highway or a road as both are dirt surfaces the entire way! Kayimit is approximately the halfway point between Pendus and Gros Morne. The original chapel had concrete walls and a tin roof but was small, only eighteen feet by thirty feet. Money was sent to replace this chapel in late 2003.

The finished chapel was much bigger, measuring thirty feet by seventy feet. It too was painted blue-with-white trim. A glass cross was embedded into the front wall just above the entrance into the chapel. Our May 2004 group celebrated Mass at this beautiful chapel.

Kayimit's chapel is called Our Lady of the Rosary. Painted around the entire four interior walls, up near the ceiling, were four complete rosaries strung end to end. Each one was a different color. Four is significant because there are four possible mysteries contemplated when a rosary is said. Depending on the day of the week there are Joyful Mysteries, Luminous Mysteries, Sorrowful Mysteries, and Glorious Mysteries. Each mystery concentrates on five various scripture readings pertaining to that topic. For example, the Joyful Mysteries focus on the Annunciation, the Visitation, the Nativity, the Presentation, and the Finding of Jesus in the Temple from Luke's Gospel.

When the new chapel opened, Martial Dareus was the sacristan. The area did not have a school. Martial displayed the admirable

Haitian trait of not wasting anything by salvaging the concrete pieces from the razed chapel. He transported them a short distance to his residence and from those remains constructed a rustic, small three-room school on his property so the local children would have a place to learn closer to their homes.

The timing of the construction could not have been better as it was our December 2004 group, stranded due to excessive rain and high rivers, which had to spend the night sleeping on the wooden pews in Kayimit's new chapel.

———◆———

Our next two projects were building schools. The first was a ten-room school at Montbayard. Father Cha Cha raised half of the $30,000 cost from a source in France. St. Mary funded the remainder. The total cost was high for several reasons. First, Montbayard is remotely located on a mountain without good vehicular access. Transporting the resources needed for construction added greatly to the overall cost. Second, the school property is adjacent to the chapel, no more than sixty feet or so away. However, the slope of the terrain is so steep that the roof of the school is level with the foundation of the chapel. This drastic drop in topography also added to the cost of construction.

St. Mary delivered the money for this project to Father Cha Cha on the December 2003 trip, and the school was completed when the May 2004 group visited. To show just how remote and difficult it was to get to Montbayard, that 2004 trip was my first time ever in Montbayard. I often teased Father Cha Cha that this chapel did not exist as he never took us there.

The second school was located at Savanne Carre. A small three-room school was on the chapel property. However, there were eight different classes taught there. Several of the classes met outside under some mango trees. If the weather was bad, those classes would simply move inside the chapel and share the space.

The new school was designed in an L-shape with eight class-rooms along the longer segment of the *L*. Two more rooms comprised the short leg of the building: one was the principal's office and one was for storage. A long overhang connected the rooms and provided extra protection from rain. As with all prior construction completed to date, there was no electrical component. Power simply was not available. For lighting and ventilation, each of the rooms simply had concrete block that was not solid, thereby letting in light and circulation of air. However, during bad storms, it would also let in rain!

The money for this school was sent to Father Wilner in early 2005. The new school was completed in time for the beginning of the school year in September!

——➤●◄——

The most unusual request for St. Mary's help came from Father Wilner in late 2005. He wanted to build a radio station in Gros Morne. Talk about thinking outside the box! With all the obvious needs in the area, I did not appreciate the necessity for a radio station. Because of his persistence and leadership, we raised the money for his visionary endeavor to be built. It has proved to be invaluable in the following years.

The church in Gros Morne is called Our Lady of the Light, so the radio station was called Radio La Chandeleur (meaning "the Light"). It was built adjacent to the rectory, within the enclosed church compound in Gros Morne.

There are twenty-four chapel areas surrounding Our Lady of the Light in addition to St. Joseph Church in Pendus and its six cha-pels. Because of its strategic location, the signal from the radio tower in Gros Morne can reach every one of these chapels. While there is no electrical power in any of these areas, many families do own a battery-powered transistor radio. Information received is then shared with neighbors who do not have radio access.

The three priests stationed at Gros Morne do most of the DJ-ing for the radio station. I teased Father that he had simply figured out a way for the priests to give more homilies! The station broadcasts daily Mass live so many of the area's elderly and shut-ins can listen. However, it produces much more than simply religious programming.

Programming topics include health and hygiene, weather, news, music, and a children's hour led by local youth. The weather and news aspects of the station have been crucial to the area. Since the station was built, there have not been any fatalities in the area from any of the many hurricanes that have hit. This was not the case beforehand. The station has been able to warn the people and provide pointers on what to do and where to go for maximum safety.

Father's foresight has since extended to Television La Chandeleur. That project is still in its infancy compared to the radio station since there are less than one hundred televisions in the entire community of over fifty thousand people.

John Sculley III, American entrepreneur and former president of PepsiCo and later CEO of Apple, once said, "The future belongs to those who see possibilities before they become obvious."

Stations of the Cross tie St. Mary and St. Joseph Churches together. The stations represent the fourteen steps of Christ's passion—from Jesus being condemned to death to his being laid in the tomb. All Catholic churches have a set inside their worship space, typically along the outer walls encircling the pews of the church. Some are painted recreations while others are elaborate three-dimensional depictions. In either case, the fourteen events depicted are the same in every church.

St. Mary Cathedral was closed for major renovation during 2000. During that time, the existing Stations of the Cross were taken down, cleaned, restored, and then reframed to match the new decor of the church interior. After the stations were refurbished, a parishioner photographed them. Dr. James Bayley spearheaded an effort to have those fourteen negatives blown up to eleven-inch-by-fourteen-inch size, dry mounted, and framed. He enlisted his "7:30 a.m. Sunday Mass group" to underwrite the cost of this effort.

We took the first set to Haiti in December 2001 to hang on the walls at St. Joseph Church. Dr. Bayley repeated this process each of the next six years so all six chapels would have a set of the Stations of the Cross. On each of those following trips, our groups would help hang the new set inside the latest recipient chapel. Each time we took a set, we also packed a hammer, a box of one-inch masonry nails, and a tape measure, all of which we left with the chapel once the stations were hung. Not only have the stations provided a theological role at each location, they have been a decorative addition as well.

The Stations of the Cross are a communal prayer. They are recited as a group during Lent, the forty days that lead up to Easter each year. What makes the stations project uniquely important is that parishioners in both Indiana and Haiti are potentially reciting the same prayers while focusing on identical Stations of the Cross simultaneously. The likelihood of this happening is enhanced by the fact that St. Mary and St. Joseph are in the same time zone, even though they are 2,200 miles apart!

Father Joseph envisioned a rejuvenation of the youth in Pendus and the surrounding areas in 2011. During his first year as pastor in the area, he decided to begin a summer camp. He invited fifteen teenagers each from Pendus and all six chapel areas. This endeavor was held at Savanne Carre's chapel because the ten-room school there allowed enough room for everyone to have floor space upon which to sleep at night.

The purpose of the retreat was to immerse the students in many aspects of formation in topics such as liturgy, sacraments, leadership, sexuality, and community citizenship. There were many talks of each of these subjects as well as role-playing, singing, and skits. Equally important, two meals provided were each day. Over the years, the cost to transport, house, feed, and educate the youth for the week-long camp averaged $20 per student. St. Mary eagerly supported this endeavor! Each year, a different set of teenagers was invited.

I talked with Father Joseph and some of the students after the first few summer camps. All agreed it was a huge success for the attendees. In the subsequent years, I have noticed many more teenagers involved at Mass, such as being a lector or member of the choir.

The last major infrastructure improvement St. Mary provided was a rectory. It was nearly completed in 2016. The Bishop of the Gonaives Diocese decided in 2013 that St. Joseph Church would become a stand-alone parish and have its first full-time priest stationed there. However, no financial support was provided after that declaration. Thankfully, Pendus has a twinning relationship with St. Mary Cathedral.

The original existing space was small and structurally unsound. It was not suitable as a residence and office for a full-time priest. Father Sylvio razed that old building in 2015 and had the foundation laid for a new rectory. The new building was adjacent to the back of the church, so it also included rooms for a sacristy and an office in addition to living space. The concrete portion of the construction was completed before our December 2015 visit, but many finishing touches such as windows, doors, and bathrooms were not yet finished. By our December 2016 visit these items were completed, leaving only exterior painting still to do.

There are three bedrooms, one for Father and two for guests; two bathrooms; and a dining/gathering room. One other small room will be used for multiple purposes. There is a concrete stairway up to the rooftop. Someday, that area could be used for expansion of the rectory if needed. In the meantime, it provides a cool, comfortable, and scenic space to gather and talk. When there is no moon, the view of the Milky Way and the nighttime sky is spectacular from that vantage.

There is a two hundred-gallon plastic container on the roof to hold water. Gravity provides the necessary pressure to supply water to the showers, sinks, and toilets below. Unfortunately, that container still needs to be filled by hand, one five-gallon bucket at a time. Still, indoor facilities in rural Haiti are quite a luxury! Now Father has an adequate space to live and work.

Built and dedicated in early 2002, this dispensary is named after the Cathedral of St Mary of the Immaculate Conception in Lafayette, Indiana. It is an exceptional facility for the northern mountains of Haiti.

36

Haiti Is Home

So then you are no longer strangers and sojourners, but you are fellow citizens with the holy ones and members of the household of God.
—Ephesians 2:19

"AYITI SE LAKAY" WAS THE title of the journal for my December 2015 trip to Pendus. Translated, it means "Haiti is Home." It became clear to me of its significance several times early in that trip. At the end of Mass on our first full day in Pendus, Father Sylvio had me speak. Among other things, I said, "I am happy to be back in Pendus. It is my second home!" When Ives Vernet, the principal at St Joseph School, spoke a bit later, he pointed out how important it was that Pendus was our second home!

When I was with Kyle in Gros Morne later that day, I asked him if he felt like he was home, as he has lived twice in Haiti—one summer in Gros Morne and then several years later for over six months in Port-au-Prince. He responded, "There are four places where I feel I am home…where I belong." Those four are Lafayette, Indiana; Johannesburg, South Africa; Washington, D.C.; and Haiti. All four are places he has lived for extended periods of his life.

That sense of belonging is one way to describe "home" to others. That concept is not quite the same in today's age where mobility is frequent and establishing roots not as common as even a generation ago. But belonging in Pendus—and in Haiti—is an appropriate description for me. After all, December 2015 was my nineteenth trip to Haiti over the prior sixteen years. I have spent more time in Haiti than nearly anywhere else, but my actual, physical residence is in Indiana. I know Sharon and Kyle share that same feeling as well.

But "belonging" isn't something measured simply by the number of days and hours spent there. It is much more. "To belong," at its deepest level, means to be affiliated, or associated, or linked with. It signifies a true connection. It is where you are supposed to be.

Sharon and I have discussed this feeling that we both have. How can we feel like home when the surroundings are so different? Everywhere you look there are mountains. There is dirt beneath our feet wherever we walk. The water for bathing comes from either collected rain water or the river. Electricity is only available at best at night when the generator is running. Yet, somehow, we have the same feelings we have when we are in Lafayette, that of being comfortable, safe, peaceful, accepted, and belonging.

Most Americans perceive these difficulties mentioned as great hardships. However, they don't matter to us when we are in Haiti. Life is brought back to its simplest form, free of the many daily distractions we all have. Without those many distractions, we are free to concentrate on the beauty of the surroundings and of the people we encounter. If we could only train ourselves to do so all the time, then we would *always* be home wherever we were! We would be content in all circumstances.

After I returned from Haiti, I read one of the daily reflections from St. Monica Church in Indianapolis written by Trina Wurst. Her thoughts were about Lent and the practice of giving up something, but they resonated with me about Haiti as well. She wrote:

> We are reminded that, as followers of Christ, we must deny ourselves daily and take up our own cross. Denying ourselves is not an exercise in willpower, but in letting go of distractions and diversions that keep us away from God.
>
> One beautiful part of Lent for me (now that I understand it) is that we are experiencing this

time of denial together. Each of us has prayerfully vowed to let go of something in order to
make room for more quality time with God. It
is at once a very personal experience, but it is
also shared with every practicing Catholic in the
world. It fortifies me to know that others are letting go of things too.

The notion of letting go of the distractions that keep us away from
spending quality time with God struck a chord with me. It captured
precisely what I was feeling about Haiti. The peace and confidence
that comes from knowing you are where you are supposed to be and
doing what you should be doing is a wonderful thing to experience.

It is always good to be home!

Sharon feels "at home" as she encounters
the beauty of Haiti and its people.

37

So What Do We Do in Haiti Part 2: Who Is Tending to Whom?

*"No one is too poor to be unable to contribute something
and no one is too rich to be unable to receive."*
—*World Vision*

IT WOULD BE VERY ARROGANT and presumptuous of me to think my trips to Haiti are so noble as to help those in need in Haiti. After all, just how much can be accomplished in about a week's time that most trips allow? From my reflections on my visits, I know that I am also being selfish when I go on these trips. I know that I get much more out of my visits with my Haitian brothers and sisters than I could possibly ever begin to deliver to them. I need that spiritual rejuvenation and growth that I receive when I go to Haiti.

I am learning many life lessons. I am learning about total dependence on God and on being thankful for what one has, even when that doesn't seem to be much at all! I am learning what it means to pray for my "daily bread" and being thankful even if bread is all there is to eat. I am learning about being thankful for another sunrise, another day. I am learning to share in proportions I had never reached before. I am learning that the joys and hopes, grief and anguish, of people who look and speak differently than me are the same as mine. We are not very different at all. I am learning that adapting to a new culture can be a very enriching and exciting experience.

I am learning that to find God, you need to go where He is. When God was present in the Old Testament, he was in the ark in a tent. The Jews came to him in the desert. He also appeared in a burning bush. Moses came to him on the mountaintop. In the New Testament, Jesus was born in a manger in Bethlehem. The shepherds and magi came to him in the stable. These were not grandiose venues fit for royalty as known by man; they were humble, secluded places where those who sought God traveled to find Him.

In chapter 25 of the Gospel of Matthew, Jesus tells us that he is that stranger, maybe we should call him an immigrant. He is that person who is hungry or thirsty. He is that person alone in his illness or in prison. Whichever mission you happen to be looking for Him within, you must go in search of Him. My search happens to take me to the mountains in Haiti.

I am learning that I can't simply give to the poor and needy from my relatively comfortable position of wealth. I must go and make contact with them; I cannot simply give from afar. I have to go to them wherever they may be. I cannot be a "have" giving to a "have-not." I need to be there. I am learning that "being there" does not have to be the same as "being far away" as your mission opportunity can arise anywhere, even right where you currently are!

Pope Francis eloquently verbalized this call to go forth, to be involved. While he was specifically talking to priests, the image he created truly applies to everyone. He said that the world's clergy must become "shepherds living with the smell of the sheep." You can't "live with the smell" if you are not up close and personal with the situation with which you are interacting. Again, it can't be from a distance.

The best lesson I am learning is that mission, or should I say life, is all about building relationships. It must be a two-way endeavor, which means that I also must be prepared to receive in return.

As shown by the many insights I have shared in this book I have truly been the "have-not" experiencing the blessings from the mutual relationships built. My travels to Haiti have taught me so many life lessons, lessons that are applicable in every aspect of my daily life. My faith has been enriched from my many trips. That should not surprise me, as we are told in James 2:5, "Did not God choose the poor of the world to be rich in faith and heirs of the kingdom that he promised to those that love him?" *Gaudium et spes* further captured this comprehension well when it stated: "It should be pointed out that many nations which are poorer as far as material goods are concerned, yet richer in wisdom, can be of the greatest advantage to others" (p.15).

Lilla Watson, an indigenous Australian, is credited with the following: "If you have come here to help me, you are wasting your time. But if you have come because your liberation is bound up with mine, then let us work together." I saw this quote on a poster at Matthew 25 Guest House. It struck a chord with me. It spelled out the essence of relationship. Don't come to do *for* me but rather come and be *with* me.

Catholics have a Penitential Act that we pray at every Mass. I am sure most of us have it memorized, but I wonder whether we really pay attention to the words:

> I confess to almighty God and to you, my brothers and sisters, that I have sinned through my own fault, in my thoughts and in my words, in what I have done, and in what I have failed to do…

Before my involvement in Haiti the most important part of that prayer to me was asking forgiveness for what I have done. Much like the Pharisees of the Old Testament, I was concerned about my checklist of "do" and "do not do" requirements. If I complied with them, I must be in good stead. I was measuring my standing with the church and with God by what was seemingly being required of me. I was following the law. I was meeting those requirements—or so I thought. I was doing what I had to do.

However, if my faith was more in line with where it should be, it really should be doing what I want to do, or better yet what I get to do. After all, the psalmist in 40:9 says, "To do your will is my delight." How could that ever be attainable? How do I get from "have to" to "want to" and finally to "get to" in the progression of my faith?

Those "do and do not" commandments are the minimalistic standard, the lowest hurdle to jump over just to get by. Jesus does not want minimalistic. He wants total commitment.

God tells us in Revelations 3:15–16, "I know your works; I know that you are neither cold nor hot. I wish you were either cold or hot. So, because you are lukewarm, neither hot nor cold, I will spit you out of my mouth."

Today the more difficult portion of that prayer to me is the second half, the part that says, "Forgive me for what I have failed to do." That list could be lengthy! How many times have I seen a situation unfurl before me and failed to act? How many times have I have I totally failed to even notice the situation happening before me and, as a result, still did nothing? How many Fessens have there been in my life who I have totally ignored or failed to bother to notice? This half of that prayer follows Jesus's commandment to "love one another." When you truly love one another, you finally reach the "get to" stage and the level of commitment Jesus seeks in all of us.

This truly is a call to action. I think that the most challenging part of the Mass used to be said right at the very end, when everyone wasn't paying close attention when they were getting ready to leave. While the wording has been changed recently, the Mass used to end with, "Go forth to love and serve the Lord!" That is a call to action, to put our faith into action. After all, faith is not a cerebral exercise but an active one!

A different way I have heard this explained is "When you pray...move your feet." Father Brenden Mbagwu, a former associate pastor at St. Mary Cathedral, often used a better, catchier way to say the same thing in his homilies: "There is more to do than sit in the pew!" Again, these are direct calls for action. My action. Not someone else's action. This must become a lifestyle. It is not easy. Pope Francis acknowledges this when he said, "Faith is not the refuge for the faint-hearted."

My favorite religious quote comes from Saint Francis of Assisi. He sums up this call to live an active, faithful life by saying, "Continually preach the Gospel…only when necessary use words."

In no way am I insinuating that I have achieved this level of commitment. Rather I am now at least aware of the calling that I need to be striving for, instead of merely getting by. I love all that I have experienced and all that I have learned in Haiti. My hope is to continue to grow and learn. I never know what God has in store for me on my next journey there!

My mother asked me a simple question upon by return from my first visit to Pendus. My response surprised her. She asked me, "What was the most difficult part of the trip?" I simply replied, "Coming home."

An immersive mission endeavor can steal your heart. It obviously has mine.

My encounter with four-year old Jevela formed the foundation
of one of the many lessons I have learned while in Haiti.

38

My Haiti Prayer

The Lord has done great things for me, and holy is his Name.
—Luke 1:49

DEAR LORD,

I give thanks for bringing Haiti into my life. Through my experiences there I have encountered Jesus firsthand and have seen with my own eyes the kingdom of God here on earth.

When I came as a stranger...I was welcomed as a brother.

When I was hungry...food was carried through mud and rain so that I might eat.

When I was thirsty...drink was shared with me, even if all that was available was coconut milk.

When I lost my luggage...clothes were provided for my return trip home.

When my son was sick...great care and concern was given to him.

When I was imprisoned in my world of me...you showed me how to break loose from those shackles and free myself from their grasp upon me.

Yes, Lord, I give thanks for allowing Haiti to become a part of me and pray that it will always remain a part of me.

Amen.

Acknowledgments

I give thanks to my God at every remembrance of you.
—Philippians 1:3

To all those in Haiti who have welcomed me into their homes, into their communities, into their places of worship, and into their lives, I say, "Mesi Anpil!" Thank you very much! Most of them were completely unaware they were teaching me so many valuable life lessons simply by sharing a few moments of their lives with me. Many of those stories are in these pages. I hope I have done them justice.

I next thank my wife Sharon and my son Kyle. They have walked nearly every step with me that I have taken in Haiti. It has been a joy and an honor to be able to share this ministry with them. I am sure they have more stories and lessons that they could add to mine and without them this book would not have been possible.

There have been others who have helped me with writing my first book, primarily my assistant Linda, as well as my great friends Art Taylor and Rod Ray. They have read multiple drafts of my manuscript as I created it over the past year. Their critiques and suggestions were always on point and appreciated. They greatly enhanced my final product. To them I owe a huge debt of gratitude.

Many others have also contributed by reading and commenting on my literary efforts. I especially want to thank Father Bob Klemme, Father Ronel "Cha Cha" Charelus, Father Ron Schneider, Father Tom Clegg, Deacon Steve Miller, John Nichols, Mike Hartman, and Fequiere Vilsaint for their insights, encouragements, and their inspiration. Over the years, they have also taught me many things about mission and ministry.

Bible Verses

(New American Bible)

Vatican II References

About the Author

BORN IN LAFAYETTE, INDIANA, JEFF Newell has been married to his wife Sharon for forty-one years, a practicing attorney for thirty-seven years, and a lifetime member of St. Mary Cathedral. He took the first of his twenty mission trips to Haiti in March 2000. Nearly every trip thereafter, Sharon and their son Kyle have accompanied him to the tiny Caribbean nation.

Jeff is the chair of the Haiti Committee at St. Mary Cathedral, the chair of Central Indiana Churches for Haiti (CINCH), and a member of the board of directors for the Parish Twinning Program of the Americas. Jeff earned two bachelor's degrees from Purdue University and his juris doctorate from Indiana University. In addition he has an Ecclesial Lay Minister certificate from the diocese of Lafayette-in-Indiana.

He worked his way through college as a newspaper sports reporter. *Open Your Eyes: Life Lessons Learned* in Haiti is the first book Jeff has authored.

CPSIA information can be obtained
at www.ICGtesting.com
Printed in the USA
LVHW052058031220
673105LV00002B/21

9 781641 918886